A HEART OF MANY ROOMS

A HEART
OF
MANY
ROOMS

Celebrating the Many Voices within Judaism

DAVID HARTMAN

JEWISH LIGHTS Publishing
Woodstock, Vermont

A Heart of Many Rooms:
Celebrating the Many Voices within Judaism

2002 First Quality Paperback Edition
© 1999 by David Hartman

For information regarding permission to reprint material from this book, please mail or fax your request in writing to Jewish Lights Publishing, Permissions Department, at the address / fax number listed below.

Grateful acknowledgment is made to the following for permission to reprint previously published material:

Aurora Press: Excerpts from *Man's Quest for God: Studies in Prayer and Symbolism* by Abraham Joshua Heschel, ISBN 0-943358-48-5, 1998, Aurora Press Inc., P.O. Box 573, Santa Fe, NM 87504

Farrar, Straus & Giroux: Excerpts from *The Insecurity of Freedom: Essays on Human Existence* by Abraham Joshua Heschel. Copyright © 1966 by Abraham Joshua Heschel. Copyright renewed © 1994 by Sylvia Heschel. Reprinted by permission of Farrar, Straus & Giroux, Inc.

Library of Congress Cataloging-in-Publication Data

Hartman, David.
A heart of many rooms : celebrating the many voices within Judaism /
by David Hartman.
p. cm.
Includes bibliographical references and index.
ISBN 1-58023-048-2
1. Orthodox Judaism—Israel.
2. Orthodox Judaism—Apologetic works.
I. Title.
BM390.H285   1999
296.8'32—dc21   98-43238
CIP

10 9 8 7 6 5 4 3 2 1

Manufactured in the United States of America

Published by Jewish Lights Publishing
A Division of LongHill Partners, Inc.
Sunset Farm Offices, Route 4, P.O. Box 237
Woodstock, VT 05091
Tel: (802) 457-4000   Fax: (802) 457-4004
www.jewishlights.com

To Bob Kogod,

a dear and devoted friend,

who shares my aspirations for a
modern renaissance of
Judaism

This book was generated as part of the ongoing research of the
Richard and Sylvia Kaufman Center for
Contemporary Jewish Thought at the
Shalom Hartman Institute in Jerusalem.

The Center explores and encourages new spiritual possibilities
emerging from the confrontation of the Judaic tradition with
modernity. The Shalom Hartman Institute, founded in 1976,
is an advanced research and teacher-training center whose
mission is to meet the new intellectual and spiritual
challenges facing the Jewish people resulting from both the
rebirth of Israel and the full participation of
modern Jews in Western culture.

"A person might think,

'Since the House of Shammai declare unclean and the House
of Hillel clean, this one prohibits and that one permits,
how, then, can I learn Torah?'

Scripture says, 'Words...the words.... These are the words....'
All the words have been given by a single Shepherd, one God
created them, one Provider gave them, the Lord of all deeds,
blessed be He, has spoken them. So make yourself a heart of
many rooms and bring into it the words of the
House of Shammai and the words of the House of Hillel,
the words of those who declare unclean and the words of
those who declare clean."

(Tosefta, *Sotah* 7:12)

Contents

PART IV

RELIGIOUS PERSPECTIVES ON THE FUTURE OF ISRAEL

ACKNOWLEDGMENTS

SINCE THE FOUNDING of the Shalom Hartman Institute in 1976, I
have had the privilege of being in the company of serious
committed intellectuals whose research agenda grew from a
commitment to affect a change in the moral and spiritual quality of
Jewish life today. Being in their company has been an inspiration
for my thinking and writing. It has been a privilege for me to
participate in a community that does not view relevance as
compromising the depth of scholarship.

Besides the congenial and inspiring atmosphere of this
community of scholars, I am grateful to the leadership of the
Shalom Hartman Institute for providing the support that makes
the Institute a compelling environment. This book is dedicated to
the president of the Institute, Mr. Bob Kogod, who is a devoted
friend and a driving force in inspiring the Institute to focus on the
central issues confronting world Jewry today. His friendship and
dedication are a source of strength for me and for the entire
community of scholars.

Dick Kaufman, president of the American Friends of the Shalom Hartman Institute and his wife, Sylvia, introduced me to their Muskegon community where I had the privilege of participating in their Jewish-Christian dialogue. My essay "Judaism As an Interpretive Tradition" grew out of a recent discussion with Father Richard Newhouse. Joan Porter, a participant at the Muskegon dialogue, believed that my work had importance for both Jews and Christians. I am grateful to her for providing the Institute with a generous grant so that I would be able to devote my time to the completion of this new work.

I am grateful to Stuart Matlins, publisher of Jewish Lights, for his support and enthusiasm; to Elisheva Urbas, for her guidance in editing the text; to Jennifer Goneau for her aid in the book's production; and to Larry Shuman for his superb promotion of the book.

My deep gratitude and appreciation go to Ruth Sherer for her kind assistance, dedication, and hard work in typing and re-typing this manuscript for publication. My wife Bobbie and my children have always been a great support through all of my work. I pray that God will bless them all with long life and good health.

PREFACE

IN PREPARING THIS volume, I decided to include, along with new essays, several reworked and revised chapters from my earlier works *Joy and Responsibility* and *Conflicting Visions*. It was very moving to reread many of my earlier essays on Israel and to sense the enthusiasm I had felt in having been given the privilege of participating in the dynamic social and religious struggles of Israeli society. In the early period of my aliyah, I believed that there was a way to build bridges between secular and religious groups in Israeli society. In presenting a covenantal appreciation of Israel's rebirth, I attempted to articulate a religious response without falling into messianic triumphalism. How optimistic and enthusiastic I was!

Coupled with my renewed enjoyment of my earlier excitement and enthusiasm, I was also deeply pained by the contrast between what I had hoped for and what was in fact the reality of Israeli society. There are tendencies within certain sectors of the Orthodox religious community in Israel and the diaspora toward intellectual insulation and sectarianism. Instead of bridges of mutual understanding, there are deep chasms of animosity and distrust between religious and nonobservant members of Israeli society. There is a demonization of North American and Israeli religious leaders not identified with certain Orthodox approaches to Torah. The "Who is a Jew?" issue refuses to go away. The delegitimization of Conservative and Reform conversions in Israel remains a live legislative option in the Knesset. Leibowitz's critique of my writings (see the chapter on Yeshayahu Leibowitz in this volume) appears more accurate as a description of Israeli society than my analysis of the possibilities of creating a shared value language.

Nevertheless, in spite of the growth of militant fanaticism, I still cherish the conviction that a committed halakhic Jew need not feel threatened by different understandings and interpretations of normative Judaism. *A Heart of Many Rooms* expresses my continuing belief in the possibility and necessity of building educational bridges between different sectors of the population in Israel and throughout the Jewish world. If we fail to build these bridges, we are in danger of splitting Israeli society and of creating sectarian forms of Judaism in the diaspora.

My refusal to give up hope is rooted deeply in my early religious upbringing. My parents were pious, observant Jews, totally committed to their children's Torah education. During all the years of my youth, I never once heard the language of demonization and exclusion ("They're heretics! They're not part of *klal yisrael!*") so prevalent in modern-day religious discourse. From my parents' home, I learned that a family dedicated to a Torah way of life can feel secure without drawing sharp lines defining the boundaries between "insiders" and "outsiders."

This work is a direct result of intense intellectual dialogue with Elliott Yagod, my friend, student, and philosophical colleague. We discussed, and worked on together, each essay. Without his devotion and cooperation, this work would not have been completed. Words cannot express adequately my appreciation and gratitude for all he has contributed throughout the years to my thinking and to my written work.

It is also important for me to mention that *A Heart of Many Rooms* focuses not only on social and religious issues that surface in Israel. Living in Israel has given me the opportunity of addressing visiting Christian theologians and pilgrims seeking a deeper understanding of Judaism. Following in the spirit of Maimonides, I am committed to the religious task of making Judaism intelligible to a wider human audience. In leaving the ghetto, Jewish thinkers were given the opportunity to articulate their faith commitment to the non-Jewish world.

Reborn Israel has created interest in the modern Israeli historical drama. In coming back to the land, we have returned not to an insulated ghetto existence but rather to a particularism informed by openness to a larger human world. I believe there is a serious Christian audience that wants to understand Judaism in its own terms and not only as a precursor to the Christian story. Many essays in this volume present a phenomenology of the Judaic experience where Jewish commitment to mitzvot is not distorted by stereotypical images of "pharisaic legalism." There is a joyful vitality in a life defined by the rigorous demands of Halakhah.

In my phenomenology of Halakhah and characterology of the faith commitment, I argue against approaches to Judaism that are opposed to offering "reasons for the commandments" (*ta'amei ha-mitzvot*). I also disagree with the claim that in order to cultivate a passionate faith commitment to Judaism, one must reject non-Jewish sources of knowledge and values.

My philosophic appreciation of Judaism was influenced by Joseph B. Soloveitchik, Abraham Joshua Heschel, and, above all, by Maimonides. All of them taught me that one can and should appropriate the richness and variety of human thought and experience regardless of its ethnic or religious source. I hope that individuals concerned with and committed to the future of Judaism in the modern world will benefit from my analysis of traditional halakhic thought and practice.

I have tried to make these essays intelligible and meaningful to a broad and diverse audience. This work is not addressed only to scholars of Judaism or theologians, but also, and primarily, to all Jews and non-Jews who would like to share the thoughts and struggles of a person who loves Torah and Halakhah, who is committed to helping Israeli society make room for and celebrate the religious and cultural diversity present in the modern world, and who believes that a commitment to Israel and to Jewish particularity must be organically connected to the rabbinic teaching, "Beloved are all human beings created in the image of God."

INTRODUCTION

THE TALMUDIC HALAKHIC tradition is not properly understood in the West. Impressions of Judaism are often compounded of elements of medieval Jewish philosophy, Martin Buber's "I and Thou," and mysticism. The religious outlook of the Talmud and Halakhah is either ignored or caricatured as "legalism."

As I have argued in my book *A Living Covenant*, the rebirth of the Jewish people in its homeland challenges us to articulate a sober and responsible religious anthropology capable of energizing Jews to assume responsibility for a total Jewish society. For a better appreciation of the significance of Israel for contemporary Jewish spirituality, it is important to briefly discuss three distinct outlooks reflected in different periods of Jewish history: biblical immediacy, talmudic postponement of gratification, and the modern resurgence of immediacy.

The biblical period may be categorized, for the purpose of the present analysis, as signifying immediacy; history and nature compose an organic unity. Morality and natural phenomena form a continuous whole; human moral failures have natural, organic consequences. The blood of the slain Abel cries out from the earth, and Cain is sentenced to a lifetime of wandering. The earth vomits forth its inhabitants in consequence of moral corruption. Heaven and earth bear witness to Israel's covenantal agreement with God. The biblical blessings and curses illustrate how nature and history mirror Israel's covenantal relationship with God.

The biblical world promises immediate gratification for compliance with the covenant. If you observe the commandments, the rains will fall in season. The rains must fall; nature must respond, for the God of nature and the Lord of history are one. Maimonides, in his *Treatise on Resurrection*, argues that the doctrine of the resurrection of the dead was not mentioned in the Bible because it signifies a blessing whose realization is not immediate and visible. The ability to accept postponed gratification is foreign to the early biblical outlook.

The harmony between moral, historical, and natural conditions stems from a worldview dominated by an omnipotent, beneficent deity. Job's problem with evil was not psychological (i.e., how to cope with suffering and deprivation) but rather ontological: How can the universe tolerate a split between God as the source of being (nature) and God as the source of morality (history)? The problem of evil, to Job, upset the unity and the order of the universe; Job's problem emerged from the matrix of the biblical outlook.

Biblical rewards and punishments were not regarded only as extraneous incentives for good behavior. Biblical man considered many descendants, abundant crops, and victories over enemies to be perfectly natural consequences of observing God's law.

In the talmudic period, however, biblical immediacy no longer dominated Jewish consciousness. Rabbinic Judaism was predominantly the product of historical defeat and exile. Biblical organic consciousness began to break under the weight of harsh historical conditions. In contrast to biblical promises of immediate gratification, a talmudic teacher, Rabbi Tarfon, said:

> The day is short and the work is great, and the laborers are sluggish and the wages are high and the householder is urgent.... The work is not upon thee to finish, nor art thou free to desist from it.... And know that the giving of the reward to the righteous is in the time to come.

The Talmud relates the story of a child who obeyed his father's instruction to send away the mother bird before removing the young birds from their nest, and subsequently fell from the tree to his death. Both in obeying his parent and in sending away the mother bird, the child was fulfilling norms for which the Bible promised long life (Exod. 20:12, Deut. 22:6–7). After verifying the precise nature of this case and concluding that such a case does, in fact, conflict with biblical promises, a talmudic teacher, R. Jacob asserts: "There is no reward in this world for observing the commandments" (*Kiddushin* 39b).

Elsewhere in the Talmud, the rabbis are presented with a series of questions meant to reveal the indifference of reality to violations of God's commandments: "If God hates idolatry, why does He not destroy the objects of idolatry? If someone stole grain and planted it in the earth, why does it grow? Why does an illicit sexual relationship result in pregnancy?" (B.T. *Avoda Zara* 54b). In response to such questions, the pronouncement is made: *Olam ke-minhago noheg* (the world conforms to its natural course). Although the Talmud concedes that *din hu* (by right) stolen grain should not grow, nevertheless, "the world conforms to its natural course." This approach is not an Epicurean negation of the unity of the God of nature and the Lord of history, for it affirms belief in a future state of harmony where one will be compelled to account for one's conduct. The crucial point of this talmudic text is the admission that natural forces and events do not mirror the moral quality of the relationship between human beings and God.

One result of the separation of nature and morality is the development of a religious personality able to tolerate delayed gratification. Biblical Jews met God in history. Momentous events, like the crossing of the Red Sea, were occasions for intense religious devotion. "And when Israel saw the wondrous power which the Lord had wielded against the Egyptians, the people feared the Lord: they had faith in the Lord and in His servant Moses" (Exod. 14:31). When God's power ceased to be apparent in history, as during the talmudic period, a new spiritual orientation began to emerge that felt Divine Presence and love for God in the act of fulfilling His normative message. Indicative of this orientation was a network of concepts, such as *li-shemah* (performing a norm for its own sake), *ahavah* (acting out of love rather than in order to receive a reward or to escape punishment), and *simhah shel mitzvah* (the joy of performing commandments), which centered religious attention on fulfilling mitzvot. In the absence of external divine confirmation and response, a talmudic teacher could assert, "The reward for performing a mitzvah is the performance of the mitzvah itself" (*Avot* 4:2).

Alongside this historical sobriety, the talmudic tradition retained the passion for biblical immediacy, although in a restrained form. It was not easy to restrict the passion for God's living presence to the realm of historical memories or eschatological hopes. The biblical portrayal of God's involvement in the daily life and needs of the community could not easily be set aside.

This was the source of great tension between the religious sensibility emerging in talmudic Judaism and the passion for biblical immediacy, which focused on God's visible power in nature and history. False messiahs represented the eruption of biblical passion despite rabbinic attempts at containment. The vulnerability of Jewish history to messianic pretenders was an outgrowth, in part, of the presence of biblical consciousness alongside rabbinic sobriety. Biblical memories served as a source of anarchy. The powerful dialectic at the heart of talmudic Judaism consisted in the tension between the anarchic passion of biblical memory and the disciplined sobriety of Halakhah.

In the talmudic tradition, the locus of divine presence in history was a memory confined to particular moments of time, such as festivals and moments of prayer. The God of history was encountered in a dramatic story with many episodes, stretching over the entire biblical period and beyond it. In prayer and in structured moments of time, the observant traditional Jew reentered the biblical world of immediacy. Symbolic time kept historical immediacy alive in the midst of rabbinic sobriety.

There are, then, two dimensions of time for the talmudic Jew: (1) empirical history, in which God's "face" remains hidden, and (2) symbolic, holy time, in which God acts as the Lord of history. In the Passover Haggadah, the ten plagues of the Bible are described in such a way that their number far exceeds ten; one teacher proves that there were sixty plagues; another, that there were three hundred. Also, after enumerating the wonders God performed for the people of Israel in the Bible, Jews read aloud *dayenu* (enough!), as if divine blessings in history are overabundant. In short, the Haggadah is the product of a people hungry for God's active intervention in history, yet compelled to focus this hunger not on their own experiences but on the vivid memory of past biblical events.

For many years I served as a rabbi in Jewish communities in the United States and Canada. God's power in history was alive to me on Passover, Shavuot, and Sukkot, the three historical festivals. On Rosh Hashanah and Yom Kippur, the imagery of the moral judge of history calling each and every human being to judgment evoked feelings of accountability and renewed commitment.

History was not problematic; however meaningful and compelling its dramatic message, it was, in the end, a symbolic history.

My theological problems were essentially outside the dramatic events of history. Kierkegaard, Freud, and existentialism were some of the foci of my intellectual and religious concerns.

Then, suddenly, I was confronted with the frightening events preceding the Six-Day War. The community of Jews in Israel was not the protagonist in a dramatic account of symbolic history but rather a real community of Jews facing the possibility of another Holocaust. And I was impotent to intervene. The reality of a living community in the very midst of the stormy currents of history suddenly invaded my consciousness. I, like most of diaspora Jewry, was paralyzed with anxiety and dread; if anything catastrophic were to happen to this community, I felt my Judaism would be strangled. Questions of theology and theodicy were beside the point; continuing to participate in the drama of Jewish history seemed unimaginable in the event of another Holocaust. How long could we be witnesses to the silent God of history?

Then, in the aftermath of the victory of the Six-Day War, I felt compelled to come to Israel to find a way of appropriating the reality of the Jewish State. After returning from Israel, when I entered my synagogue on the Ninth of Av, a fast day commemorating the destruction of Jerusalem and the exile, I was struck by the incongruity of my congregants' sitting downcast on the floor reading and mourning for Jerusalem. In the Jerusalem from which I had just returned, Jews were rejoicing in the streets with dance and song. The contrast was astounding and spiritually maddening. Before the service began, I announced to the "mourners for Jerusalem": "The Jews in Jerusalem are presently jubilant." I was uncertain about whether this meant that identifying with Jewish defeat and suffering, and mourning for the past, had now become meaningless. Mourning, after the liberation of Jerusalem, seemed to me like the case of a parent who continues praying for a child to get well even after the child's recovery because he or she fell in love with the prayer. All I knew then was that my task was to tell my congregation of a reality that could not be easily contained within the confines of the story of Jewish suffering.

Fearing that Jews would lose the powerful significance of the experience of the Six-Day War, I went enthusiastically to my Rav (teacher), Rabbi Joseph B. Soloveitchik, with this request: "Proclaim a religious festival; proclaim God's revelatory presence in history! Must God be revealed only in stories? Can we not celebrate the living God of our directly felt redemption?"

R. Soloveitchik responded by referring to a talmudic passage that says that the festival of Hanukkah, which celebrates the Maccabean victory and the miracle of lights, was not proclaimed immediately after these wondrous events, but rather only in the following year (B.T. *Shabbat* 21b). Pointing out the significance of "the following year," R. Soloveitchik counseled me to wait and not to react in the heat of excitement.

His sobriety and restraint were out of tune with the enthusiasm and passion I felt as a result of the experience of liberation. I passionately wished to respond religiously to events, whereas he chose to be satisfied with worship mediated by halakhic sobriety.

Shortly afterward, in December 1971, I left my pulpit and, with my family, went to settle in Israel. After living in Israel, I rediscovered the age-old experience of Jewish history: uncertainty, loneliness, isolation, and the concern for survival. In contrast to the triumphant experience of redemption following the Six-Day War, after the Yom Kippur War I rediscovered the tragic dimension of Jewish history. I felt like writing to R. Soloveitchik and saying, "Perhaps you were right. We must wait for 'the following year' before giving an enthusiastic religious response to events in history."

This haunting thought continues to influence my approach to Judaism. On one hand, the living God of Judaism is revealed in Halakhah, in the disciplined religiosity of the normative framework of Judaism. On the other hand, the reality of present-day Israel mediates the living God of the Torah and places Jews within the context of a living community's active response to God's involvement in their history. Choosing either option exclusively is dangerous. To focus attention solely on a living God whom you believe is acting in history leads to a manic-depressive syndrome: one day God is your liberator; the next day, your enemy. On the other hand, choosing the safety of a traditional halakhic orientation that perceives God in the ancient story empties contemporary history of its evocative religious power. Is the Jewish presence in Israel similar to the Jewish presence in the United States, Canada, or Europe, or does the Jewish presence in Israel somehow mediate the God of the covenant for contemporary Jews?

My approach to contemporary images of traditional Judaism moves between these two poles. In choosing to make the reality of Israel revelatory and to sense God in the vicissitudes of history, I gave up the security of the story. Nevertheless, I did not adopt a messianic posture or abandon the realism of the halakhic (legal) mind. I cannot return to biblical immediacy. I live in Israel as a Jew in the spirit of the talmudic tradition who, nevertheless, is open to the events of history as potential organizing moments mediating the living presence of God. In participating in the rebuilding of a nation, I do not feel compelled to announce the beginning of redemption. I have no theology of history, nor do I consider the rebirth of Israel a providential event ushering in a new messianic era in history.

In contrast to Yeshayahu Leibowitz, I respond with religious enthusiasm to our nation's rebirth without claiming (as he suggests) a knowledge of or belief in a divine blueprint for history. I make no historical judgments in the spirit of the biblical prophets.

Mine is a logic of human responses, not of metaphysical truth claims.

Three responses to the rebirth of Israel stand in contrast to the outlook I am advocating:

1. There are those in the Orthodox Jewish community who regard Israel as a spiritual danger, insofar as the rebirth of Israel threatens to undermine the sacred story of God's intervention in Israel's history. According to this point of view, history (i.e., symbolic history) must be safeguarded, and we must forever live in anticipation of God's decision to have mercy on His people and to create a modern Passover drama. Present history, according to this view, is opaque and insignificant. The universe we inhabit is bounded by "the four cubits of Halakhah." History is none of our business; the Lord, when He sees fit, will invite us to reenter history (albeit a new history).

   The practical consequences of this viewpoint include barricading one's subcommunity off from the broader community, including those Orthodox Jews who view Israel positively. Television, newspapers, secular education, and universities, not to mention interaction with other points of view and cultural traditions, are dangerous foreign influences to be shunned. The walls of separation must be extended higher and higher. The task is to safeguard the purity of the traditional belief in messianism. Nothing must change. You pray and dress in Jerusalem in the Middle East as Jews did two hundred years ago in the wintry climate of Eastern Europe. Nothing must change, because nothing has changed.

2. Another response to Israel is based on a particular interpretation of the course of history. It stems from the teachings of Rabbi Abraham Isaac Kook, the first Ashkenazi

Chief Rabbi during the British Mandate in Palestine. According to this view, the secularism of the Zionists who rejected traditional Judaism reveals the cunning of the Divine mind in furthering the plan of redemptive history. Israel is the beginning of the end. The rebirth of the nation of Israel and the eschatological realization of the dreams of countless generations are but two stages of the same process. Those who believe in the wisdom of *realpolitik* and are concerned about how the nations of the world react to Israeli policies are not unlike the fool in biblical literature: they fail to detect God's providential presence. The Bible is the touchstone of reality. You consult the Bible to determine Israel's borders and to prepare the biblical home for God, Who is about to reenter history triumphantly. In the end, we are pawns in the divine game plan; the great destiny of the Jewish people is about to be revealed, and no power on earth can change this in any way.

3. The third response, characteristic of ultra-secularists, celebrates the "normalization" of Jewish society in Israel, including the abolition of a Jewish covenantal consciousness. "To be like all the nations" can become a motto for an indiscriminate acceptance of contemporary modern culture and mores. Pride in Jewish "normalcy" reflects the danger of embracing contemporary history totally, without a traditional historical identity to provide a critical posture toward modernity.

The outlook I am proposing does not celebrate normalcy and assimilation, nor does it announce the imminent eschatological triumph of Judaism. Rather, it attempts to be in history and to accept responsibility for building a total society, while retaining the sobriety of certain features of the talmudic religious sensibility. This approach is, I believe, rabbinic, without a mystical or biblical organic consciousness and without an eschatological dimension. My picture of a genuinely religious person is one who is not averse to getting hands dirty; one who does not await divine intervention but who experiences God's presence in efforts to discharge the responsibilities he or she feels for the welfare of a total society. No aspect of social involvement is beyond the domain of service of God: "In all your ways, know Him." In extending the concept of service of God into countless areas of social behavior, we are, so to speak, breaking open the story to the flow of reality. We allow the rhythms of modern history to enter into our normative relationship with God.

The exposure of a total people and its tradition to modernity is filled with great opportunities as well as risks. The reality of Israel has created the opportunity to educate and to open Jews to Judaism as a way of life. Failure to inspire those who seek a Jewish content for their communal existence would reveal the weakness and the intellectual bankruptcy of contemporary religious leadership. Secular Zionism has created the social and political conditions for the entire Jewish people to renew its ancient covenant at Sinai.

One aspect of the significance of Zionism for the modern Jew lies in its enabling us to rediscover the vitality of Torah as a way of life. The religious value of events in history is measured not solely in terms of their relationship to a future messianic age, but by how they expand the area of responsibility for the implementation of mitzvot. Unlike the diaspora, Israel contains a public domain for which Jews, as Jews, are responsible. In Israel, Jews have the opportunity to bear witness to the sanctifying power of Torah in the mundane marketplaces of life.

I do not subscribe to the belief in linear progress in history. What the tradition asks of Jews is that in each generation they renew the covenantal moment of Sinai. Though I am ignorant of how contemporary Israel is related to the *end* of history, I do know how the rebirth of Israel is related to the *beginnings* of covenantal history.

Israel provides a framework for recapturing the spirit of the fundamental organizing principles of Jewish spirituality: Creation, Exodus, mitzvot, and the Promised Land. My concern with using past models to interpret present conditions grows out of my belief that Israel offers Jews an unprecedented opportunity to regenerate the primary roots of Judaism. As a traditional Jew I am grateful to Zionism and to Israel for renewing the significance of the beginning, not necessarily for bringing about the end.

My search for a way to renew the Sinai covenant leads first of all to "Egypt"; in other words, to solidarity with a suffering people seeking liberation. Solitary lonely individuals with no sense of community cannot appropriate the spiritual way of life that emanates from Sinai. Judaism is unique in that rather than beginning with a leap of faith, it demands a leap of identification with a people and its history.

The internalization of "We were slaves to Pharaoh in Egypt" leads, in our generation, to identification both with the tragic dimensions of the Holocaust and with the struggle for the peace and security of the State of Israel. This sense of solidarity with peoplehood implies that love and concern for all Jews must be independent of faith commitments and levels of mitzvah observance.

According to the Midrash, the Jewish slaves in Egypt had abandoned the covenantal faith of Abraham. Participation in the suffering and the yearnings for security of the Jewish people imbues the solitary individual with a deep sense of collectivity. The "I" is transformed into a "we" through participation in the historic destiny of the Jewish people.

Religious Jews who are deeply concerned about the fate of all Jews must not only share the burdens of survival but also strive to build spiritual bridges among Jews. The sense of community that precedes mitzvah must also influence one's approach to the observance of the commandments. Halakhah is addressed not to the singular individual but primarily to the individual rooted in the historical destiny of a community.

The quest for community ought not to be expressed solely in terms of survival. Religious educators who stress the centrality of Jewish peoplehood must strive to formulate an approach to mitzvah that would enable their students to share a common spiritual language with the rest of the Jewish people. The need to formulate a shared spiritual language is most evident in the State of Israel, where the common struggle for survival loses much of its meaning in the absence of belief in the significance of Jewish communal existence.

Providing spiritual understanding for Jews in the modern world is not an easy task. Whereas in the past we shared a common framework of religious authority, today the daily lives of most Jews are not organized by the principles of Halakhah. How, then, shall we teach Talmud, mitzvot, and Halakhah to a community that does not acknowledge the basic presuppositions of traditional normative Halakhah? What does a believer share with a so-called nonbeliever?

My years in the rabbinate taught me to seek ways of talking about Judaism that would be meaningful to Jews of various backgrounds. Although I had been an Orthodox rabbi in the Bronx and in Montreal for seventeen years, my congregations were made up of people of many different backgrounds and levels of observance and belief. During my rabbinic training at Yeshivah University, I was taught to answer halakhic questions. The details of the laws of *kashrut* (Jewish dietary laws) and similar mitzvot were studied with rigor and devotion. Upon entering the rabbinate, I was anxious to answer the great halakhic questions of the Jewish community. I waited with anticipation, but to my dismay there were no questioners. Finally I realized that the role of the rabbi was not so much to provide answers as to create questions.

I found that people were not engaged with Judaism; it did not demand their serious attention. It was not, in William James's words, a "live option." I realized then that my task was to fight indifference and to convince Jews to confront the Judaic tradition as an option that could not be easily dismissed.

My years in the rabbinate also taught me that a teacher must begin where the students are. The task of the teacher is to listen before speaking, to hear and to share in the deep estrangement of Jews from their tradition, to enter that alienation and try to understand its roots. I had to postpone my answers in order to hear the new questions.

Maimonides' approach to Torah as expressed in *The Guide of the Perplexed* has been a permanent source of inspiration and guidance for me. In Maimonides I beheld a master halakhist, whose authoritative halakhic works have guided Jews for generations, who was prepared to understand many mitzvot of the Torah in the light of the particular historical conditions of the community of slaves who left Egypt (see *Guide*, III:32). God, says Maimonides, speaks in the language of human beings and takes into account the lived reality of people when formulating norms and directives. God listens carefully and sympathetically before speaking.

In addressing a generation estranged from and indifferent to traditional frameworks of Jewish spirituality, one must not begin by demanding a leap of faith or a commitment to mitzvah observance. To a generation that has lost an appreciation of the significance of mitzvot, one should not emphasize a theocentric orientation to Halakhah. Rather than articulating the dogmatic foundations of Judaism, I focus on how the practices and conceptual frameworks of Halakhah can influence a person's character and perspective on life. I am not concerned with proving that God created the universe in six days, but rather with understanding the human implications of accepting the doctrine of a creational universe. Belief in creation leads one to reject passivity and to adopt an active, self-reliant attitude to history. According to R. Soloveitchik, the idea of God the Creator serves as a model for the Jew to imitate. One must imitate God not only by internalizing His moral attributes but also by becoming an active and responsible agent attempting to perfect an imperfect reality.

I try to correct the mistaken notion that halakhically observant Jews are naive, arrogant, and spiritually complacent. The demand that individuals assume responsibility for community cannot be met if people are afraid to fail. One who cannot tolerate the thought of failure, but requires constant success in order to confirm one's dignity and worth, cannot live with the innumerable demands of Halakhah. One who seeks absolute certainty will not find comfort in a spiritual tradition whose response to the disagreements between the schools of Hillel and Shammai was that both schools of thought were the words of the living God.

Rabbinic Judaism was fully aware of the various risks that Jewish communal spirituality entailed. When one strives to build one's spiritual life within a living community, one must give up viewing religion in terms of salvation of the soul; one must be spiritually prepared to take great risks and make compromises. If one does not do that, one cannot build a relationship to God within the framework of community. In Judaism, love for God must lead to a love for real people. One who can love only an idealized community of the elect remains the victim of messianic abstractions, unable to embrace the community of real Jews in this imperfect world.

The joy of Torah emerges from feelings of adequacy, responsibility, and solidarity with a community. The description of the community of Israel in the Bible is for some theologians a shocking account of rebellion and sin; for me, it is an inspiring testimony to the fact that God gave the Torah to human beings and not to angels. The continuous renewal of divine demands, despite repeated human failures, indicates that God did not operate with an idealized concept of the covenantal Jew. The giving of the Torah to a people who were prepared to return to slavery in Egypt the first time they were thirsty fills me with feelings of deep joy—fragile human beings are deemed capable of becoming responsible and mature. The revelation of the Torah reflects God's belief in the human capacity to obey the mitzvot. Rabbinic Judaism's expansion and elaboration of Halakhah further illustrate the belief in the community's ability to realize the historic task of becoming a holy people. The joy of mitzvah stems from recognizing that God is prepared to give limited, imperfect human beings a great covenantal task. The election of Israel testifies to the willingness of the Teacher of Torah to take a stiff-necked, rebellious people and to educate them, step by step, toward the ideal of becoming "a nation of priests and a holy people." The continuous normative authority of Torah confirms God's continuous love and patience for His people.

We may hope that the shift in emphasis from dogmatic theology, leaps of faith, and eschatological pronouncements to an analysis of the significance of religious concepts will provide the ground for a shared spiritual language for a society seeking to understand the covenantal foundations of Judaism.

Modern Jewish history has created strong existential bonds among Jews. Standing before the *kotel* (the Western Wall), one hears the echoes of Jewish hopes resounding throughout history: "Next year in Jerusalem!" When one walks through the streets of Jerusalem today, one is accompanied by all those Jews throughout history who yearned for and believed that one day Jews would return to Jerusalem. Israel is home for all Jews, both of the present and of the past. The urgent question is whether, in coming home, "children," "parents," and "grandparents" can share a common spiritual language so that Judaism can once again become a live and compelling option.

PART I

FAMILY AND MITZVAH WITHIN
AN INTERPRETIVE TRADITION

JUDAISM AS AN
INTERPRETIVE TRADITION

A LIVING TRADITION can provide a person with a critical perspective on contemporary social reality by pointing to alternative possibilities and by providing a sense of distance that enables one to evaluate current beliefs and practices. Being anchored to a tradition that predates modernity, such as Judaism, gives one access to an alternative vision of human possibilities. It thus counteracts the ideological prejudice of modernity that equates "the now" with "the good," and "the latest" with the important and valuable.

Yet, tradition is itself challenged when people become aware of new values and possibilities in the surrounding culture, which invariably affect their moral intuitions and attitudes. Morality does not develop in abstraction from the lived reality into which human beings are born. Our moral sense and conscience are nurtured by life—be it social, economic, or cultural—and not necessarily by books and formal education.

I myself feel this kind of paradoxical relationship to modern culture, this complicated alternation between attraction and repulsion, affinity and estrangement. On one level, I embrace modern culture; on another level, I am often critical of and repelled by it. I relate to modernity with both openness and reservation. Both moves define my soul. I am very deeply rooted in the classical talmudic tradition, which was perpetuated in the modern world by the yeshiva (talmudic academy) Torah culture. I thus can be a kindred spirit with the Orthodox Haredi community in Jerusalem, the "black hat community" who have chosen the culture of the *shtetl* over modernity. At times, I can truly say that I share their love of and devotion to Torah, their music, their spiritual yearnings. Yet, at other times I can join the ranks of the Zionist rebels who have rejected traditional Judaism. My soul moves in multiple and diverse directions.

While this phenomenon is a natural consequence of the interaction of different cultural traditions at any time in history, the modern situation makes a person particularly susceptible to the destabilizing effects of competing cultures and values. The modern world, as distinct from some other periods of human history, is characterized by a widespread ambiguity of moral insights and attitudes. Conflict and disagreement characterize the domain of values and human options. There is hardly any universal consensus about moral beliefs and judgments. There are deep conflicts among individuals and cultures about the meaning and role of gender, of family, and of the political, legal, and religious institutions of modern life.

This situation differs dramatically from the medieval world, where Aristotelian philosophy was considered the most perfect intellectual tradition available to human beings. Maimonides felt no qualms about reinterpreting all anthropomorphic biblical texts as metaphors because of his belief that corporeality was incompatible with what the unity of God entails. He would have been prepared to reinterpret the biblical story of creation if

4

Aristotle had provided a valid demonstrative proof for the eternity of the universe.

> For if creation in time were demonstrated—if only as Plato understands creation—all the overhasty claims made to us on this point by the philosophers would become void. In the same way, if the philosophers would succeed in demonstrating eternity as Aristotle understands it, the Law as a whole would become void, and a shift to other opinions would take place. (*Guide of the Perplexed*, II:26)

Our moral discourse today is filled with ambiguity, conflict, and uncertainty. And this is what makes the issue of reinterpretation of the tradition in light of modern moral insights so problematic. Ethical dilemmas in the modern practice of medicine, for example, indicate the uncertainty and indeterminacy of applying the values of respect for human life and dignity in concrete situations. How does one measure "quality of life"?

Even though we lack intellectual certainty, I would argue that our situation is not unique or without precedent in the history of the Jewish tradition. The interpretive tradition, which defined Judaism in the past, was acquainted with ambiguity and controversy. In fact, rabbinic Judaism can best be described as a bold interpretive culture amidst disagreement. I shall discuss this claim on two levels: the legal and the theological. The former involves halakhic thought and practice, Judaism's central concern as a religious and cultural phenomenon, while the latter relates to a theology of history, or more precisely, a theology of exile.

How does the tradition understand exile, and how can it respond to Zionism, a movement aimed at overcoming the reality and psychology of exile? After explaining the meaning of Judaism as an interpretive tradition from both legal and theological perspectives, I shall defend my characterization of the rebirth of the State of Israel in terms of "covenantal renewal" and of other such concepts that, I believe, reflect the deep structure of Judaism.

RABBINIC CULTURE:
THE TEXT AS THE WORD OF GOD

The idea of love of God is often contrasted with the legalism of "Pharisaic Judaism" in terms of the spontaneity and passion associated with the religious experience. The terms *religious* and *halakhic* are thus differentiated with reference to whether God or law is at the center of one's religious concerns. Before evaluating this religious stereotype, I would like to draw attention to Psalm 119, where God and the word of God are often indistinguishable. The writer's love for and worship of God are channeled toward God's commandments.

> I have turned to You with all my heart;
> do not let me stray from Your commandments. (10)
> I am racked with grief;
> sustain me in accordance with Your word. (28)
> I shall have an answer for those who taunt me,
> for I have put my trust in Your word. (42)
> Do not utterly take the truth away from my mouth,
> for I have put my hope in Your rules. (43)
> Teach me good sense and knowledge,
> for I have put my trust in Your commandments. (66)
> Those who fear You will see me and rejoice,
> for I have put my hope in Your word. (74)
> May Your mercy reach me, that I might live,
> for Your teaching is my delight. (77)

I long for Your deliverance;
I hope for Your word. (81)
I will never neglect Your precepts,
for You have preserved my life through them. (93)
I am Yours; save me!
For I have turned to Your precepts. (94)
My flesh creeps from fear of You;
I am in awe of Your rulings. (120)
I rise before dawn and cry for help;
I hope for Your word. (147)

According to the letter and spirit of this text, the word of
God is interchangeable with God. Torah, therefore, conveys the
immediacy of God's presence, as if it were an incarnation of God's
will and love. The language of worship, which in other biblical
contexts is directed toward God,

Pour out your heart like water before the face of the
Lord; lift up your hands (*se'i kapaiyich*) toward him for
the life of your young children. (Lamentations 2:19)

is here directed, with no less intensity, toward the commandments:

And so will I lift up my hands (*ve'esa kapai*) unto Your
commandments, which I love; and I will meditate on
Your statutes. (Ps. 119:48)

This perspective is necessary for an understanding of the
passional religious dimension of rabbinic culture. When you learn
Torah, you "meditate" on the divine word, you, so to speak,
suspend belief in the written medium separating you from the
author of the word and imagine yourself talking with and hearing

God directly. You therefore experience the existential immediacy of being in the presence of God. The author of this psalm relates to the word and to the law in the same personal and emotive language that religious poets usually reserve for impassioned references to God. The speaker feels "hope in the word," is "comforted" and "revived" by God's laws, and is able to "rejoice in," "delight in," and "love" the commandments.

The word, then, at the deepest, most fundamental level of Torah culture, embodies the living reality of God. Rejoicing in the word is rejoicing in God. And, contrary to the standard interpretation of Paul's description of mitzvah and Halakhah (Jewish law), the phrase that best describes the essence of rabbinic religiosity is not the "burden of the law" but "*simcha shel mitzvah*," the joy of mitzvah. As in Psalm 119, the law was not considered to be a burden in any pejorative sense, because it mediated and expressed God's love and concern. In the daily liturgy, Jews declare, "You have loved the house of Israel with everlasting love," and then proceed to substantiate this theological statement with "You have taught us Torah and precepts, laws and judgments." The prayer then concludes with

> Therefore, Lord our God, when we lie down and when we rise up we will speak of Your laws, and rejoice in the words of Your Torah and in Your precepts forevermore.

God's love is embodied in the giving of the Torah. Torah and mitzvot convey divine love and are thus a source of joy and comfort. One of the first benedictions traditional Jews say every morning refers to their being commanded "to be engaged in the words of the Torah," and, following that, they express this hope:

8

Lord our God, make the word of Your Torah sweet in our mouth and in the mouth of Your people, the house of Israel, so that we and our descendants and the descendants of Your people, the house of Israel, may all know Your name and study Your Torah for its own sake. Blessed are You, O Lord, who teaches the Torah to Your people Israel.

"Learning," the talmudic involvement with the interpretation of the law, is misrepresented by such derogatory labels as "pharisaic legalism" or "rabbinic casuistry" that totally ignore the phenomenological experience of fascination with and rejoicing in the richness and complexity of the divine word and, by implication, of the divine reality. The biblical text is understood to contain multiple layers of meaning and subtlety. Torah, no less than nature, conveys the immensity and richness of the divine reality.

It is no wonder, therefore, that not only the semantic significance of the words themselves but also their syntactic and even their physical form became objects of interpretation. Rabbi Akiva was noted for his imaginative, ingenious interpretations not only of the meaning of the words and sentences of the biblical text but also of the *tagim* (crownlets atop the Hebrew letters) and the *ethim* (particles of speech indicative of the objective case).

This seemingly extreme example of rabbinic biblical exegesis was not the result of a philological obsession but reflects the specific religious context in which the biblical text was understood. Rabbi Akiva read the Bible as an intimate love letter. He read and reread the words; he, so to speak, felt the parchment and examined the handwriting, the shapes of the letters, and the marks on the page, always looking for signs and clues to hidden meanings and secret messages.

9

To use modern terminology, the medium became a part of the message, conveying the rich and subtle complexity of the divine word. Consequently, the term legal text only partially and incompletely describes the text that the Torah scholar scrutinized. Even today, in yeshivot, academies of Torah learning, the student sings the words of the text and, on the holiday of Simchat Torah, dances ecstatically with the scrolls of the law. Enigmatic legal cases and narratives are recited with a characteristic chant and bodily sway as the talmudic student struggles to decipher the mysteries of the divine text.

In order to understand this interpretive tradition from within, one must go beyond its hermeneutics and methodologies to the distinctive mode of consciousness of this text-oriented worldview, where the presence of God was filtered through an engagement with the words of Torah.

It is highly significant that the most mystical and religiously impassioned figure of this tradition, the person who claimed that the love poem *Song of Songs* was the Holy of Holies of the Jewish canon, the man who later died a martyr's death while proclaiming, "Hear, O Israel, the Lord our God, the Lord is One," was that same hero of the interpretive tradition, Rabbi Akiva. In this tradition, textual analysis and interpretation are informed by the same religious ethos that produced heroic commitment, devotion, piety, and mystic passion.

One can try to explain the inner religious and theological significance of such a culture at this stage of Jewish history by saying that despite the reality of defeat and exile, rabbinic Judaism refused to succumb to the sense of being abandoned by God. Instead, it created a culture that gave meaning to the idea of continuous revelation. In contrast to Martin Buber's notion of spontaneous, existential encounters with the eternal "Thou," rabbinic "formalism" counteracted God's apparent absence from history by turning the text into a carrier of God's ever-present concern. In the interpretive tradition, God never abandons you, because His word is always with you.

> When ten people sit together and occupy themselves with the Torah, the Shekhinah [divine presence] abides among them, as it is said: "God stands in the godly congregation." (Ps. 82:1) Whence do we know that the same applies even to five?...Whence do we know that the same applies even to three?...Whence do we know that the same applies even to two?...Whence do we know that the same applies even to one? It is said: "In every place where I have My name mentioned I will come to you and bless you." (Mishnah *Avot* 3:7)

INTERPRETATION AND CONCEPTS OF GOD

If, as I have just tried to show, the reality of God is mediated by Torah study, then there is bound to be a relationship between your approach to interpretation and your conception of God. How you relate to the text is affected by how you relate to God. And if interpretive strategies are in some ways outgrowths of a person's conception of God, then one would expect to discover that the same fundamental religious paradigms that inform one's approach to God and revelation also inform one's approaches to human understanding and textual analysis.

The organizing metaphors that filter and shape one's sense of the Divine also influence the epistemology and hermeneutics that inform one's reading of the biblical text. The scope of my claim will extend beyond the literary and legal levels of the reading of texts to the broader area of the "reading of history," an area of life no less affected by these same modes of thought and experience.

The biblical narrative of Abraham is, for example, a source of two different organizing images of God. (The worldview that evolved with the appearance of political Zionism is, as I shall argue later, a third option, which is both opposed to and continuous with these fundamental motifs in the Jewish tradition.) There are thus two classical models of religious consciousness that can claim the biblical narrative of Abraham as their source. The first is expressed in the bold conversation between God and Abraham concerning the divine decision to destroy the city of Sodom:

> Will You sweep away the innocent along with the guilty? What if there should be fifty innocent within the city;...Far be it from You to do such a thing, to bring death upon the innocent as well as the guilty, so that innocent and guilty fare alike. Far be it from You! Shall not the Judge of all the earth deal justly? (Gen. 18:23–25)

Given that there was no prior revelation instructing Abraham about the meaning or the rules of applying the concepts of innocence, guilt, and justice, Abraham must be seen as appealing to some generally accepted moral mode of discourse that allowed, or rather, compelled him to exclaim: "Far be it from You! Shall not the Judge of all the earth deal justly?"

Abraham's appeal to principles of morality and compassion reflects his overwhelming sense of their inherent normative force and validity. He can judge God's intended actions without "quoting scripture" or authoritative tradition because of a deep intuitive sense of justice and love, which neither God nor human being may violate. While for some the Christian "natural law" tradition is helpful in explaining such theologically independent moral intuitions, I maintain that the text itself reveals the integrity and consistency of Abraham as a deeply religious and ethical personality. The words "Here I venture to speak to my Lord, I who am but dust and ashes" (18:27) are not those of a Promethean challenger to God but of a lover of God, a humble and reverent religious personality with a strong sense of moral autonomy. In this context, moral autonomy is not an expression of hubris or of the need to assert human independence, but is compatible with and integral to a religious consciousness that believes that the God you worship would never violate your fundamental moral intuitions of justice and of love.

This biblical paradigm contrasts dramatically with another narrative account of Abraham, which presents a radically different model of the meaning of religious life and of human understanding and independence. After being promised by God that his desperate hope for an heir would be realized—"None but your very own issue shall be your heir" (Gen. 15:4); "Sarah your wife shall bear you a son, and you shall name him Isaac; and I will maintain My covenant with him as an everlasting covenant for his offspring to come" (17:19)—Abraham is told: "Take your son, your favored one, Isaac, whom you love, and go to the land of Moriah, and offer him there as a burnt offering on one of the heights which I will point out to you" (Gen. 22:2). Offering no explanation, let alone justification, God orders Abraham to forget past promises, hopes, and natural expectations and to sacrifice his beloved son: his long-awaited heir and the carrier of his legacy and covenantal history. Does the divine command not violate Abraham's moral intuitions, his fatherly sensibilities and feelings, and even God's own promise?

Given the earlier account of Sodom, one would have expected Abraham to respond by pleading for the life of his innocent child. Instead he is silent. He expresses no argument, or even a request for an explanation, let alone a justification. He simply obeys without uttering a word. His response is one of total submission and unconditional surrender. According to the rabbis, Isaac also knew about his intended sacrifice, and he too went along compliantly.

The God of Abraham, therefore, takes two very different forms in the book of Genesis: a God who demands total surrender to His command and a God who invites independent moral critique and judgment. These two paradigms have informed religious life as well as interpretation and exegesis throughout Jewish history. For many teachers from the time of the Talmud to the modern period, including Yeshayahu Leibowitz and my own teacher, Rabbi Joseph B. Soloveitchik, the *akedah*, the binding of Isaac, was the dominant paradigm of religious life and thought. For them, the survival and continuity of the tradition require the unconditional surrender and loyalty that the *akedah* represents. To be claimed by God, I must be willing to sacrifice my intellect and intuition, to give up everything I know and cherish as a human being, in deference and obedience to the word of God.

Contemporary critiques of those who appeal to moral considerations in questions of religious practice and change often invoke an *akedah* mode of reasoning, arguing (or implicitly presupposing) that religious life would lose all credibility if submission and surrender were any less than total. The belief that "if you change anything, everything will collapse" owes its logic and conviction to the silence of Abraham in the binding of Isaac story.

Yet, Abraham, in pleading for Sodom, felt that God was not beyond his own understanding of moral argument and persuasion. This other paradigm, therefore, says: "Bring your moral intuitions, your subjective sense of dignity and justice into your understanding of the reality of God." Not only does it not threaten or undermine religious consciousness, but it is actually necessary for recognizing the validity and applicability of the divine command.

INTERPRETIVE STRATEGIES AND THE RELIGIOUS IMAGINATION

Echoes of the two religious models derived from Abraham's two responses to God in the Sodom and the *akedah* narratives are discernible in different interpretive strategies in the talmudic tradition, as for example in the following interpretive analysis of the biblical law of the stubborn and rebellious son:

> If a man has a stubborn and rebellious son who does not heed his father or mother and does not obey them even after they discipline him, his mother and father shall take hold of him and bring him out to the elders of his town and the public place of his community. They shall say to the elders of his town, "This son of ours is disloyal and defiant; he does not heed us. He is a glutton and a drunkard." Thereupon the men of his town shall stone him to death. Thus you will sweep out evil from your midst: all Israel will hear and be afraid. (Deut. 21:18–21)

The Talmud in Sanhedrin (72a) reads this text with the kind of free, seemingly playful, yet intensely serious attention I described at the beginning of this essay. At what point, the rabbis ask, does one become liable as "a stubborn and rebellious son"? In other words, what exactly did the guilty son described in Deuteronomy do? He was, they answer, citing the words of the parents in the above text, "a glutton and a drunkard." He ate this kind and amount of meat; he drank wine of such and such a vintage. He had, as they then proceed to describe, the biblical equivalent of a serious teenage alcohol and drug problem. His sin, in other words, was not total rebellion but a destructive addiction to eating and drinking and to related delinquent behavior.

But then, asks one of the talmudic teachers in rhetorical fashion,

> It has been taught: R. Jose the Galilean said: Did the Torah decree that the rebellious son shall be brought before *beth din* [court] and stoned merely because he ate a *tartemar* [weight measure] of meat and drank a *log* [liquid measure] of wine? (Sanhedrin 72a)

In contrast to a biblical text that could be taken to mean that parental control over children was as absolute as over property and other possessions, the rabbis, in light of their assumption that parental authority over children must be limited, insist that the law in question be justified by weightier reasons than parental prerogative or by gluttony and drunkenness. The talmudic discussion continues:

> But the Torah foresaw his ultimate destiny. For at the end, after dissipating his father's wealth, he would [still] seek to satisfy his accustomed [gluttonous] wants but, being unable to do so, would go forth at the crossroads and rob. Therefore the Torah said, "Let him die while yet innocent, and let him not die guilty." (72a)

Although an earlier opinion had invoked an *akedah* mode of argument—"it [the text] is a divine decree"—to rule out an interpretation of biblical law that went beyond its literal meaning, this opinion alludes to suggestive aspects of the language of the text to bring broader social and moral considerations to bear on the issue at hand. First, the precise wording of the question: "Did the Torah decree that the rebellious son shall be brought before *beth din*" indicates the existence of a changed biblical social reality where parental authority was no longer absolute and independent of social institutions such as the courts ("They shall say to *the elders of his town*"). This requirement stands in sharp contrast to the situation described in Genesis, where Judah, when learning of his daughter-in-law Tamar's alleged harlotry, proclaims: "Bring her out, and let her be burned" (Gen. 38:24). Judah's paternal status gave him the peremptory authority of "judge and executioner" over his family. By drawing attention to this subtle exegetical point, the talmudic interpreter adopts a strategy aimed at deriving a morally defensible interpretation from an otherwise morally questionable biblical law.

According to the talmudic reference to the dangerous nature of the delinquency in question, the crime for which the son was so severely punished was not only rebellion against parents but also what were believed to be the inevitable consequences of his current behavior. He is so addicted to his destructive habits and way of life that it is better for him to die now, while still relatively meritorious, than later, after he becomes a compulsive thief, murderer, and enemy of society. It is not, therefore, parental authority that is being so zealously protected but the social fabric of society.

This interpretive strategy is then extended to argue that only if the son's habitual behavior is of the type and intensity that invariably leads to the aforementioned criminal consequences is the law implemented. Here, then, is an interpretive move that preserves the legislative force of the text but shifts the context and meaning of the law away from the authoritative hierarchy of the family to the broader framework of social order and welfare. A third and more radical interpretive strategy makes the implementation of the law virtually impossible:

There never has been a "stubborn and rebellious son" and there never will be.... R. Simeon said: "Because one eats a *tartemar* of meat and drinks half a *log* of Italian wine, shall his father and mother have him stoned? But it never happened and never will happen. Why then was this law written?—That you may study it and receive reward." (71a)

The talmudic discussion supporting this remarkable conclusion consists of a series of legal qualifications making implementation all but impossible. Both parents must be present at precisely the same time, each must resemble the other in voice, in height, and in other ways that stretch the probability of implementation toward the zero point. Finally the law is declared to be a theoretical case worthy of jurisprudential analysis ("Study it and you will receive reward"), but as a law to be implemented, never!

There are, then, three different responses to a text that was considered *prima facie* morally problematic. One teacher said categorically: "This is what the text says and this text is the authoritative word of God. Therefore, put aside your moral intuitions." The second view mitigates the dissonance between our moral intuitions and our commitment and love for the text by shifting the point and rationale of the law from parental authority to the order and welfare of society in general. The third interpretation moves the problematic law out of the realm of actual practice. The stoning of the stubborn and rebellious son, like several other "difficult" cases of biblical law, never will be (and never were!) implemented, even though they warrant careful analysis and discussion.

These different interpretive strategies reflect different evaluations of the relative weight of traditional texts compared with our own moral intuitions and with our understanding of the particular social reality in which Torah law is to be implemented. Some talmudic teachers felt that the authority of the family was primary and that punishing such a child was both feasible and justified. Others felt that rebellion within the confines of the family was not currently a threat to society in general and that parents should not have authority over the lives of their children.

It is clear that this law was not universally regarded to be a potentially "bad law," yet it was sufficiently controversial and problematic to inspire a rich diversity of interpretive possibilities. Those who chose to neutralize the practical impact of this law realized that their position was not self-evident or without legitimate alternatives. Other moral arguments had to be taken into account—for example, those that focused on the dangers to the family unit and to social stability, pointing to the relationship between the weakening of parental authority and the erosion of social order and stability.

One should bear in mind that we are dealing with a traditional society where reverence for parents was compared and even equated with reverence for God. The logic of "spare the rod, spoil the child" coupled with a family ethic based on a disciplined, hierarchical parent–child relationship (you weren't allowed to sit in your parents' regular seats or to interrupt them when they spoke) must have created a strong case for linking parental authority with the stability of the social and theological superstructures.

Yet, there were others who were willing to compromise on the formal conditions of respect for parents by allowing individual choice to determine how parental authority would be expressed. There was a legal opinion that permitted a parent (but not a king) to forgo the honor due him or her, *mochel al kvodo*, thus giving parents the freedom to determine the amount of formality and authority in their relationship with their children. In other words, the interpretive strategies that emerged in response to the law of the "stubborn and rebellious son" probably reflect the same social and moral attitudes and opinions that must have informed other discussions about the nature and future of the family during the talmudic period.

And yet, I am suggesting that these talmudic scholars allowed themselves the right to interpret according to their judgments, knowing full well that their views were less than necessary and self-evident and that there were risks in accepting the positions they advocated. It is often instructive to characterize the full implications of an argued point of view by clearly specifying the implicit risks they entail. In our case you could say that one group—those most inspired by an *akedah* religious mentality—might have warned against the danger of undermining divine authority, while their opponents might have argued, in the spirit of Abraham's defense of Sodom, that the punishment did not fit the crime. The strict traditionalists might have shot back: "How dare you question God's wisdom?" only to be countered by an equally earnest statement of religious commitment: "God's laws must reflect, in some way, my understanding of reality and morality. Not sacrificing what I believe to be fair and just is not a violation of my belief in God or in divine authority. My moral intuitions have been nurtured by the study of Torah!"

TOLERANCE AND AMBIGUITY IN THE INTERPRETIVE TRADITION

In contrast to the Bible, the Talmud is filled with disagreements and differences of opinion. The Talmud itself was aware of the problem this might create for people seeking religious certainty.

> "The masters of assemblies": these are the disciples of the wise, who sit in manifold assemblies and occupy themselves with the Torah, some pronouncing unclean

20

and others pronouncing clean, some prohibiting and others permitting, some disqualifying and others declaring fit.

Should a person say: How in these circumstances shall I learn Torah? Therefore the text says: "All of them are given from one Shepherd." One God gave them; one leader uttered them from the mouth of the Lord of all creation, blessed be He; for it is written: "And God spoke all these words." Also make your ear like the hopper and get yourself a perceptive heart to understand the words of those who pronounce unclean and the words of those who pronounce clean, the words of those who prohibit and the words of those who permit, the words of those who disqualify and the words of those who declare fit. (B.T. *Hagigah* 3b)

There is a beautiful metaphor in the Tosefta that describes the kind of religious sensibility the Talmud tried to nurture: "Make yourself a heart of many rooms and bring into it the words of the House of Shammai and the words of the House of Hillel, the words of those who declare unclean and the words of those who declare clean" (*Sotah* 7:12). In other words, become a person in whom different opinions can reside together in the very depths of your soul. Become a religious person who can live with ambiguity, who can feel religious conviction and passion without the need for simplicity and absolute certainty.

In this type of interpretive tradition, awareness of the validity of contrary positions enhances, rather than diminishes, the vitality and enthusiasm of religious commitment. So while the law may be decided according to the views of one teacher or school of thought, alternative views are not discarded as if falsified but are retained and studied and may even become law at some later date. The Mishnah or the Talmud may determine the official law by choosing among opposing views on the basis of accepted mechanisms of decision making, but they never eliminate the rich variety of opinions or diminish the creativity of the moral imagination that is able to make sense of alternative positions.

Perhaps it is owing to the specific nature of legal reasoning, which recognizes the need for and the validity of decision-making procedures to resolve disagreements (in contrast to science or philosophy, where majority rule or any other extrarational mode of determining truth is an absurdity), that the participants in a talmudic debate do not present their views as evident and necessary, i.e., as the only valid truths. It is with this in mind that the Tosefta says "make yourself a heart of many rooms" so that your heart can contain a variety of conflicting opinions.

This, then, is the distinctive legacy of the talmudic interpretative tradition: an understanding of revelation in which God loves you when you discover ambiguity in His word. He loves you for finding forty-nine ways to make this pure and forty-nine ways to make it impure. Revelation is not always "pure and simple" but may be rough and complex.

Since you may find yourselves arguing interminably, you may decide the law according to such principles as majority rule. But even if God, the Law Giver, were to intervene in a legal debate among scholars and were to reveal that this interpretation was correct or that legal formulation should become law, the rabbis would object and say: "Sorry, God. You may not interrupt and terminate discussions among students of Torah. If our minds appreciate and conceive of the ambiguity of the human situations in which your word must be implemented, you may not interfere to change our minds. Torah is not in heaven."

In other words, the religious personality this system tries to produce is able to interpret situations in multiple ways and to offer cogent arguments for opposite positions and points of view. This orientation reflects a particular kind of religious humility. What has often been portrayed as legalism and pilpulism (casuistry) is a superficial misrepresentation of the deep joy in study and fascination with the rich complexity of the Torah.

The test of excellence of the Torah scholar was the ability to read and analyze a talmudic text, to explain and defend both sides of a disagreement by offering imaginative and compelling reasons for both positions. The student's interest in and competence at reproducing both argument and counter-argument convincingly were often rooted in a genuine appreciation of the moral and intellectual complexity of the subject matter.

I would even say that there was a distinctive sense of humor that typified the classical Jewish tradition: a sense of humor—and therefore of humility—about your certainties, about what you believed "could not be otherwise." In all my years of study with Rabbi Joseph B. Soloveitchik, I never once heard him call someone a heretic or dismiss a soundly argued opinion as illegitimate. You argued, you discussed, you disagreed with intensity, but you understood that you were defending a human point of view, not the final word of God. And even then (according to the midrash), we would not hesitate to reprimand God for exceeding the limits of divine authority in the domain of halakhic debate. Revelation gives you the word of God, but the interpretive strategies necessary for implementing that word are "not in heaven."

THE INTERPRETIVE COMMUNITY AND HISTORY: THE ZIONIST CHALLENGE

The most radical situation to confront Jewish consciousness rooted in the interpretive rabbinic tradition was the emergence of Zionism in the nineteenth century. The idea of Jewish history that passed through the political-theological conceptual filter of rabbinic Judaism, especially following the trauma of the Bar Kochba revolt, taught Jews to submit to exile and political powerlessness as God's will. In contrast to the intellectual independence and theological audacity of the talmudic scholar in the academies of Torah study, the passivity of Jews in the domain of mundane politics and history was indicative of a kind of split personality insofar as Jews were educated not to ask questions or to rebel against their historical fate. The contrast between these two opposite attitudes is sharply captured in the following midrash:

> Rav Judah said in the name of Rav: "When Moses ascended on high, he found the Holy One, blessed be He, engaged in affixing coronets to the letters of the Torah. Said Moses, 'Lord of the Universe, who compels You?' He answered, 'There will arise a man, at the end of many generations, Akiva ben Joseph by name, who will spin out of each tittle heaps and heaps of laws.' 'Lord of the Universe,' said Moses, 'permit me to see him.' He replied, 'Turn you round.' Moses went and sat down at the end of the eighth row and listened to the discourses upon the Law. Not being able to follow their arguments, he was ill at ease, but when they came to a certain subject and the disciples said to the master, 'Whence do you know it?' and the latter replied, 'It is a law given to Moses at Sinai,' he was comforted.
>
> "Thereupon he returned to the Holy One, blessed be He, and said, 'Lord of the Universe, You have such a man and You give the Torah by me!' He replied, 'Be silent, for such is My decree.'
>
> "Then said Moses, 'Lord of the Universe, You have shown me his Torah; show me his reward.' 'Turn you round,' said He. Moses turned round and saw them weighing out his flesh at the market-stalls. 'Lord of the

Universe,' cried Moses, 'such Torah, and such a reward!' He replied, 'Be silent, for such is My decree.'" (B.T. *Menahot* 29b)

The rabbis were bold and innovative with respect to revelation and the word of God in a typically loving and reverent manner. Moses, the prophet of the revelation at Sinai, attends the academy of Rabbi Akiva and sits down unnoticed among the students discussing Torah. He fails to comprehend their debate and feels saddened until he hears his own name mentioned as an authoritative source of the interpretive tradition in terms of the legal category "a law given to Moses at Sinai." After thus being comforted, Moses asks to see the reward in store for this remarkable and creative teacher of the Oral Law and is shown the mutilated, martyred body of Rabbi Akiva. He is dumbfounded with astonishment ("such Torah, and such a reward!") but nonetheless remains silent after being told by God: "Such is My decree."

As a revealing parable on the inner contradictions of rabbinic society, this midrash uses dramatic juxtaposition to set the voice of the innovative teacher of the interpretive tradition against the silence of Moses before God's decree. In that culture at that time, it was as if you lived on two levels of experience. In trying to understand the workings of history, you were quiet, submissive, and passive. In learning, however, you found your voice; you were active, innovative, and assertive. In the academies of learning, you were masters. You had the authority to play with the word, to interpret it, even to silence God if He broke the rules of talmudic debate. But as far as the divine scheme in history was concerned, you were speechless; you had nothing to say. "Moses, be silent. Such is My decree."

Spinoza charged Judaism with creating an emasculated personality, and in the *Tractatus* he suggested that renewed statehood for Jews was conceivable only if the effeminate nature of Jewish political consciousness could be healed. Yet, the dominant image of the Jew in exile continued to be one of passivity and accommodation until well into the nineteenth century, when the Zionist movement proclaimed the time had come to liberate Jews from the "disease" of historical passivity and accommodation. The early Zionists were not prepared to continue internalizing the traditional explanation of *galut* (exile).

Ample texts are quoted in the rabbinic tradition that reinforce this stereotypical submissive attitude to political exile. The following verses from Jeremiah were often cited in this context:

> Put your necks under the yoke of the king of Babylon, and serve him and his people and live. Why die, you together with your people, by the sword, by famine and by pestilence? (Jer. 27:12–13)

Then, referring to the vessels of the Temple, Jeremiah says:

> They shall be brought to Babylon, and there shall they remain until I take note of them, says the Lord, and I will bring them up and restore them to this place. (27:22)

"Until I take note of them" is the keynote expression of this conception of history. *You* must wait and submit until *I* intervene to change your situation. This view, which was deeply ingrained in the rabbinic tradition, can be traced directly to the biblical understanding of Israel's role in history, where Israel was to be a symbol of God's reign in history. God's election of Israel was also a political act, which entailed (a) God's total sovereignty and (b) Israel's total dependency. This is the primary reason for the spontaneous opposition to the monarchy in the book of Samuel and for Gideon's refusing kingship. Wanting a king and a standing army meant wanting to become "like all the nations" rather than God's elect. God was king, and Israel, as God's people, mediated God's lordship in history. Seeking autonomous political power was tantamount to rebellion, because Israel would then cease being the transparent symbol of God's lordship in history.

The biblical accounts of a people's wandering forty years in the desert and of receiving the manna are perhaps the most eloquent metaphors describing Israel's political destiny. Israel was not a natural community but a metahistorical, covenantal people meant to bear witness to God's rule in history. Its weakness, no less than its strength, was laden with transcendental meaning. "Submit to the yoke of Babylon," says Jeremiah to the exiled community of the first Temple, "for you are God's people."

The Talmud in *Ketubot* (111a) adds an additional figurative element to the words of Jeremiah by alluding to the divine promises forbidding Israel to rise up collectively to reconquer its homeland or to rebel against the nations of the world. The political message of exile was clear and unambiguous: "Do not seek to end your exile by military means or any other human initiative."

Therefore, when Zionism began to emerge in the late nineteenth century with its radical message of self-determination, political activism, and national rebirth, it was viewed with deep mistrust and derision as a dangerous threat to an essential principle of traditional Judaism. Not only were the Zionists sinning; they were undermining the very foundation of the Jewish people's historical destiny. How could you change the condition of Jewish history through natural means? Ours is not an ordinary human history. We are a messianic people, the children of the prophets. Our weakness is our strength. We are not warriors or farmers. The book, not the gun or the shovel, is the instrument of our survival. Only God's intervention in the course of history can bring about our redemption. "I swore you," says the Talmud, "not to rebel

27

against the nations." Submit and you will overcome the nations because you are an eternal people, an eternal symbol of God's presence in history.

While this was the response of the majority of the rabbinic community to Zionism, a minority responded in a diametrically opposite manner. Rather than viewing Zionism as a rebellion against our metahistorical destiny, its members interpreted this secular challenge as a dialectical unfolding of the messianic drama. Israel's return to the land, the rebirth of Hebrew, and the renewal of political and national life would safeguard the Jewish people in modern history and would nurture and release new historical forces necessary for Israel's spiritual redemption. The land and the language of the Bible would reunite Jews with the historical, prophetic consciousness of their tradition. As they dug their shovels into the land of the prophets, Jews would begin to hear the prophetic message from the past.

The great secular Zionist revolution was thus transformed into an integral part of a great religious drama, "the beginning of redemption." The secular pioneers who turned against the tradition of the past, who gave up Sabbath, *kashrut* (dietary laws), prayer, and other aspects of Torah culture, would be the ones to usher in the messianic redemption. Rabbi Kook appealed to a Hegelian type of dialectical model of history to explain this apparent contradiction. As he explained, when the Temple was under construction, workers walked freely throughout the Temple mount paying little attention to whether they were dragging mud through the Holy of Holies or treading on the site of the sacred altar. Yet, the ordinary and mundane nature of their activities did not detract in any way from the Temple's final sanctity. Analogously, he argued, the emergence of secular Zionism was part of a dialectical process leading toward a renewed religious vitality and empowerment of the people of the book. It was as if he and others like him were arguing that embracing secularism, or at least this secular historical phenomenon, would release new and important spiritual energies.

The opponents of the "beginning of redemption" interpretation vehemently attack this enthusiastic embracing of Zionism as an illegitimate and suicidal religious conceit. For them, Zionism calls for weeping and mourning for the great loss we suffer whenever Jews become a "normal" people. The whole notion of normalization—the very banner that Zionism carried proudly into its battle against the tradition—is a dangerous heresy, a deathblow to our religious destiny. According to this form of traditional Jewish orthodoxy, the most appropriate way of celebrating Israel's Independence Day is by reading the Book of Lamentations.

There are thus two vastly different and contrary perceptions of modern Israel. One sees the State of Israel as a satanic heresy; the other, as an unfolding drama of redemption. Two interpretations; two antithetical postures to the tradition and to the modern world. Submission or assertion? Political passivity or activism? Faith or rebellion? Is taking responsibility for your national destiny rebellion? Is normalization the giving up of covenantal identity?

THREE STAGES OF THE COVENANTAL IDEA

My own view is based on the concept of the covenant as a process comprising three stages. The Biblical narrative is the source of what I call covenantal theology, a theological framework that presupposes the paradoxical notion of divine self-limitation (a metaphysical metaphor necessary for making sense of the notion of the covenant).

The story of Genesis begins with God as the Lord of creation, the single, all-powerful architect of life and nature. His presence overshadows all else, and His will is absolutely free and unimpeded. The world He creates reflects His power and dominance. The Garden of Eden is the perfect home for human beings—innocent creatures totally dependent on God, totally aware of His presence, totally responsive to His will. This idyllic world, however, is God's dream. When innocence turns into rebellion, then God (pardon the anthropomorphism) has "great difficulty" accepting the fact that His creation did not turn out as He had planned. He rages at human ambivalence and disobedience and, in a moment of anger, decides to destroy the world because of human corruption.

Through Noah, God preserves life on earth and makes a fresh start, only to meet failure again with the Tower of Babel. A universal language and a human community driven by hubris and conceit threaten God's rule on earth, leading this time to expulsion by means of linguistic and geographical dispersion.

It is only with the advent of Abraham that God's response to failure and disappointment changes and a covenantal theology emerges in place of a theology of the Creator God. Instead of divine rage and the unilateral use of power, God "admits" that the Lord of Creation cannot become the Lord of History unless human beings become responsible and accountable. God's presence in the world becomes conditional on human beings sharing the burden of history. This, then, is the meaning of covenantal mutuality. As I argued in *A Living Covenant*, covenant (*brit*) reflects the divine decision to share responsibility for history with human beings. The underlying metaphysical notion of self-limitation sets a new theology of history in motion wherein God is not the unilateral redeemer of history.

The central norm of the covenantal framework is the assumption of moral responsibility. "I have put before you life and death, blessing and curse. Choose life" (Deut. 30:19). The biblical sense of responsibility is essentially normative responsibility. The first stage of the covenant consists in responsibility for fulfilling and implementing the revealed word of God. When a question of law arises in the Bible, God is called upon to resolve the dilemma.

> Once, when the Israelites were in the wilderness, they came upon a man gathering wood on the sabbath day. Those who found him as he was gathering wood brought him before Moses, Aaron, and the whole community. He was placed in custody, for it had not been specified what should be done to him. Then the Lord said to Moses, "The man should be put to death: the whole community shall pelt him with stones outside the camp." So the whole community took him outside the camp and stoned him to death—as the Lord had commanded Moses. (Num. 15:32–36)

In another situation, when the daughters of Zelophehad confront Moses with a difficult question involving the laws of inheritance, Moses similarly receives instruction directly from God and "the daughters of Zelophehad did as the Lord had commanded Moses" (Num. 36:10). In the Bible, revelation was the source of both the law and its interpretation.

The second stage of the covenant idea is not limited to obeying commandments but also includes responsibility for interpreting the word of God. This stage goes beyond fulfilling the word of God to actually determining its meaning and content. Revelation is thus incorporated into the human realm of responsibility, with the once clear-cut line between divine author and human interpreter becoming increasingly blurred. Consider the following example of the merging of legislative and interpretive functions in the Mishnah, especially the subsequent talmudic discussion of its metalegal, theological implications.

All who are liable for *karet* [the divine punishment of being 'cut off' from one's people], if they are flogged they are no longer liable for *karet*; for it is said, "He may be given up to forty lashes, but no more, lest being flogged further, to excess, your *brother be degraded before your eyes*" (Deut. 25:3), [which shows that] after being flogged, then he is *your brother*.

In the ensuing discussion in the Talmud, Rabbi Joseph questions this virtual annulment of *karet* and, on the basis of a fine semantic dissection of the text, asks sardonically: "Who went up to heaven to confirm this cancellation of divine punishment in such situations?" Abbaye replies by citing Rabbi Joshua ben Levi, who stated that on three occasions the decision of a human court was subsequently confirmed by the heavenly court: the institution of the festival of Purim, the greeting of people in the name of God, and the ruling that the tithes of Levites should be brought to the Temple and also distributed to the priests.

"Who," continues Abbaye "went up to heaven in these cases?" He then concludes by arguing that just as Rabbi Joshua ben Levi inferred the heavenly confirmation of these three rabbinical rulings on the basis of interpretation, so too the grounds for rescinding the *divine* punishment of *karet* in cases of flogging was also due to interpretation.

To paraphrase Abbaye: We know how God punishes the sinner because we know how to read the Torah. We anticipate God's moves through learning and interpretation. The Torah is now our property. It is ours. In other words, the rabbinic scholar talks about God and about God's role in administering Torah law, because, in this phase of the covenantal tradition, the word and judgment of God are mediated by interpretation.

R. Isaac ben Shila said in R. Mattena's name in the name of R. Hisda: If a father renounces the honor due to him, it is renounced; but if a Rabbi renounces his honor, it is not renounced. R. Joseph ruled: Even if a Rabbi renounces his honor, it is renounced, for it is said, "And the Lord went before them by day" (Exod. 13:21). Said Raba: How can these be compared! There, with respect to the Holy One, blessed be He, the world is His and the Torah is His; [hence] He can forego His honor. But here, is then the Torah his [the Rabbi's]? Subsequently Raba said: Indeed, the Torah is his [the scholar's], for it is written, "and in his law does he meditate day and night" (Ps. 1:2). (B.T. *Kiddushin* 32a,b)

Talmudic Judaism thus appropriated the word of God, internalized it, played with it, sang with it, made it its own. The rabbis became the shapers of revelation. That is, they became an interpretive community.

The third stage of the covenantal tradition is expressed in part by the growth of Zionism. According to my view, when the Jewish people took responsibility to end their exilic condition, when homelessness ceased being a defining category of Jewish history and the wandering Jew decided to build a home, then covenantal consciousness evolved to yet a further level of human responsibility. The interpretive community, which showed such remarkable independence and freedom of thought during and following the talmudic period, had left history exclusively in the hands of God. While it was true of this phase of covenantal history that "Torah was not in heaven," *history*, on the other hand, definitely was. The solution to the exilic condition of their history remained in heaven insofar as historical change was conceivable only in terms of God's intervening to create the long-awaited messianic, redemptive moment.

The third stage of the covenant began when Jews felt responsibility for their own history and not only for implementing mitzvot (the biblical stage) or for their intellectual, interpretive autonomy (the talmudic stage).

The interpretive community set the precedent by becoming a culture in which loyalty to tradition was combined with self-corrective processes of reinterpretation. The Talmud offered none of the certainties of classical appeals to self-evidence and logical demonstration, but provided abundant illustrations of how a tradition could be sustained and reinvigorated in the midst of disagreement, argumentation, and reinterpretation. Analogously, the variety of responses to modern Israel today—ranging from enthusiastic celebration, to indifference, to branding it a satanic scheme—has created a situation in which religious responses to events and to moments in history cannot expect to be confirmed by the kind of absolute certainty and incorrigibility that is promised by eschatology.

The crux of the religious worldview I am discussing can be summarized as follows: I find joy in serving God in this incomplete, fragmentary world with my limited and fragmentary mind. The only God I know is the God mediated in the everyday rhythms of the temporal world. While I would surely accept the gift of divine grace if God were to choose to redeem history, this, however, is not the operative hope that informs my religious life.

My reality is essentially temporal and limited; I make religious choices and decisions without the benefit of perceiving life *sub specie aeternitatis*. I leave messianism and eschatology to God and try to get on with life as an incomplete, finite human being building a religious life without knowledge of whether there is a secret divine scheme for history.

The acceptance of finitude and limitation and the absence of metaphysical certainties do not entail a weakening of conviction and passion. Love can grow out of partial understanding and an appreciation of the knowledge that our convictions and beliefs are inherently limited and incomplete.

Although I live in a world where disagreement is widespread and acute, I do not admit to a lack of strong convictions. The strength of your convictions is not dependent on a belief in their absolute status, which would condemn those who disagree with you to blindness to self-evidence or to stubborn ill will. A framework of rational moral argumentation without absolutes is not equivalent to relativism. Not every point of view is equally legitimate simply because it is someone's point of view. A point of view must always be subject to and vulnerable to counterargument and evaluation.

Also, taking part in a discussion within a tradition requires that a person know how to argue within that particular tradition. This means that you have to master its language, its literature, and its history in order to participate actively in its cultural debate. Unless you listen carefully to the voices that make up a tradition, you will be unable to think intelligently about its central issues and concerns, let alone present meaningful interpretations that can be organically integrated into its interpretive discussion. The intellectual experience of the Torah scholar is not an isolated, lonely one. There is a community to which you are responsible and with which you are engaged in an ongoing conversation.

A traditional Jew earns the right to speak by listening. Learning is a condition for being taken seriously as a discussant in this tradition. If you don't study or listen with reverence, if you don't feel the burden of the tradition or speak with trepidation about your certainties, you will never gain credibility. The voices of the sages and scholars who participated in the interpretive tradition speak to me. I must be careful and responsible in my interpretations because I have to answer to all those voices that spoke in the past.

As I have argued throughout this discussion, loyalty to tradition need not suspend critical intelligence. One should not feel paralyzed because of doubt or inhibited from entering an interpretive process because of the realization that one's moral intuitions are not self-evident and universal. The legacy of the interpretive community requires its contemporary heirs to be fully awake to the possibility that the interpretive strategies they adopt may not be shared by all, and that diversity and disagreement are not signs of inauthenticity. If we can rid ourselves of the obsession with certainty and finality—if we can internalize the spirit of the covenantal idea—then the uncertainties of the modern world will not deter us from renewing the vital interpretive processes that define our religious heritage.

2

THE JOY OF TORAH

I HAVE OFTEN been asked to address Christian theologians who have difficulty grasping the notion of the joy of Torah. While accepting the possibility of joy in a Buberian-Hasidic approach to Judaism, they cannot imagine any sense of joy in approaches to Judaism that emphasize the centrality of mitzvah (divine commandment) and an intellectual involvement with talmudic texts. They automatically identify this type of Judaism with "pharisaic legalism"—with submissive obedience to the merciless letter of the Law and with guilt.

In this chapter we shall analyze the notion of the joy of Torah with the intention of illuminating how the underlying principles of halakhic practice provide conditions for the experience of joy. Many features of Halakhah appear to militate against the experience of joy. For example, in commenting on the talmudic statement "commandments were not given for your enjoyment" (B.T. *Rosh Ha-Shanah* 28a), Rashi explains that commandments were given to Israel not to be a source of pleasure but rather to be a yoke around their necks. Similarly the *Tosafot* commentary suggests, with regard to the statement "greater is one who does an act because of being commanded, than one who does an act without being commanded" (*Kiddushin* 31a), that being commanded makes an act greater because one must overcome the added anxiety and fear of failure.

The picture of halakhic observance reflected in these statements seems totally at odds with the experience of joy. More generally, the expression "yoke of the commandments" (*ol mitzvot*) conveys the idea that mitzvot are a heavy burden. "Pharisaic legalism," with its allegedly submissive obedience to the letter of the law, hardly seems conducive to joy, which is normally associated with ease and spontaneity.

In addition to the weights of commandment and authority, another feature of Halakhah that appears to be incompatible with joy is the emphasis in the tradition on uniform practice. Individual uniqueness and spontaneity seem to be ignored by a spiritual life that elaborates detailed patterns of behavior for all to follow.

GOD AS TEACHER

The Torah begins not with the account of the Sinai revelation but with the story of creation. From a theological perspective, Sinai and creation are the most significant moments in the Torah. Both involve divine speech: the Word that constitutes creation out of nothing, and the Word that constitutes the covenant of Sinai. To Maimonides, creation is a moment of divine self-expression—*olam hesed yibaneh*, the world emerges out of an overflow of divine creative power. Being and nature are the products of the divine overflow. In creation, divine speech is divine self-expression. To Maimonides, reflection on nature heals human grandiosity because comprehension of God's revelation in nature leads to the awareness that humanity is not the center of creation.

Whereas human beings are not at the center of the cosmic drama expressing God's power and wisdom in nature, they are crucial to the revelation at Sinai. Reflection on the laws of the Torah leads to an anthropocentric worldview, for the covenantal speech of Sinai is addressed essentially to human beings. For Maimonides, divine speech at Sinai followed divine "listening" to the physical and spiritual conditions of the community enslaved in Egypt. One cannot understand biblical legislation without taking into account the influence of Egyptian pagan culture on the Hebrew slaves. The particular social and historical conditions of the Jewish people (the "students") influence the approach of the divine educator at Sinai.

It is not surprising, therefore, that one way divine speech at Sinai is understood by the rabbinic tradition is through the model of a teacher:

> Because the Holy One appeared to Israel at the Red Sea as a mighty man waging war, and appeared to them at Sinai as a teacher who teaches the day's lesson and then again and again goes over with his pupils what they have been taught, and appeared to them in the days of Daniel as an elder teaching Torah, and in the days of Solomon appeared to them as a young man, the Holy One said to Israel: Come to no false conclusions because you see Me in many guises, for I am He who was with you at the Red Sea and I am He who is with you at Sinai: I am the Lord thy God. (*Pesikta de-Rab Kahana, piska* 12)

In the daily *birkat ha Torah* (the blessing over Torah), God is identified as "He who teaches Torah to His people Israel."

Halakhic authorities viewed the teaching of Torah as *imitatio dei*, an imitation of God, the teacher *par excellence* (B.T. *Nedarim* 34a; M.T. *H. Talmud Torah* I, 7).

DIVINE "SELF-EDUCATION" AND REVELATION

The unfolding of the biblical narrative connecting creation with the covenant at Sinai may be interpreted in a way that supports the rabbinic image of God as teacher. In the beginning, amidst the exhibition and the excitement of the creation of the universe, the Creator God proclaims majestically: "Let us make a human being!" The God Who is limited by nothing, Who need but say: "Let there be..." for anything to come into being, creates humanity with the intention that human beings reflect the image of God. The Torah then describes God's punishing response when humanity fails to live up to divine expectations. The corruption of the generation of the flood results in God's nearly destroying all of creation. In the early chapters of Genesis, God is portrayed as reacting violently to human moral failures.

As Yochanan Muffs has shown, the covenant and Halakhah emerge when God's aspirations for humanity come to terms with the reality of human nature. God's saying "Never again will I doom the earth because of human beings, since the devisings of the human mind are evil from youth..." (Gen. 8:21) is the first sign of a process of divine self-education culminating in the giving of the Torah. In contrast to the rage of the flood, the giving of the Law reflects God's acceptance of human beings with their imperfections and their weaknesses. God no longer looks at them simply as the embodiment of the divine image, but as complex creatures for whom perfection is the rare and often momentary result of much effort and concentration. Torah legislation should not be understood as the embodiment of divine perfection; rather, it reflects a dialectical tension between divine aspiration and human imperfection.

The Torah was given in the desert, where human frailty and limitations are exposed. God proclaims: "You shall be unto Me a kingdom of priests and a holy people" (Exod. 19:6). Yet, in the desert, where there is neither food nor water, the people cry out: "Why do we need to put up with the insecurity of freedom? We may as well go back to Egypt!" The desert reveals basic human fears and weaknesses in the face of hunger and deprivation. To Martin Buber, the "Eagle Speech" of Exodus expresses the essence of the covenant between God and Israel:

> You have seen what I did to the Egyptians, how I bore you on eagles' wings and brought you to Me. Now then, if you will obey Me faithfully and keep My covenant, you shall be My treasured possession among all the peoples. Indeed, all the earth is Mine, but you shall be to Me a kingdom of priests and a holy nation. (Exod. 19:4–6)

In contrast to Buber, and in the spirit of Yohanan Muffs, I suggest that the biblical account of God's giving manna in the desert (Exodus 16) is a more poignant prelude to the covenantal moment at Sinai. God tells the people: "I will give you food sufficient for each day, but please do not hoard extra. Trust Me to provide for the next day." How do the people respond? They go out and gather for additional days. On Friday, God provides double the amount so they will not have to gather on the Sabbath. Nevertheless, people go out on the Sabbath to gather even more. The manna story reveals the problematic nature of the relationship between God and Israel. "You shall be unto Me a kingdom of priests and a holy nation" reveals what God dreams for the chosen people; the manna incident reveals the human reality with which God must come to terms.

The desert repudiates the romanticization of human beings, and the Torah is given in the desert. Revelation thus expresses divine realism in God's acceptance of human beings with their limitations. The following midrash beautifully expresses the idea that the Torah is an attempt to educate and guide people with passions and jealousies:

> R. Joshua b. Levi also said: When Moses ascended on high, the ministering angels spoke before The Holy One, blessed be He: "Sovereign of the Universe! What business has one born of woman among us?" "He has come to receive the Torah," He answered them. They said to Him, "That secret treasure, which has been hidden by You for nine hundred and seventy-four generations before the world was created, You desire to give to flesh and blood! 'What is man, that Thou art mindful of him? And the son of man that Thou visitest him? O Lord our God. How excellent is Thy name in all the earth! Who has set Thy glory [the Torah] upon the Heavens!'" "Return them an answer," the Holy One, blessed be He, said to Moses.... He [then] spoke before Him: "Sovereign of the Universe! The Torah, which You give me, what is written in it?" "I am the Lord thy God, who brought thee out of the Land of Egypt." He said to them [the angels]: "Did you go down to Egypt; were you enslaved to Pharaoh? Why then should the Torah be yours? Again what is written in it? 'You shall have no other gods.' Do you dwell among peoples that engage in idol worship? Again what is written in it? 'Remember the Sabbath day, to keep it holy.' Do you then perform work, that you need to rest? Again what is written in it? 'You shall not take (tissa) [the name...in vain].' Is there any business

dealing (*massa*) among you? Again what is written in it? 'Honor thy father and thy mother.' Have you fathers and mothers? Again, what is written in it? 'You shall not murder. You shall not commit adultery. You shall not steal.' Is there jealousy among you? Is the Evil Tempter among you?" Straightway they conceded to the Holy One, blessed be He. (B.T. *Shabbat* 88b)

The essential point of this midrash is expressed in concepts used widely in talmudic discourse, such as *deha lo dibra Torah ela keneged yetzer ha-ra* (the Torah speaks in relationship to the evil inclination). In other words, Torah is not a heavenly law addressed to perfect beings, but rather a response to what human beings in fact are: people who steal from one another, who covet one another's property, etc. Whereas Nature reflects the divine creative overflow, the Torah reveals God's address to a community of people in their imperfect human condition.

Halakhic discussions are not always spiritually uplifting and beautiful; they often presuppose harsh and brutal realities. People are often puzzled or embarrassed by the section in Deuteronomy 21:10–14, dealing with a soldier who takes a woman captive. The situation involves a person away from home, family, friends, and familiar social context, who is engaged in the violence and brutality of war. Addressing this context, the Torah says: If you desire her, you may have her, but you must wait, you must take her home, etc. The significance of this biblical legislation as understood by the Talmud lies in the fact that God does not abandon a person in the jungle, but goes into the jungle to try to salvage whatever is possible.

Our Rabbis taught: "And you see among the captives"— when taking her captive; "a woman"—even married; "of beautiful countenance"—the Torah only addressed the *yetzer ha-ra* [lit. evil inclination, human passion]; it is better for Israel to eat flesh of animals about to die yet [ritually] slaughtered, than flesh of dying animals which have perished [without ritual slaughter]; "and you desire"—even if she is not beautiful; "her"—but not her and her companion; "and you shall take"—you have marriage rights over her; "to yourself a wife"— [teaching] that he must not take two women, one for himself and another for his father, or one for himself and another for his son; "then you shall bring her home [to your house]"—teaching that he must not molest her on the [field of] battle. (B.T. *Kiddushin* 21b–22a)

Rather than pretend that human beings will transcend their desires and hungers no matter what the circumstances, the Torah aims at retaining some degree of dignified conduct within an otherwise brutal and anarchic situation.

Much halakhic discussion deals with the minute details of everyday life. When one studies the legal minutiae of the case of someone's ox goring someone else's ox, or of a person lighting a fire that destroys another person's property, one encounters the idea of a God Who is involved in the world of ordinary human beings. In their attempt to have the Law address almost every aspect of life, the authors of the Talmud and those who followed in their tradition refused to regard any aspect of the human condition as unworthy of divine concern. Halakhic discussions anchor the dialogue with God within the multiple possibilities of the concrete. They reflect a sustained struggle to achieve *kedushah* (sanctity) within everyday human life. The courage to establish partial meaning in an unredeemed world is one of the most profound dimensions of rabbinic spirituality.

The divine acceptance of limited human beings is a fundamental philosophical presupposition for understanding Judaism. This idea is the ground for the belief in the permanent possibility of *teshuvah* (repentance, renewal). The following prayer expresses the Jew's experience of divine love and acceptance:

> You have loved the house of Israel Your people with everlasting love; You have taught us Torah and mitzvot, laws and judgments. Therefore, Lord our God, when we lie down and when we rise up we will speak of Your laws, and rejoice in the words of Your Torah and in Your mitzvot forevermore. Indeed, they are our life and the length of our days; we will meditate on them day and night. May You never take away Your love from us. Blessed are You, O Lord, who loves Your people Israel. (Daily Evening Service)

The giving of the Torah in the desert confirms God's love as a response to our humanity, and not only as an expression of divine aspirations. Biblical descriptions of Israel in the desert allow for no illusions about the unique "spiritual genius" of Israel. Even Moses, in his final speech to the people, recognized how far they were from embodying their covenantal mission. The Bible does not allow even an old, dying leader to have illusions about the spiritual grandeur of Israel! Still, God "loved the house of Israel" by giving them the Torah. And the people rejoice in it. Mitzvah, thus, is inherently related to the joy of feeling accepted and confirmed by God. Not only are realism and responsibility not antithetical to love and joy, they are their very grounds.

The joy of personal adequacy and dignity liberates a person from having to manipulate relationships in order to gratify personal hungers. Human fears and deprivation can imprison people by preventing them from recognizing and appreciating that which is

45

independent of their needs. To Maimonides, the study of philosophy—that is, of physics and metaphysics—liberates a person to appreciate objective reality. Philosophy, by clarifying how nature mediates divine wisdom, provides the liberating power for a person's moving from a relationship motivated by reward and punishment to one based upon *ahavah* (love) (M.T. *H. Teshuvah* 10:5–6).

I claim that an understanding of the halakhic process itself may provide the existential impetus to worship God out of *ahavah*. When one internalizes the affirmation of worth and dignity implicit in a relationship to God built upon mitzvah, one may discover the psychological resources that enable one to respond to mitzvot with love. Sensing the presence of God in the legal minutia of talmudic halakhic discussions may provide the psychological conditions for the modern Jew's learning to worship God out of love.

The centrality of petitional prayer in rabbinic Judaism expresses the same motif of divine acceptance as my understanding of the Sinai revelation. In petitional prayer, you bring your full human situation into the life of worship. Your humanity—its frailties, needs, and longings—is not an embarrassment. In contrast to Maimonides, for whom love of God grows out of the liberating experience of the philosophic quest wherein your personal, physical identity is transcended, I claim that consciousness of your full humanity and awareness of God's loving acceptance of your corporeal self generate the spiritual power for love.

In receiving mitzvot, we experience joy in knowing that God accepts human beings in their limitations and believes in their capacities to shoulder responsibility. In fulfilling mitzvot, we experience joy in performing mitzvot for their own sake (*li-shma*). Just as there is joy in our acceptance *by* God, there is joy in our acceptance *of* God and *of* the mitzvot for their own sakes. Divine acceptance empowers human acceptance in the form of our serving God with joy. We manifest our love for God by performing the commandments with joy—that is, for their own sake, and not as a means to have God gratify our needs. When I sense God's love, I realize that the reward for doing a mitzvah is the mitzvah itself (*Avot* 4:2).

THE JOY OF STUDY

Our analysis of the joy of the Torah has so far dealt only with mitzvot, the joy of the commandments. The term "Torah" also denotes a body of material that is studied and analyzed. In the *beit ha-midrash* (study hall) of a yeshivah, one often finds people singing while studying Talmud. On seeing such people swaying and singing, one might mistakenly believe them to be praying, when in fact they are engaged in a profound intellectual activity. I have had the rare privilege of studying with a talmudic master who experienced total joy while intellectually grappling with Talmud and with the vast corpus of legal and aggadic material. Within the world of learning, often referred to as "the world of Torah," one discovers concepts of joy similar to those discussed above. The Judaic emphasis on study began with talmudic Judaism, with the oral tradition. The centrality of learning in rabbinic Judaism, as expressed in the saying "*talmud torah keneged kulam*" (Torah study above all else), has characterized Jewish values and practice throughout history.

The covenant experience truly emerges when Israel, the listener, turns the spoken Word into an open-ended creative word. The content of Torah can never be exhausted; it must be received and expanded in each generation. The student experiences the presence of God even in those aspects of Torah created through human interpretation. A student recites *birkat ha Torah* (the blessing over the Torah) even when studying the writings of contemporary teachers. Prophets are no longer the sole mediators of the word of God. Scholars and students of Torah are now the main actors in the ongoing drama of revelation.

The covenant, which is predicated on human responsibility, is strengthened when Israel feels adequate to expand the implications of the spiritual guidance that began at Sinai. Revelation at Sinai then becomes a *derekh* (a pointing, a way, a direction) and not the final consummation of the word of God. Intense intellectual engagement with Torah transforms the individual from a passive recipient to an active shaper of the future direction of Torah. Cognitive dignity and intellectual adequacy provide the foundations of the joy of Torah.

The tradition of Torah learning reflects a fundamental acknowledgment of human adequacy and dignity. Within this tradition, the importance of learning is closely linked to the model of God as the accepting, loving teacher. A student is encouraged and empowered to develop the implications of what was received. God's love liberates students of Torah to create, and to regard their creation as an elaboration of what the original teaching contained. The claim to originality is not the highest aspiration when love characterizes the teacher–student relationship. It is in this spirit that we should understand the talmudic ascription of all rabbinic and later creativity to the founding moment of Sinai.

> Scripture, Mishnah, Halachot, Talmud, Toseftot, Haggadot, and even what a faithful disciple would in the future say in the presence of his master, were all communicated to Moses at Sinai; for it says, "Is there a thing of which it is said: See this is new?" (Eccl. 1:10) and the other part of the verse provides the reply to this: "It has been already." (*Midrash Rabbah, Leviticus, Achare Mot*, 22:1)
>
> What relation does the Sabbatical Year [*shmitah*] have to Mount Sinai? Were not all the commandments

48

stated at Sinai? Rather, just as [the laws of] the Sabbatical Year were stated in their general principles and in their specific details, so too were all the laws stated in their general principles and in their specific details. (*Sifra, Behar* 9, *parshata* A)

"Let him kiss me with the kisses of his mouth" (Song of Songs 1:2)—R. Yochanan said: An angel carried the utterances at Mount Sinai from before the Holy One, blessed be He, each one in turn, and brought it to each of the Israelites and said to him, Do you take upon yourself this commandment? So and so many rules are attached to it, so and so many penalties are attached to it, so and so many precautionary measures are attached to it, so and so many precepts and so and so many rulings from minor to major. The Israelite would answer him, Yes. Thereupon, he kissed him on the mouth. The Rabbis, however, say: The commandment itself went to each of the Israelites and said to him, So and so many rules are attached to it [etc.] and he would reply, Yes, yes. And straightaway, the *commandment* kissed him on the mouth. (Song of Songs *Rabbah*)

Instead of viewing rabbinic statements attributing halakhic discussions and interpretations to the founding moment of Sinai as attempts to provide authoritative foundations for the learning tradition, I believe these statements can be understood as expressing the experience of love of God that characterized the interpretive tradition, where the distinction between what is the Word of God and what is humanly derived loses all significance. Just as in human relationships of intense love, one often feels that all one is or has achieved is due to the beloved, so too a student intensely committed to a teacher may not always distinguish between what was received and what he or she has created.

It is important to differentiate between creativity grounded in love, which flows from an intense relationship, and the creativity of one who is conscious of separation and of individuality. Midrashic writers reflect the relationship of a lover to a beloved; the feeling that the Torah is a gift of love from God permeates all their writings. Because the Torah was given in love and is studied with love, it contains all that future generations will "discover" to have been "included" in God's message.

> "The words of the Lord are...silver tried in the open before all men refined seven times seven" (Ps. 12:7). R. Yannai said: The words of Torah were not given as clear-cut decisions. For with every word which the Holy One, blessed be He, spoke to Moses, He offered him forty-nine arguments by which a thing may be proved clean, and forty-nine other arguments by which it may be proved unclean. When Moses asked: Master of the Universe, in what way shall we know the true sense of a law? God replied: The majority is to be followed: when a majority says it is unclean, it is unclean; when a majority says it is clean, it is clean. (Midrash on Psalms, I, 12)

With the development of the oral tradition, Israel becomes a co-partner in the creative process of the Word; revelation ceases to be a Word given once and for all at Sinai, but becomes a Word that is continuously discussed and developed by students. The Word that mediates divine love becomes integrated with the human response. God's revelation at Sinai and the creative development of the Torah by Israel become one Torah. The written Torah and the oral tradition become one.

THE INDIVIDUAL AND COMMUNITY

The revelation of the Torah did not take place in the lifetime of Abraham. According to Maimonides, the concept of mitzvah and the normative system of Halakhah are fundamentally related to Moses, the liberator and political founder of the nation of Israel. Mitzvah is not rooted in the leap of the "alone to the Alone" in the Plotinian sense. Mitzvah is the spiritual road of an individual who serves God within the context of community. Mitzvah and Halakhah give expression to the spiritual concerns of a person whose sense of "I" is infused with a broader sense of "we."

I do not deny that an individual can discover a unique personal way to God, but this is not the way of Halakhah. In other words, mitzvah is not a private spiritual language but rather a collective language embracing the spiritual needs and capacities of the community. Consequently, one finds throughout history repeated attempts to elaborate mitzvot in a clear, precise, and detailed manner and to codify Halakhah for widespread popular use. The importance of such elaboration, clarification, and specification can be only appreciated in light of the fact that Halakhah constitutes a collective language giving expression to a shared spirituality. Individuals meet through the medium of the shared form; mitzvah creates the basis on which individuals build a joint spiritual life. In this manner, Halakhah mediates a collective spirituality and leads the individual to the joy of solidarity with community.

In the traditional prayer book, prayers are in the first person plural, because it is not "I" as a single individual but "we" as a collective community that prays. The liturgy symbolizes this connection to the collective in the requirement of the *minyan* (quorum of ten), for it is only in the midst of community that one can give expression to a collective identity.

While recognizing how central uniform practice and community are to the joy of Torah, one cannot ignore the stultifying dangers of halakhic spirituality to individual spontaneity and joy. The Jewish tradition was awake to this risk and sought ways to minimize its effects. The joy of learning described above expresses not only a general sense of intellectual adequacy but also a deep sense of individuality. On one level, the total community stands as one before God; on another level, individuals develop according to their particular sensibilities and abilities.

The emphasis on learning loosens the grip of collective uniformity by making room for individual spirituality. Although participating in shared, communal forms of behavior, through learning and understanding an individual can discover new layers of meaning in these very shared concepts and practices. One acts, to begin with, as a collective person (*halakhah*); one understands and internalizes mitzvot, however, as a single person (*aggadah*). Learning, then, is one way a collective, covenantal people allows for the possibility of individual spirituality.

> Said R. Jose bar R. Hanina, "The Divine Word spoke to each and every person according to his/her particular capacity.... Now if each and every person was enabled to taste the manna according to his/her particular capacity, how much more and more was each and every person enabled according to his/her particular capacity to hear the Divine Word." (*Pesikta de-Rab Kahana, piska* 12)

The emphasis on learning in Jewish tradition may be one of the reasons why the Torah, throughout history, has been able to address so many types of individuals despite vast differences in background and mentality. Commitment to the collective past need not negate your own way of hearing and accepting the Torah from within your own human reality. It is in this sense that I understand the rabbinic teaching that the Torah must be received in every generation as if it has been given to you directly.

> Let the Torah never be for you an antiquated decree, but rather like a decree freshly issued, no more than two or three days old.... But Ben Azzai said: Not even as old as a decree issued two or three days ago, but as a decree issued this very day. (*Pesikta de-Rab Kahana, piska* 12:12)

Learning moves the individual beyond collective solidarity to individual appropriation. Individuality, however, finds expression in Halakhah not only in the meaning and purpose one ascribes to mitzvot, but also in the scope of obligation. The concept of halakhic obligation has both a collective and a singular meaning. Halakhah is a system of laws that prescribes specific behavior for every member of the community. But obligations based on the legal authority of God do not exhaust its full scope. Besides the detailed and specific norms that obligate every individual in the community, Maimonides' *Mishneh Torah* also includes a different perspective on the meaning of a halakhic life:

> A man should aim to maintain physical health and vigor, in order that his soul may be upright, in a condition to know God.... Even when he sleeps and seeks repose, to calm his mind and rest his body, so as not to fall sick and be incapacitated from serving God, his sleep is service of the Almighty. In this sense, our wise men charge us, "Let all your deeds be for the sake of Heaven" (*Avot* 2:17). And Solomon, in his wisdom, said, "In all your ways acknowledge Him, and He will direct your paths" (Prov. 3:6). (*Hikhot De'ot*, III, 3)

53

This description of how the halakhic Jew relates all human activities to God is not a description of behavior grounded in legislative authority. The statement "Let all your deeds be for the sake of Heaven" is not a formula yielding explicit legal norms of behavior. "In all your ways acknowledge Him" reflects the human aspiration to sanctify every aspect of conduct. These statements reflect the aspiring movement to God, rather than the legislative movement from God. In attempting to endow all of human action with religious significance, they inspire the individual to seek a way of life that would enable him to say, "I have set the Lord before me continuously."

This single-minded quest for God indicates that Halakhah is more encompassing than a collection of specific legal commandments addressed to a community. In endowing sleep and physical exercise with religious significance, one is not merely following explicit legal rules. An all-pervasive longing for God, not only an obedient posture to specified norms embodying God's legislative will, are necessary features of a comprehensive understanding of the goals of Halakhah. Singular individuals understand that what God requires of them cannot be confined to and exhausted by a precise, delimited set of normative rules. (See *Guide*, III, 54; Nachmanides' commentary on Lev. 19:2). They are drawn to a God Who inspires action not only by divine legislative will but also by God's perfection. They do not look solely to what is required of the community to determine what is expected from them.

> When a man great in the knowledge of the Torah and reputed for his piety does things which cause people to talk about him, even if the acts are not express violations, he profanes the Name of God. As, for example, if such a person makes a purchase and does not pay promptly, provided that he has means and the

creditors ask for payment and he puts them off...or if his mode of addressing people is not gentle, or if he does not receive people affably, but is quarrelsome and irascible. The greater a man is, the more scrupulous should he be in all such things, and do more than the strict letter of the law requires. And if a man has been scrupulous in his conduct, gentle in his conversation, pleasant towards his fellow-creatures, affable in manner when receiving them, not retorting, even when affronted, but showing courtesy to all, even to those who treat him with disdain, conducting his commercial affairs with integrity,...and doing more than his duty in all things...—such a man has sanctified God, and concerning him, Scriptures saith, "And He said unto me, 'You are My servant, O Israel, in whom I will be glorified'" (Isa. 49:3). (*Hilkhot Yesodei ha-Torah*, V, 2)

Whether the possibilities for joy and individual self-expressions presented here are sufficiently broad to satisfy the great variety of spiritual sensibilities in modern society is a serious question. While not attempting to resolve this problem, I propose that in spite of the concept of "the yoke of the commandments," joy is an integral part of a religious life grounded in mitzvot. The joy of being intellectually engaged in the study of Talmud, the profound intellectual autonomy found in halakhic creativity, and the self-respect and the dignity of being a commanded person before God must not be ignored in our understanding of normative Judaism.

3

MEMORY AND VALUES

A Traditional Response to the
Crisis of the Modern Family

ANY DISCUSSION OF the family within a Jewish context must recognize the basic reality that Judaism is fundamentally a communal spiritual system. Judaism's distinctive institution, Halakhah, is best understood within the categories of social and political order. It is not by chance that the revelation at Sinai, the spiritual foundation of Judaism, followed the liberation from Egypt. Moses and the revelation at Sinai cannot be fully understood unless one appreciates what is involved in forging a community.

The law is not addressed to the individual seeking personal salvation; mitzvah (divine commandment) is not designed for a Plotinian leap of the "alone to the Alone." The Torah is significant to the Jew who seeks spiritual fulfillment within the context of community. "You stand this day, all of you, before the Lord your God—your tribal heads, your elders and your officials, all the men of Israel, your children, your wives, even the stranger within your camp, from woodchopper to waterdrawer" (Deut. 29:9–10).

It is instructive to note the context within which Maimonides discusses the family in his code of Jewish law, the *Mishneh Torah*. His discussion does not appear in *Sefer Nashim* (the Book of Women), which deals with such issues as marriage and divorce. Rather, it is included in the last book of his code, *Sefer Shoftim* (the Book of Judges), in the section called *Hilkhot Mamrim*, which deals with questions of authority (courts, the *Sanhedrin*, the role of the Oral Law, and the case of the "rebellious child.") Chapters five, six, and seven, which treat laws pertaining to parents and children, follow four chapters on the authority of the *Sanhedrin* and on procedures for dealing with insubordination to legal decisions.

The integrity of the family unit and the authority of parents are relevant to the wider issue of authority in community. Concern for the institutional welfare of the community (the theme of *Hilkhot Mamrim*) demands careful attention to the family structure. When the family is weakened, an essential element of political community is undermined.

The family in Jewish experience emerges against the background of a religious framework inextricably tied to community and to history. The collective nature of Jewish spirituality cuts across generations, stretching from the distant past into the emerging future. ("I make this covenant...not with you alone, but both with those who are standing here with us this day before the Lord our God and with those who are not with us here this day" [Deut. 29:13–14]). The family—the essential link between generations—is vital for sustaining the covenantal community's covenantal consciousness.

CHALLENGES TO THE FAMILY

The modern family is challenged on four fronts: technology, universalism, despair, and radical individualism. Technological civilization looks to the future for salvation; it promises something better for tomorrow and encourages severance from the past. Technological culture educates the individual to give up the old and customary and to adapt to the new. Its vocabulary of commendation focuses on terms such as "modern," "contemporary," "novel," and "latest." New and unimagined ways of being happy, unprecedented forms of material satisfaction, the most recent modes of gaining pleasure are at once descriptions and evaluations of the superiority of advertised products. In a technological society, one is expected to be prepared for the radically new and therefore superior way of satisfying human needs and wants.

Technological consciousness is memory-less, for to remember is to connect the present to the past. Continuity and process build on what is and was. Market technology, however, calls for shifting styles, new beginnings, a ruptured perception of time. In the area of human relationships, this discontinuity is mirrored in the social norm of defiance and breaking of ties. There is a positive attitude toward rebellion. The child who does not revolt deviates from the expected norm; failure to rebel requires explanation and analysis.

Furthermore, constant expectation of and hunger for novelty has made the feeling of dissatisfaction a characteristic feature of modernity. If people are not discontented, they lose desire. Against this background of dissatisfaction, there sometimes emerges a profound adult resentment of the child's ability to become immersed in novelty. In technological society, aging is one of the worst things that can happen to a person; growing old deprives you of the ability to seek novelty and to consume incessantly. Thus, in a very profound way, the child emerges as the vicarious redeemer ("My child will have everything that I missed!").

59

Young people growing up with this type of experience become persons without memories, constantly in search of identity. "Who am I?" is the question that haunts this generation because part of the answer has to do with tradition and continuity. The language of youth reveals the malaise: "I've got to put myself together," "I'm in pieces," "I feel lost." Even while driven by the search for the new, young people are internally frightened because they do not know where a future severed from a past will lead to. Modern youth exude an aura of freedom, but at the same time they suffer from profound fear and disquietude. Their bodies are perpetually in motion; their eyes are never at rest.

When there is no sense of the importance of memory and tradition, the foundations of the family are undermined. Parents are significant when the past is important. If what happened before is of little interest, and if memory is of no account, parents lose their value as adults. Thus, one discovers in technological societies a shift from the parent-centered to the child-centered family.

The child emerges as the herald of a better future and educates the parents as to what really counts. The juvenile messenger brings the news of tomorrow to a family without memory; since the dominant orientation is futuristic, he or she must teach about the new, unfolding world. Thus, technological society not only promotes rupture and rebellion; it may also emotionally overburden children by making them the final judges of the family's significance and direction.

A second challenge to the family is the quest for global universality. The liberal universalist often accuses the family of being provincial and restrictive because commitment to family diminishes one's involvement with the greater community of humankind. Loyalty to a particular family is confining and limiting. When you believe that the future offers a totally unprecedented solution to the problems of the human condition, anything that anchors you to the past becomes reactionary. The family is an

60

anachronism to the radical activist who is activated by the all-embracing vision of a united humanity.

On the other hand, people with memories and traditions tend to be more conservative because they realize that radical change is not simple. The romantic utopian hates anyone who raises doubts and difficulties regarding the redemptive possibilities of the future. He or she despises "old men" who speak about "experience" and "complexity" and about the naiveté of believing in the creation of a "new man" in history. A person convinced that a new human world will emerge in the future cannot have much regard for parents and tradition.

A third challenge to the integrity of the family derives from a very different source: pessimism and hopelessness. Despair and despondency have gripped college campuses that were once centers of militant activism. Instead of anticipating and planning a radically new tomorrow, students turn inward to sensitivity groups to try to "put themselves together." Families, however, are not reared on despair. Children are not born out of hopelessness. Despondency traps an individual within the self, whereas the longing for a child is an expression of self-transcendence.

Out of despondency, some people have turned to individual self-realization as their framework for human redemption. Unbounded meanings are said to be available within each individual; there are no internal borders to what is possible. Despair is thus overcome in the discovery and expression of one's uniqueness; yet, the family is again excluded. The family becomes an intolerable burden in a culture that exclusively values self-realization.

JEWISH TRADITION AND THE FAMILY

The family is thus challenged on four fronts. Technology confronts it with a sense of temporal discontinuity. Utopianism opposes it with its vision of disconnected, revolutionary possibilities. Despair robs the family of its child. Radical individualism eradicates familial roots and structures. Nevertheless, even in such an environment, one must raise families and encourage children to marry and bear offspring. How can one possibly talk about the family in a positive way?

There are no quick and easy solutions to complex social problems. Traditions, with all the reverence they deserve, do not provide formulas that automatically resolve every human dilemma. "I-have-the-answer; What's-your-problem?" reveals a shallow misunderstanding of the relationship of religious traditions to the problems of modern society. Nevertheless, the Jewish tradition can be a source of possible directions to consider.

The following midrashic analysis of a talmudic description of parental duties may offer some insight and guidelines to the dilemma of the modern family. What are the responsibilities of parents to children?

> With respect of his son, a father is bound to circumcise [him], redeem [him, if he is firstborn], teach him Torah, take a wife for him, and teach him a craft. Some say to teach him to swim too. (B.T. *Kiddushin* 29a)

The Talmud thus imposes six parental obligations. The first duty is *brit milah* (circumcision). The Jewish infant must be introduced into the covenant of Abraham. The task of the parent is to demonstrate that a Jew is the progeny not only of biological parents but also of a person who, thousands of years ago, entered into a covenant with God. Jews are the descendants of Abraham, whose identity was based not on family biology but on a transformation of values. Abraham is defined not by his past but by a spiritual conversion, which made him the carrier of the divine hope for human history.

> And I will bless those who bless you and curse that curse
> you; and all the families of the earth shall bless
> themselves by you. (Gen. 12:3)

The symbolic significance of the change in name from
Abram to Abraham

> As for Me, this is My covenant with you: You shall be
> the father of a multitude of nations. And your name
> shall be Abraham, for I make you the father of a
> multitude of nations. (Gen. 17:4,5)

is that the recognition of Abraham as one's father is not restricted
to biological lineage but extends to a commitment to a way of life.
The family is not only a biological survival unit but also a
framework for developing identity grounded in the covenantal
aspirations of Judaism.

Furthermore, a child who identifies with Abraham learns
about the strength and dignity of being an iconoclast in history.
Abraham personifies the courage to say "no" to the corruptions of
one's time. But negation must not become a compulsion. The
person who says "no" only because another says "yes" is ultimately
a conformist whose responses are defined by others. People raised
in the tradition of Abraham can stand alone against their
environment out of profound conviction and love for a particular
way of life. Their "no" grows out of their "yes."

The second duty, *pidyon ha-ben* (redemption of one's child),
indicates that parents must not simply bring their child into the
covenant of Abraham but must also introduce the child to the
memory of Egypt. The child shares in the memory: "We were
slaves to Pharaoh in Egypt."

One of the most important functions of parents is to
transmit knowledge of realities beyond the child's own experience.

63

The father and mother must provide frames of reference rooted in the history and the memories of the covenantal community of Israel.

Torah demands *yir'ah* (respect, awe, reverence) for parents:

> The honoring of father and mother is a weighty positive command; so too, is reverence for them. The Bible attaches to the duty of honoring and revering parents an importance equal to that which it attaches to the duty of honoring and revering God. What does reverence imply? What does honor imply? Reverence requires that the son should not stand in the place in which his father usually stands, or sit in his place, or contradict his words, or decide against his opinion, or call him, living or dead, by his name. (M.T. *Hilkhot Mamrim*, VI, 1,3)

Yir'ah expresses distance. The parent is never wholly accessible, for in the parent, the child meets a person from outside of his or her world. One's identity is not grounded only in one's immediate experience; it is enriched by memories and by a past mediated by one's parents. One of the essential tasks of the parent is to be a storyteller who narrates experiences that the child never knew.

In recalling Egypt, Jews are exhorted to remember they were once slaves. Rather than deny it, they are to incorporate their history of slavery into their consciousness. Thus, love the stranger because you too were outcasts in Egypt; have regard for the poor because you too were destitute; care for the oppressed because you too were persecuted; help the defenseless because you faced annihilation; be careful with the use of power because you suffered from its misuse.

The poor person who achieves wealth after difficult struggles but then blocks out the memory of his or her previous poverty can become a harsh overseer. The "self-made man" can remain sensitive to others only if he is not ashamed to face his former destitution. If you cannot bear to acknowledge your former degradation, you will act with cruelty to those who remind you of your past. Haman, an archetypal demonic figure in Jewish history, was understood by the Midrash as a former slave who, having become a master, tried to forget his previous servitude. He therefore needed others to bow down to him in order to confirm his dignity; anything less than total subservience led to rage and violence.

In the Jewish tradition, it is crucial to create the recollection of former slavery and helplessness. Integrating memories of past suffering and humiliation and not repressing them secures one's moral identity. When the prophets wanted to return the Jewish people to moral conduct, they attempted to restore its memories. In contrast to Socrates, who believed that the source of evil was ignorance ("knowledge is virtue"), the prophets identified moral depravity with the loss of identity and of covenantal memory.

The role of parents is to help children develop a sense of history and an empathic identification with the world of experience beyond their own. Whether these memories will be relevant and meaningful to the child is another issue. The mother's and father's task is not to decide how the child will use these memories; their obligation is to see to it that the child does not enter into the future without the burden of the past.

A sense of historical memory provides children with a filter through which they can evaluate their own experiences. They need not be inextricably bound to modernity if other life options become part of their consciousness. Current values and lifestyles need not be perceived as inevitable and necessary. Historical memories can help them develop the distance necessary for critical reflection on contemporary culture.

Having elaborated on the need to introduce the child into both covenantal and historical solidarity with the people of Israel, the Talmud presents a third obligation: to teach Torah. The tradition viewed the family not only as a link to what was, but also as the transmitter of values to guide the child in everyday life.

Even though the tradition permits transference of the role of parent-as-teacher to the formal educational framework of the teacher-student relationship, there nevertheless remains unique significance to the parent's own role as teacher. The parent imparts information while creating an environment that embodies moral and spiritual values. Values are transmitted not only through formal learning but also through the living, intimate community of the family.

The danger of formal education is that the student may perceive a gap between life and learning. The child, to recognize the intimate bond between learning and action ("great is learning because it leads to practice") and to sense that ideas make a difference in the way one lives, needs parents seriously committed to their roles as educators.

Moral education is limited if one's source of norms derives only from textbooks. Law and morality, however cognitively convincing they may be, are incomplete if they do not grow out of living images that embody values and give them concrete expression. In moments of crisis, one derives the strength to overcome weakness and temptation by reflecting not only on moral rules but also on "significant others." Parents as living models can inspire courage in moments of moral crisis.

The Midrash narrates that when Joseph was managing Potiphar's household in Egypt, his master's wife tried to seduce him. When Joseph was about to succumb to her enticements, he did not recall the prohibition against adultery; rather, he saw the image of his father, Jacob. And he overcame temptation. Joseph's decision to uphold his loyalty to his master resulted not so much from the normative force of certain rules, as from the compelling influence of his father's memory. The image of the parent concretizes the normative claims of Judaism.

It is interesting to observe that, halakhically, the command of teaching was addressed not only to parents but also to grandparents. One might view this as a mere expansion of educational responsibilities. One can also, however, consider the uniqueness of a grandparent's role in teaching Torah to children.

The Talmud finds biblical support for the role of grandparents in *talmud Torah* (teaching Torah) from the text "And you shall make known to your children and your children's children the day you stood at Horeb" (Deut. 4:9–10). One might teach one's children Torah to help them find immediate meaning and guidance for everyday living, for the teachings of Torah are "our lives and length of our days and we shall meditate on them day and night." On the other hand, Torah is also to be studied in order to introduce a child to his or her collective historical roots. This kind of teaching might be the task of grandparents, for they are symbolically closer to the historical moment of Sinai. Grandparents can relate instruction not simply to the present and future; they can also imbue the study of Torah with a sense of continuity from Sinai.

Learning blossoms beyond a pupil's desire for guidance in his or her own life; it can also expand into a sense of responsibility to the normative dreams of the community of Israel. The intellect becomes saturated with historical commitments. Not only is there a quest for self-realization (the parents' role in *talmud Torah*), but also there is a challenge to place the individual within the covenant of Israel's collective existence (the grandparents' role).

Another possible distinction between the educational role of the family and formal education involves the relationship between learning and ethical responsibility. A school achieves its goal if it instills intellectual curiosity and a hunger for knowledge. Schools cultivate intelligence by introducing the student to the ocean of the

Talmud, with its logical intricacies and subtle distinctions. But the joy of intellectual creativity and of being totally engaged in a difficult passage of Talmud may lead to a severing of the intellectual personality from ethical responsibility. The family, on the other hand, relates learning to mitzvah. Familial education enriches the personality of the child by teaching that learning for its own sake loses significance if it does not enhance one's sensitivity to others.

These, then, are the three foci of the Jewish heritage: the covenant (*brit milah*), Egypt (*pidyon ha-ben*), and Sinai (*talmud Torah*). The Talmud, in quoting the Tosefta, adds that parents must find their son a wife (cf. Jer. 29:6) and teach him a trade (cf. Eccl. 9:9).

The attention paid to marriage in Tractate *Kiddushin* indicates a great concern for a child's bodily needs. It is the responsibility of parents to recognize that their children have physical and emotional needs. Moral education becomes an abstraction if it ignores the reality of the physical body.

Thus, a boy's bar mitzvah is at age thirteen and a girl's bat mitzvah is at age twelve because, according to the Talmud, these are the times when sexual awareness begins in males and females, respectively. The connection between normative responsibility and sexual consciousness means that sexual self-awareness should be integrated into a person's normative mitzvah consciousness.

The duty to provide for the marriage of one's children should not to be understood solely in economic and material terms. It indicates the importance of creating family conditions that foster the psychological capacity to love the "other." The task of modern parents, broadly speaking, is to build a family structure that instills feelings of adequacy that enable the mature son or daughter to function within the framework of marriage.

With regard to the obligation of teaching one's child a trade, there were two opinions in the Talmud: (1) to teach about business and (2) (that of R. Judah) to teach a trade that could withstand market fluctuations. The common goal was to provide for a child's economic dignity and welfare so that he or she would not be overwhelmed by financial crises.

The last obligation, to teach a child how to swim, may imply that part of the role of the parent is to teach a child to cope with the unpredictable. Does your child know how to handle unforeseen crises and have the resources to deal with unanticipated misfortune?

From a Judaic perspective, the family is an instrument of history; the parent is significant for the child not because of the latter's helplessness and incompetence but because, without the parent, the child has no Sinai, no Egypt, no Abraham—in a word, no memory. When the family loses its significance as a source of history, it centers increasingly on the psychological dynamics of dependency. Psychologists replace prophets as the key figures providing for the health of the family. Parents often feel needed only because their children cannot survive economically without them. In a tradition-oriented family, they feel—and are—needed because the next generation cannot live in the future without a past.

Judaism imposes a vital task on parents: to tell the Jewish people's story. What the child does with this past, no parent can decree. Parents provide their children with luggage. Whether they open up this luggage in the future and use its contents is beyond the knowledge and control of parents. It is sufficient for parents to aim at instilling memories that "haunt" children an entire lifetime; their bequest is a weight of generations, an awareness that a Jew's biography begins with Abraham.

4

TORAH AND SECULARISM

REFLECTIONS ON THE ACTIVE AND PASSIVE DIMENSIONS (*DIN* AND *RAHAMIM*) OF JEWISH SPIRITUALITY

ONE OF THE disturbing characteristics of Jewish identity in the modern world is the loss of historical memory and tradition. Modernity in many respects can be characterized by "discontinuous consciousness," a lack of rootedness in the past, a conception of the present as an instant locked into itself. The modern "triumphant" secular person believes that tradition is unnecessary because the autonomous self has within it sufficient resources to solve the problems of the human condition.

Another offspring of modernity is the disillusioned person who reflects the failures of human efforts to bring about the just society. It is difficult to inspire faith in radical schemes to recreate the world, in view of repeated disillusionment with totalistic political movements. Modernity thus lacks the resources to provide us with a future in which to believe.

If technology has eliminated the past, and the failures of secular revolutions have aborted the future, then people are caught in a single temporal dimension. How can they respond to the loss

of history? By losing themselves hedonistically in the moment—
"It's later than you think; enjoy yourself now!"—or by adopting a
religious response that promises to connect human beings with a
deeper dimension of spirituality?

One religious response to the frustration at human failures
to establish a just society involves withdrawing into privacy by
building a world out of the inner life of the individual. This
religious outlook offers meaning and spiritual fulfillment for an
individual outside the social and communal structures of society.
One may characterize this option as an *escape response* to modern
secular civilization.

Another response that typifies modern spirituality can be
characterized as a *retreat response*. Rather than escape from history
to the haven of the private self, one who chooses this response
retreats from the broad stage of history to the confines of a
community or sect. Alasdair MacIntyre speaks of the "religion of
the enclave," a religion in which a remnant develops some form of
earnest communal religious life. One might call such a group a
communion that prays together, or a fellowship that shares the
Sabbath together, but not a true community, responsible for its
total collective existence. It is a mode of social involvement and
spiritual intensity in isolation from the total rhythm of life, where
the sacred is severed from the profane.

A possible example of this phenomenon is the modern
house of worship where people meet on a Sabbath to share a
common life of worship that is sharply separated from their
mundane life during the rest of the week. The temple or church can
act as a corrective to the anxieties and pains of everyday life. Going
to a house of worship can be a moral holiday, an oasis in a desert
of busyness and anonymity, where one escapes the impersonality of
the marketplace. There was a time in America when large
synagogues were thought to be the sign of the Jews' entering
modernity. Today, many believe that large synagogues are failing,

and they seek instead smaller congregations that allow for deeper interpersonal experiences.

Religious institutions often justify themselves by claiming to offer a form of leisure and peace of mind that secularism cannot. Indeed, religion as enclave prospers by emphasizing its separation from the profane and by pointing to the failures of secular human efforts. Sermons tend to harp on the ill-conceived consequences of technology, reveling in the hazardous ecological effects of industrial society, the breakdown of the family and of parental authority, and the spread of drugs, promiscuity, and AIDS. The more the failures of secular society are emphasized, the more religious institutions justify their place in the modern world. Ritual and tradition are preached as the only proven antidote to the anarchic, violent spirit of secular society.

The religion of the retreat is not a mystical escape in search of eternity within the self, but a framework for a religious community alienated from secular society.

A third response to secularism is the identification of religion with prophetic social criticism. Here, religion moves to the margins of history; there, from an aloof, isolated vantage point, safe from involvement with the material and social forces that shape life, it condemns and criticizes. In the role of relentless critic, religion abandons its role in history, giving to Caesar what is Caesar's and, in effect, turning its back on the collective world. The use of the biblical prophets to validate this form of social criticism is a perversion of prophetic consciousness. The prophet is a messenger of a God seeking embodiment in all aspects of communal life, but the God of these modern "prophets" remains transcendent and fosters alienation from community and history. Transcendence is expressed in the refusal to translate the spiritual vision into a concrete involvement with lived human history.

These different religious orientations can be understood as responses to the remarkable growth of human power in the modern world. This power is often viewed as a threat to religion because it fosters human pride and feelings of self-sufficiency. Science and technology are products of human knowledge and initiative. The responses discussed above share a common inability to cope with the success of secular power.

Classic Judaism, however, can offer a different response to secularism. Halakhic thought and practice suggest a religious orientation that carefully balances feelings of human adequacy and dependence. The Sabbath–weekday metaphor can provide us with a fuller understanding of these two countervailing senses of self. "Remember the Sabbath and keep it holy. Six days you shall labor and do all your work, but the seventh day is a sabbath of the Lord your God; you shall not do any work" (Exod. 20:8–10).

An analysis of the nature of the Sabbath and of the Jewish approach to creation, revelation, and redemption will reveal a consistent concern with balancing a sense of human power and assertiveness with an awareness of human finitude and limitations.

CREATION

In Genesis, the biblical narrative begins with a description of God who creates for six days, who manifests His will by shaping the world. In fashioning a finite being who is free, God creates a being in His own image. The human ability to structure the social and the natural environments, and to create a home in the midst of hostile or indifferent natural conditions, embodies the dignity of the religious person conscious of having been created in the image of God.

Rabbi Joseph B. Soloveitchik, in *Halakhic Man* and *The Lonely Man of Faith*, claims that creation is not simply a cosmological event but also a model to be imitated by human beings. As God is Creator, so shall you be a creator. Creation is not the exclusive prerogative of God.

A person whose religious sensibilities are nurtured by the biblical creation model cannot sit passively and watch a child die of leukemia. He or she must reject the myth that hunger, sickness, and exploitation are inevitable or tolerable because of the doctrine of divine providence. To R. Soloveitchik, feelings of responsibility and belief in the efficacy of human efforts characterize biblical anthropology. He also argues that one of the profound spiritual implications of secular technological progress is an increase in the scope of human responsibility:

> The brute's existence is an undignified one because it is a helpless existence. Human existence is a dignified one because it is a glorious, majestic, powerful existence.... Dignity of man expressing itself in the awareness of being responsible and of being capable of discharging his responsibility cannot be realized as long as he has not gained mastery over his environment.... Man of old who could not fight disease and succumbed in multitudes to yellow fever or any other plague with degrading helplessness could not lay claim to dignity. Only the man who builds hospitals, discovers therapeutic techniques, and saves lives is blessed with dignity.... Civilized man has gained limited control of nature and has become, in certain respects, her master, and with mastery, he has attained dignity, as well. His mastery has made it possible for him to act in accordance with his responsibility. (*The Lonely Man of Faith*, pp. 14–15)

Technology expands human ability to affect the environment, and by doing so it also expands the range of human obligations. If only because of the media, one can no longer claim ignorance of suffering even in remote corners of the earth. Coupled with scientific and technological know-how, this knowledge extends the range of responsibility beyond one's immediate environment. Industrialization disturbs the complacency of the morally insulated individual; it universalizes moral obligation and challenges abstract sermonizing by presenting concrete opportunities for action.

Secularization—in the sense of the expansion of the domain over which human beings can take responsibility—can thus be described as an instrument of God. God does not issue a mandate to establish justice and love on earth without providing human beings with the ability to fulfill this task. Technological consciousness can, therefore, be regarded as an instrument of the willful God of history.

THE SABBATH

The cycle of six days of the week and the Sabbath expresses the dialectical relationship between creator and creature. The Sabbath enables us to experience human power and assertion as gifts of God. R. Hoshayah, in *Midrash Rabbah*, comments on the paradox of human beings being created in the image of God:

> When the Holy One, Blessed be He, created Adam, the ministering angels mistook Adam for a divine being and wished to exclaim "Holy!" before him. What does this resemble? A king and a governor were riding together in a chariot. The king's subjects wished to greet their king with cries of "Sovereign!" but they did not know which was the king. What, then, did the king

do? He pushed the governor out of the chariot and, thus, the subjects knew who was the king.

"Similarly," said R. Hoshayah, "when God created Adam, the angels mistook him [for God]. What did the Holy One, blessed be He, do? He caused sleep to fall upon him and thus all knew he was a human being...." (*Midrash Rabbah*, Genesis, VIII, 4,5)

This midrash addresses the danger of human self-deification. Because of human greatness as manifest in willful control and power over the rest of nature, the gap between God and human beings can be blurred. Sleep, however, destroys the illusion of omnipotence, forcing us to recognize our humanity. Sleep symbolizes a state of consciousness in which human beings give up control and mastery.

The dialectic between control and power, on one hand, and letting go and rest, on the other, characterizes the tension the religious person faces in the confrontation with advanced technological society. Because human beings are accorded such majesty and given so great a task in history, technology can correctly be perceived as an invaluable extension of humanity's God-given charge. The danger is that this nobility and majesty may lead to the human usurpation of the role of God

On the Sabbath, the Creator God ceases to act as an independent willful agent. Similarly, on the Sabbath, a person may not stand over and against the universe as a Promethean figure. On the Sabbath, one is expected to relate to the world not in terms of subject–object mastery. The seventh day is informed by an existential rhythm in which human beings and the world participate equally as creatures of God.

The halakhic notion of the holiness of the Sabbath aims at controlling the human impulse to mastery by setting limits to human dominance of nature. Nature is transformed from an "it" into a "thou"; the world is no longer the object of human gratification. The halakhic norms of the Sabbath affirm the value of existence outside of an anthropocentric perspective.

The setting of the sun ushers in a unit of time when the flowers of the field and I are equal members of the universe. Halakhah prohibits my plucking a flower from my garden or doing with it as I please. At sunset the flower becomes a "thou" with a right to existence irrespective of its instrumental value for me. I stand silently before nature as before a fellow creature and not as before a potential object of my control. By forcing us to experience the meaning of being creatures of God, the Sabbath aims at healing the human grandiosity of technological arrogance.

As the sun sets we dramatically experience our inability to control the holy. Human beings may not decide when the Sabbath begins. As I race against time on Friday afternoon and fight like Joshua to hold back the sun so as to complete some unfinished work, I realize that despite my efforts, I must respond to that which is beyond my control. As the sun sinks silently and relentlessly, God, as it were, announces: "You are no longer a creator; you are a creature." And as the Sabbath night blessing over wine—"Blessed are you, O Lord, Who sanctifies the Sabbath"—indicates, the holiness of the Sabbath is independent of human initiative.

This view of Creation and of the Sabbath reflects the relationship between human will and assertion, and human limits and creatureliness. On the day of rest, a mortal being experiences its limits. The Sabbath brings peace by healing the human inclination to manipulate and control. The "willful" person of the six weekdays acknowledges human finitude in the restful joy of "Sabbath sleep" (as in the midrashic association between sleep and creature-consciousness).

DIN AND *RAHAMIM*

The tension between willful assertion and quiet receptivity is a central motif of rabbinic thought. The pair of concepts *rahamim* (mercy, compassion) and *din* (judgment, justice) gives expression to this dialectic. According to the midrash, God initially thought of creating the world with the quality of *din*, and then, realizing that the world could not endure with *din* alone, introduced the quality of *rahamim*.

> "The Lord God [made earth and heaven]." This may be compared to a king who had some empty glasses. Said the king: 'If I pour hot water into them, they will burst; if cold, they will contract [and snap].' What then did the king do? He mixed hot and cold water and poured it into them, and so they remained [unbroken]. Even so, said the Holy One, blessed be He: 'If I create the world on the basis of mercy alone, its sins will be great; on the basis of judgment alone, the world cannot exist. Hence I will create it on the basis of judgment and of mercy, and may it then stand!' Hence the expression, 'The Lord God (Adonai [the Tetragrammaton] Elohim).' (*Midrash Rabbah*, Genesis, XII, 15)

Din as a behavioral quality suggests willfulness and assertiveness. As the original foundation of reality, *din* symbolizes a world of human responsibility and accountability before a God Who responds on the basis of merit. *Din* expresses the idea of human adequacy and dignity because of the implied assumption that human beings are capable of shouldering responsibility for their actions. Justice and responsibility (*din*) presuppose the capacity to act or to refrain from acting; *din*, therefore, is linked to human will and assertion.

79

The Midrash claims that the quality of *din* would be disastrous if it were not coupled with *rahamim*, or unconditional love. In order for *din* not to become a destructive force, it must be balanced by a principle of love that does not depend on merit.

Rahamim is a feature of relationships that cannot be controlled. *Din* alone can create a person who feels the need to be in charge of every situation. The fear that unless you have total control you will be ignored leads to a self-defeating obsession with constantly inducing the responses of others.

Hence the significance of conjoining *din* and *rahamim*. Mercy, or the exclusive reliance on Divine Grace, is a response to the belief that human beings are depraved or incapable of bearing responsibility for their conduct. A theology of grace alone best fits the helpless child who is unable to survive without the unconditional care of its parent. On the other hand, the principle of *din* as assertiveness alone excludes trust, gentleness, and openness to others. *Rahamim* and *din* together join responsiveness, irrespective of human assertion, with human initiative and responsibility.

REVELATION

Revelation in Judaism is first and foremost the giving of the Torah. An analysis of the nature of Torah reveals the interplay of principles similar to *din* and *rahamim*.

The revelation at Sinai differs from the mystic experience. The Torah does not present human beings with esoteric mysteries but with a clear task. God's disclosure is in the form of mitzvah (divine commandment). As opposed to the spiritual urge to withdraw from human history, the receiver of Torah is thrust into the affairs of humanity. Revelation at Sinai is an encounter with a mission to sanctify the earth and to construct a covenantal community: "And I will be sanctified among the people of Israel."

A second aspect of Torah follows from the law-giving nature of revelation, namely, acknowledgment of the possibility of failure. The task of implementing the Torah is spelled out in a system of norms, and norms as commands or laws presuppose the possibility of nonobedience. Sinai does not present a romantic conception of humanity; rather, it addresses real people, who are vulnerable and weak. The Torah was given in the desert, where people are exposed to failure and defeat, where they are prepared to give up their freedom and sacred destiny to satisfy their momentary desire for bread and water.

The Jewish tradition acknowledges this human reality and accepts it as the price of the divine decision to be revealed within human history. Unlike the god of Aristotle, who is wrapped in blissful self-contemplation, the God of the covenant forgoes the serenity of self-sufficient perfection by wedding divine fate to the vicissitudes of human history. God chooses to be involved with human society despite the real possibility of failure.

Sinai thus reveals a God Who is present with human beings no matter what their failures and shortcomings. In the Talmud, R. Meir argues that the people of Israel are considered "children of God" even when they violate the covenant and do not act as children. In contrast to R. Yehudah, who maintains the conditional nature of being called children of God, R. Meir argues for the endurance of the intimate relationship with God irrespective of merit. Demand and responsibility are conjoined with love and acceptance.

The prophet fulfills a dual role that embodies these two principles. The prophet speaks to human beings in the name of God and transmits the uncompromising demands of the Almighty. Yet, at other times, the prophet approaches God and tries to temper divine anger at human failure. Instead of rejecting the people out of hopeless despair, the prophet intercedes on their behalf and tries to protect them from divine fury (see Yochanan

Muffs, "Who Will Stand in the Breach? A Study in Prophetic Intercession," in *Love and Joy: Law, Language and Religion in Ancient Israel* [New York & Jerusalem: The Jewish Theological Seminary of America, 1992]).

On one level, the prophets protect the people of Israel by engaging the Almighty in dialogue on their behalf. Yet, they are never patronizing. Strict in their demands, they view Israel through the eyes of justice and accountability. *Din* implies a heavy burden of responsibility. You stand in judgment before God ("the yoke of the commandments"); you are accountable for all your actions. At the same time, the prophet communicates love and *rahamim* in encouraging people to persevere despite failures and setbacks. Divine *rahamim* makes it possible for you to believe that "The gates of *teshuvah* (return, repentance) are never closed. One can begin anew."

The classic response of rabbinic Judaism to failure and suffering is *teshuvah*. People educated in the spirit of Judaism should not celebrate the failures of technological society. Rather than make religious capital out of human setbacks, they should feel personally pained when the "Great Society" fails to materialize. The religious response should not be discouragement but, on the contrary, encouragement to try again—that is, a *teshuvah* response. Perseverance in the historical struggle to extend human responsibility by eliminating sources of suffering and chaos is the religious response called for by the biblical and rabbinic traditions.

MESSIANIC REDEMPTION

The dialectic between *din* and *rahamim* influenced rabbinic conceptions of hope and redemption. In *Sanhedrin* 97b, two views of the conditions for historical redemption are presented. Shmuel maintains that "it is sufficient for the mourner to persevere in mourning"—that is, that redemption will take place even if we suffer passively. This view reflects the quality of *rahamim*; redemption will "erupt" irrespective of human efforts. In contrast, Rav and R. Eliezer make *teshuvah* a condition of *geulah*, redemption. The principle of human will and initiative, the quality of *din*, defines the nature of this approach.

In *Hilkhot Teshuvah*, Maimonides combines these two views into a single formulation that subtly balances the qualities of *rahamim* and *din*. Like Rav, Maimonides says that redemption depends on human initiative—that is, on *teshuvah*—yet, he adds that the Torah communicated a divine promise that "in the end" people will in fact do *teshuvah*. The divine promise provides the certainty of redemption that only the quality of *rahamim* can provide; yet, the insistence on *teshuvah* retains the willful, *din*, perspective. Even when offering Jews the precious guarantee they long for, Maimonides refused to be seduced into a passive, apocalyptic eschatology.

THE HOLY AND THE PROFANE IN THE SABBATH AND THE FESTIVALS

In the Jewish tradition, weekdays do not have distinct names (such as Sunday, Monday) but are referred to as successive units in a progression leading to the Sabbath: the first day to the Sabbath, the second day to the Sabbath, and so on. When the traditional Jew is located in *hol* (the mundane, everyday), time is not a closed collection of discrete units but a continuity pointing toward the holy. The Sabbath thus introduces anticipation and aspiration into the struggles of each weekday.

Now, although the holiness of the Sabbath is exclusively God's gift, the holiness of the festivals introduces the motif of human assertion into the concept of the holy. The holy, therefore, is not necessarily the complete antithesis of the profane. In the language of dialectics, there is a productive interaction between these opposing elements. Accordingly, even within the holy, there is an aspect of human assertion. Not only is *hol* (the weekday) the domain of human initiative and dignity, but holiness too may bear the marks of human assertion.

This point is suggested by the difference between the *Kiddush* (blessing over the wine) recited on the Sabbath and on the festivals. The blessing "Blessed are You, O Lord, Who sanctifies the Sabbath" indicates that the holiness of this day is independent of human initiative. The blessing recited on the festivals, however, is "Blessed are You, O Lord, Who sanctifies *Israel* and the festivals." As rabbinic commentaries indicate, the sanctification of the festivals is a product of *Israel's* activity. In other words, God sanctifies Israel, who then becomes a holy people and a co-partner in the sanctification of time.

When celebrating the Sabbath as a memorial to creation, we perceive holiness as God's creatures, who have received a divine gift. When celebrating the historical festivals, on the other hand, we perceive holiness as a covenantal, historical people that has become an active participant with God in history.

THE STATE OF ISRAEL

The categories discussed above shed light on the religious significance of the reestablishment of the State of Israel. Israel restores to Judaism the full spiritual potential of the everyday; it adds new dimensions to the tension between the holy and the secular. Holiness is not achieved in withdrawal from reality; sanctity is reflected in the way we deal with the everyday. "Six days you shall labor and do all your work" has far-reaching normative significance for the spiritual person. The right to experience the holy comes only after a person has accepted the challenge of "six days."

"Six days you shall labor..." R. says: Behold this is a separate decree, for just as Israel was commanded the positive mitzvah of resting [on the Sabbath] so too were they commanded regarding labor [on the rest of the week]. (*Mekhilta D'Rabbi Simon b. Jochai, Yitro*, Exodus 20:9)

The difference between Judaism in the land of Israel and in the diaspora is that Israel demands that Judaism be significant as a way of life for an entire community. Judaism cannot simply offer Jews a retreat or an enclave to protest against an estranged world. Israel enables Jews to overcome religious compartmentalization by providing us with a state in which Jews are responsible for all they do and for all the social and political institutions they build. Jews can no longer remain the prophetic critics in the marketplaces of others.

The challenge facing twentieth-century Jews was either to choose a Jerusalem of heaven, which one entered only in one's prayers, or to build a Jerusalem of the earth, for which one would be responsible seven days of the week. Where was God to dwell? In a mystic rapture? Or in a living community? The revolution of secular Zionism created the conditions in Judaism for the "return" of the Lord to the fullness of everyday life, with all its problematic features.

CONCRETENESS: THE SPIRITUAL SIGNIFICANCE OF THE EVERYDAY (*HOL*)

Religious talk is often identified with lofty phrases and ideals. People enjoy the beauty and drama of descriptions of spiritual beings and situations, and they protect these fantasies by insisting on untestability. One of the most serious criticisms of religious language is its unfalsifiability. A common caricature of the theologian is of a person who qualifies what he says, then qualifies again and again until, after qualifications of the hundredth degree, he empties his claim of any significance.

The decision not to put one's ideals to the test is, in effect, a decision to be safe at the risk of one's words becoming vacuous. In one sense, Judaism's return to the concrete discloses its imperfections and exposes it to the watchful eye of others. Reality tests convictions and, in the testing, reveals the weaknesses and delusions of unproved ideals. In its return to the land, Judaism has been compelled to abandon the realm of verbal purity.

For hundreds of years, Jews concluded the Passover Haggadah with the words "Next year in Jerusalem," symbolizing the capacity of a people to dream irrespective of historical conditions. The ability to remember the Exodus in times of unspeakable misery and oppression enabled Jews to rise above their political circumstances. They viewed themselves as free, regardless of how others viewed them.

What happens to that vision when one actually returns to Jerusalem, walks her streets, and lives in her houses? The question is, can we continue to dream on Jaffa Road? Can we experience transcendence within the mundane? Can we hope from within reality? Or must we Jews live on the periphery of human history in order to offer a vision for those at the center?

Jews have often lived on the margins of history. There are Jews who are most comfortable as protesters or outcasts. It is easy to be the conscience of the world when you do not have to implement your moral ideals and aspirations in concrete reality.

Jews who embraced Zionism abandoned the role of the sideline conscience of humanity. We thus chose to speak from within the concreteness of life, to see whether Judaism would reveal its strength when faced with ordinary human problems. In choosing to get our hands dirty, we decided to let Judaism grow from the earth. But when an organism is rooted in the soil, it does not always remain unsullied and clean. When a people is responsible for a total society, others see its flaws. The world press exposes our failings to public scrutiny.

What courage it took for Jews to abandon the safety of our prayer books and classical religious texts! The people of the book became the people of the earth. We now are often pained and disillusioned by having to know ourselves by what we do. People prefer to be inspired by prayers for Jerusalem and for the ingathering of the exiles, over having to face the social and cultural problems of living together with the exiles.

In Leviticus 22:32, God says, "I will be sanctified," but only after warning the people of Israel not to profane His holy Name. "You shall not profane My holy name, that I may be sanctified in the midst of the Israelite people." The decision to sanctify God (*kiddush ha-shem*) in the midst of community exposes us to the danger of failure and profanation (*hillul ha-shem*).

CONCRETENESS: THE HEALING OF GRANDIOSITY

The return of Judaism to the concrete, and the acceptance of the challenge to embody its spiritual vision within ordinary everyday reality, may engender a new perception of the relationship between Judaism, Christianity, and Islam. Today there is an opportunity to heal one of the most devastating diseases spread by religion in human history: hatred of the outsider and inability to share and validate the spiritual vision of others. Religions often speak of love and brotherhood. Repeatedly, Jews have invoked the rabbinic statement "Beloved are human beings created in the image of God." The events of history, however, have tested monotheistic religions, which, unfortunately, have often failed to appreciate the dignity of the stranger. The "Fatherhood of God" has not led to the "Brotherhood of Man."

The claim to exclusive authenticity is a form of violence. So, too, is the infantilization of others by confining them exclusively to one's own faith categories. The assimilation of other religious traditions to one's own theological faith system, regardless of how they view themselves, is religious hubris of the worst kind.

To heal spiritual tyranny, one must enter the self-perception of the other. "Do not judge your fellow human beings until you have entered into their place" (*Avot*, 2:5) implies that one must try to perceive others as they perceive themselves. This is a precondition of genuine listening and respect.

Reducing a "subject" to an "object" leads to aggression. You heal your aggression when you see the other person as a being who sets limits to your conduct. In experiencing these limits, the "I" discovers its creatureliness. An individual who acquires the power and strength not to be reduced to an object of manipulation can heal the disease of spiritual tyranny in others.

Israel's return to history as a political community constitutes a proclamation to the world that Jews are no longer a wandering exilic people. Judaism is not an idea. It is the way of life of a people. Here, then, is an opportunity to redeem the violence of categorical monism: Christendom is challenged to listen to Judaism not only as the forerunner of Christianity but from within Judaism's own self-understanding. Islam is asked to see more than a vestigial corruption of Semitic monotheism. Israel's particularity may be spiritually redemptive because it heals hubris. It humbles grandiosity; it banishes the illusion that religious ways of life demand universalization.

Secular Zionism has inspired and given Jews the means to return not to a spiritual and secure heaven but to an unredeemed and uncertain earth. Zionism is a rejection of the belief that Jewish sovereignty must be the expression of a messianic reality. Political Zionism expresses the power of a community to act as a nation in an unredeemed world. We do not know whether our return to history harbors a messianic renewal. But as bearers of the Sinai covenant, we know that we are responsible and challenged to discover ways of making Judaism a live option in a secular world.

PART II

EDUCATING TOWARD
INCLUSIVENESS

5

CREATING A SHARED SPIRITUAL LANGUAGE FOR ISRAELI AND DIASPORA EDUCATION

THIS ESSAY WILL argue against the claim that an educational system grounded in a commitment to Torah and Halakhah must educate toward the spiritual insulation of its students. Opportunities exist within the tradition to educate toward sensitivity to other viewpoints and openness to dialogue. I shall attempt to indicate possibilities for a shared spiritual language between different sectors of the Jewish community. First, I shall consider how a halakhically committed student can find support within the tradition for an appreciation of values not grounded on traditional sources of authority. Second, I shall suggest philosophic approaches to Halakhah and God that may help create a shared universe of discourse between halakhic and nonhalakhic Jews. Finally, I shall argue for an approach to mitzvot that stresses the urgency of realizing one's individual spiritual aspirations within the matrix of community.

Zionism in the twentieth century has created a framework for Jewish political activism. It expresses the revolutionary thrust of the Jewish people to become politically autonomous. It reflects the will of the Jewish people to determine, as far as possible, its own historical destiny. Zionism has provided a cause around which Jews with different ideologies and lifestyles have forged a minimum basis for community. The yearning for liberation from exile, however understood, is a vital source of Jewish self-understanding and collective action.

Rabbi Joseph Ber Soloveitchik, in his article "The Voice of My Beloved Knocks" (*Kol Dodi Dofek*), uses traditional covenantal categories to explain the religious significance of community forged by common political destiny. He describes the resurgence of Jewish political autonomy in terms of *brit goral* (covenantal destiny). His attempt to understand the secular Zionist revolution and the State of Israel in traditional, covenantal categories indicates how deeply Israel's political existence has permeated the spiritual consciousness of contemporary Orthodox Jews. R. Soloveitchik is not satisfied, however, with community based on a common historical and political fate. He argues that the Jewish people must strive to become, as in the past, a community of shared spiritual goals. His article reflects the hope that beyond shared political destiny, the soil of the Israeli reality may nurture a renewal of *brit ye'ud* (covenantal spiritual aspiration).

One can appreciate the pathos of R. Soloveitchik's yearning that *brit goral* be consummated with *brit ye'ud*. But, while the shared values of Jewish society were quite clear during long periods of history, today, unfortunately, there is no consensus as to how the Jewish people ought to express *brit ye'ud*. Given the contemporary breakdown of traditional Jewish society, is it possible to create a community of shared values? Or will the sense of Jewish community be limited to the struggle for survival?

94

TRADITION AND THE VARIETIES
OF RELIGIOUS EXPRESSION

Let us examine some of the stumbling blocks to creating a community of shared values among Jews. Creative encounters change people. New ideas and concepts may force you to reevaluate your initial beliefs and views, casting doubt on previously unquestioned certainties. In his introduction to *The Guide of the Perplexed*, Maimonides realized that once the student addressed in the *Guide* encountered other philosophic positions, he would not be able to ignore their challenges to traditional Judaism. Intellectual repression is not an option if one's goal is to serve God out of love.

In suggesting that students in our traditional educational system engage in dialogue with Jews who live according to different lifestyles and value systems, we, too, realize that such encounters may create serious doubts and questions. Previously accepted certainties may have to be rethought. Recognizing this, we must help our students overcome such potentially paralyzing doubts by providing them with tools that will sustain them through periods of intellectual struggle.

What educational approach will help our students realize that a religiously committed person can live with conflict and doubt? What insights can turn the turmoil of encountering others to creative use? How can we convince students that doubt can contain the seeds of new insights into untapped depths of the tradition?

Too frequently in traditional education, religious convictions are conveyed through human models of dedicated, unquestioning, simple faith. Too seldom do we indicate the dark nights of the soul that precede the certainty of faith. Can one imagine Maimonides' *The Guide of the Perplexed* having been written by a person who had not struggled with profound religious issues? It is inconceivable that Maimonides wrote the *Guide* only for others but not for himself. One cannot guide the perplexed without having felt the anguish of doubt oneself. In his legal works, Maimonides created sufficient complexity and confusion to bring the traditional reader of his halakhic works to the threshold of the philosophical, spiritual world of *The Guide of the Perplexed*.

Students must be taught that insulation from differing views and experiences need not characterize a spiritual worldview grounded in revelation. It is essential for students to be shown that religious personalities in our tradition confronted, and often welcomed, challenges that forced them to rethink accepted beliefs and practices. Instead of viewing the tradition as immune to novelty, the student must be taught to appreciate the profound dialectic between continuity and innovation in the rabbinic tradition. A religious education that provides an appreciation of the thought processes of the rabbinic mind and the dynamic tension between continuity and novelty in our foundational texts would encourage today's students to continue in the tradition of bold yet loyal *parshanut* (commentary, interpretation) without fear.

A generation that has to grapple with intellectual challenges and to grow spiritually within a pluralistic society that is often indifferent to its deepest commitments must be provided with models of how creative possibilities can emerge out of doubt and uncertainty. We pay a heavy price for not revealing the struggles of faith. The dropout rate from religious circles into pluralistic secular society reflects the weakness of an educational approach that hides the reality of religious confusion.

We must also correct the mistaken image that religious individuals in the past were of one cloth. We must give due recognition to the variety of religious sensibilities expressed in the tradition. Our students should be exposed not only to uniform halakhic practice but also to the vital, inner spiritual life of halakhic personalities. They must be made aware of the rich diversity of approaches to *ta'amei ha-mitzvot* (reasons for commandments) in the tradition. We present a distorted picture of religious practice if we divorce the description of an action from the intention of the actor. To the uninformed observer, the Kabbalists and Maimonides perform the same mitzvah. One who understands their respective approaches to *ta'amei ha-mitzvot*, however, realizes that they are not doing the same thing. The performance of mitzvot should not be reduced to an external, mechanical behaviorism.

Exposure to multiple aggadic approaches to mitzvot gives meaning to the traditional saying that although the Torah was *given* once; it is *received* differently in each generation. What happens when an educational system emphasizes the variety of spiritual options? The student comes to realize that the tradition is more than shared practice and behavioral obedience, and that the practice of Halakhah involves the fullness of one's personality. Our educators, therefore, must present a broad range of authentic religious models. Such a multiplicity of models provides breathing space for the variety of intellectual and psychological sensibilities among their students.

In an attempt to achieve religious certainty, contemporary halakhic education tends to emphasize one model of authenticity. It attempts to gloss over and harmonize the teeming variety of religious sensibilities and approaches contained in our tradition. The religious security that a monolithic approach attempts to achieve is often hollow and atrophic. Halakhic monism deprives the student of the opportunity of developing his or her own *ta'amei ha-mitzvot*, a responsibility one must shoulder even in a system with a detailed *Shulhan Arukh* (code of law, lit. "a set table").

When one is exposed to the playful mythic imagination of the mystics; the sober, rational passion of Maimonides; and the love of imagery in Halevi, one recognizes that the tradition was able to accommodate many different spiritual sensibilities. In the tradition, aggadic teleology was never normative. A fuller understanding of Judaism must therefore contain an appreciation of the interaction between pluralistic aggadot (nonlegal, narrative sections of rabbinic literature) and uniform halalakhic practice. It must reflect the interplay between obedience and conformity to authority, on one hand, and a spontaneous, freely chosen, personal spiritual teleology, on the other (see A. J. Heschel, "The Problem of Polarity" in *God in Search of Man*).

Emphasis on the subjective elements within Halakhah will help mitigate the monistic harshness that frequently accompanies a highly structured spiritual system. Students whose understandings of Halakhah are informed by the variety of *ta'amei ha-mitzvot* will find richness in their spiritual lives even while recognizing that others draw meaning for their halakhic practices from different spiritual sources.

HALAKHIC ARGUMENTATION

Thus far I have tried to show that Halakhah has never freed the individual from the need to develop a personal spiritual worldview. Emphasis on the broad aggadic options available within the tradition may be helpful in developing students who feel secure with their approaches to religious practice even while recognizing other valid perceptions of Halakhah. I should now like to indicate how such a sensibility might also be nurtured by the study of the logic of halakhic argumentation.

What is the relationship of halakhic argumentation to revelation? What are the logical tools needed to understand legal disagreement in the Talmud? How can two opposing views both be considered "the words of the living God"? What is the cognitive status of a rejected, minority opinion? Is divine truth revealed in the opinion of the majority, or is majority rule a procedural, juridical principle, which does not imply exclusive truth in the application of law?

A serious study of the epistemology of halakhic argumentation may help the student realize that halakhic reasons never provide the cognitive certainty of a deductive syllogism. Legal decisions are not necessarily inferences drawn from true premises. In other words, decision making in a legal system is not a mechanical process. The relative weights granted to principles and values, and the appreciation of the particularity of different situations and historical contexts, all participate in halakhic decision making (see my essay "Judaism As an Interpretive Tradition" [p. 3], and Moshe Halbertal, *People of the Book: Canon, Meaning, and Authority* [Cambridge: Harvard University Press, 1977]).

A traditional understanding of *Torah mi-Sinai* (Torah from Sinai), that is, Torah as Divine revelation, cannot be divorced from the way in which talmudic scholars applied Torah to life. The halakhic process clearly shows that there was more than one path leading from belief in revelation to halakhic practice and decision making.

One who has a deep appreciation of the logic of halakhic argumentation can never be certain that current practices represent the only possible response to the Torah of God. Alternative ways of practice are present in a living tradition that applies *Torah mi-Sinai* to everyday life. "These and these are the words of the living God" is an enduring description of halakhic thinking. In the tradition, the ultimate source of halakhic authority is God; yet, the application of Halakhah to life is contingent on human reasoning and judgment. *K'nesset yisrael* (the congregation of Israel) was and always will be responsible for the way of life it develops.

Both halakhic and aggadic components of the tradition can support the development of a pluralistic spiritual sensibility. Commitment to practice and a passionate concern with action need not be grounded in an epistemology that provides certainty. It is a

99

profound educational mistake to teach texts that do not acknowledge different halakhic arguments and *ta'amei ha-mitzvot*. Learning based on the *Kitzur Shulhan Arukh* (Abridged Code of Jewish Law) can have a quality of rote catechism. Compared with the study of Talmud, the codes of law and "how-to" books are like a bathtub compared with an ocean. In an ocean, multiple strokes and movements are possible. In a bathtub, you can only immerse yourself and passively soak in the water without movement or maneuverability. There is a spiritual adventure and diversity in the ocean of Talmud. There is a limited spiritual monism and passivity in the study of halakhic rulebooks.

I appreciate the concern with educating toward the importance of halakhic practice. This should not, however, be achieved at the expense of the rich adventure of being exposed to multiple points of view.

A SHARED SPIRITUAL LANGUAGE:
POSSIBILITIES AND STRATEGIES

Let us now consider ways of creating a shared language between observant and nonobservant members of the Jewish community. We shall explore the question of whether Halakhah and religious faith necessarily create private worlds of meaning unintelligible to those who do not share their faith commitments. Is it possible to translate a way of life based on belief in revelation into categories intelligible to those who do not share this belief?

What approach to *ta'amei ha-mitzvot* would enable such a translation? An approach that insists that *kabbalat ol malkhut shamayim* (acceptance of the yoke of the commandments) must be the sole motivation for observance of the commandments creates an insurmountable barrier to dialogue. The statement "I do this solely because God commanded it" ends any further discussion between believer and nonbeliever. The Jewish tradition, however, provides other approaches to halakhic practice, which open up possibilities for a shared language of appreciation among individuals, irrespective of a common commitment to Halakhah.

Maimonides suggests such an approach:

> There is a group of human beings who consider it a grievous thing that causes (reasons) should be given for any law; what would please them most is that the intellect would not find a meaning for the commandments and prohibitions. What compels them to feel thus is a sickness that they find in their souls, a sickness to which they are unable to give utterance and of which they cannot furnish a satisfactory account. For they think that if those laws were useful in this existence and had been given to us for this or that reason, it would be as if they derived from the reflection and the understanding of some intelligent being. If, however, there is a thing for which the intellect could not find any meaning at all and that does not lead to something useful, it indubitably derives from God; for the reflection of man would not lead to such a thing. It is as if according to these people of weak intellects, man were more perfect than his Maker; for man speaks and acts in a manner that leads to some intended end, whereas the Deity does not act thus, but commands us to do things that are not useful to us and forbids us to do things that are not harmful to us. But He is far exalted above this; the contrary is the case—the whole purpose consisting in what is useful for us, as we have explained on the basis of its dictum: "For our good always, that He might preserve us alive, as it is at this day." And it says: "Which shall hear all these statutes

[*hukkim*] and say: Surely this great community is a wise and understanding people" (Deut. 4:6–8). Thus it states explicitly that even all the statutes [*hukkim*] will show to all the nations that they have been given with wisdom and understanding. (*Guide*, III, 31)

In this chapter, Maimonides argues against an understanding of mitzvot that insists that religious passion must be nurtured by unintelligibility. According to that approach, mitzvot must isolate you cognitively from those who do not believe in revelation. Without such isolation, one cannot appreciate the uniqueness of mitzvot. The greater your separation from nonbelievers, the more deeply do you experience the religious significance of Halakhah.

One may call that religious sensibility an *akedah* (binding of Isaac) consciousness, which ascribes great religious importance to surrender, regardless of the commandments' unintelligibility. If the *akedah* model symbolizes the highest rung of spiritual development, then mitzvot that appear unintelligible to others become paradigmatic expressions of religious faith. No shared language is possible if the nonrational is the main source of religious passion.

Maimonides attempted to correct what he believed to be a religious "sickness of the soul." He insisted that belief in revelation does not preclude rational discussion of the values and practices of religious life with those not committed to *Torah mi-Sinai*. Maimonides used the proof text "for it is your wisdom and your understanding in the sight of the peoples" (*ki hi hokhmatchem u'vinatchem l'einei ha'amim*) to demonstrate that the Torah assumes that other nations can appreciate the wisdom of a way of life they do not obey. Appreciation by others presupposes our ability to explain the purpose of one's norms in rational terms. He thus offers his reader universal criteria of understanding the purpose of Halakhah.

> Every commandment from among these six hundred and thirteen commandments exists either with a view to communicating a rule of justice, or to warding off an injustice, or to endowing men with a noble moral quality, or to warning them against an evil moral quality. (*Guide*, III, 31)

Given these universally intelligible criteria, a halakhic Jew can begin to communicate with those who do not share the same authoritative presuppositions. In his introduction to *Helek*, the tenth chapter of Tractate Sanhedrin, Maimonides again uses the proof text quoted above with respect to the cognitive claims of the Jewish tradition. He argues against those who do not subject the truth claims of aggadic teachers to universal criteria of rationality. Neither the knowledge claims of Aggadah nor the behavioral norms of Halakhah need isolate one from participating in a universal culture of rational human beings. To Maimonides, commitment to tradition is not fed only by nonrational leaps of faith. Cognitive isolation is not the price one must pay for commitment to a particular way of life.

The educational implication of Maimonides' orientation to mitzvot is that students of Torah must not revel in their distinctiveness and separation from the world. They must be taught to discover *ta'amei ha-mitzvot* grounded in values that can be understood and appreciated by Jew and non-Jew alike. Exclusive reliance on faith can easily become an excuse for not thinking about the human significance of a Torah way of life.

The psychological and intellectual comfort of living only with those who think and behave the same way as you is shaken by

Maimonides' orientation to the commandments. One must constantly oscillate between two powerful poles, the universal and the particular, striving always to integrate both. One must evaluate one's spiritual growth not only in terms of the *akedah* but also in terms of Abraham's impassioned prayer for the people of Sodom. Abraham demands that God be intelligible within universal criteria of morality. Abraham at Sodom corrects the one-sided notion that religion is a private language. God does not demand of Abraham that he sacrifice his sense of morality (see Gen. 18:16–33).

In exploring the possibility of a shared language for believer and nonbeliever, we must also consider the following question. Can observant Jews recognize in the practice of secular Jews the same aspirations that Halakhah aims at realizing? If so, then both communities can share common aspirations despite different means of implementation. Again, let us turn to Maimonides.

Maimonides begins chapter 4 of *Shemonah Perakim* (The Eight Chapters) with a discussion of Aristotle's ethical theory. He discusses the meaning of virtue as moderation, and the relationship between action and character, and then shows that Halakhah aims at realizing the same virtues as those contained in Aristotle's *Nichomachean Ethics*. Aristotelian ethics and the halakhic system share a common conception of moral health. Although they do not share a common Halakhah, Maimonides indicates that to a great extent they share common goals.

In the first chapter of *Hilkhot De'ot* (Laws Concerning Character Traits), we find the same approach as in *Shemonah Perakim*. Here, Maimonides analyzes the concept of virtue in terms of moderation, but again, he does not derive this approach from the authority of tradition.

In *Shemonah Perakim*, Maimonides shows how the detailed specification of Halakhah aims at the formation of healthy character dispositions. In *Hilkhot De'ot*, he identifies the divine attributes, such as mercy and graciousness, with the virtues of the healthy human soul. In Judaism, one strives for the ideal of a healthy soul by following halakhic prescriptions or by imitating the moral attributes of God. Halakhic practice and the imitation of God aim at developing specific virtues. Although these pursuits are perceived as religious commandments by the halakhic Jew, Maimonides does not hesitate to make halakhic practice intelligible in categories not grounded in mitzvah and revelation.

If one were to follow in the spirit of Maimonides, one could argue that today, individuals can share halakhic aspirations without sharing the same halakhic guidelines for their implementation. A student trained in this spirit could share a spiritual language with people without sharing common theological presuppositions. Halakhah would thus expose its students to the possibility of aggadic discourse independent of halakhic practice.

I have thus far attempted to show how halakhic practice need not isolate a person from sharing common goals with others who are not committed to the behavioral prescriptions of Halakhah. A much more difficult question is whether a shared theological language is possible between a believer and an agnostic or an atheist.

I suggest that such discourse is possible if a believer has a clear understanding of what constitutes, in modern terms, the battle against the seductive powers of *avodah zarah* (idolatry). I use the evocative term "seductive" intentionally, so as to indicate that the rejection of idolatry is important only if what is rejected has a luring power. Our convictions gain vitality when we understand the significance of what they are incompatible with. The negative can thus ignite the power of the positive. If our belief in God sometimes appears hollow and superficial, it may be due to our limited understanding of what constitutes modern idolatry. Abraham, the iconoclast in history, is diminished if the only idols he smashes are those in his father's idol factory.

Maimonides sets the rejection of idolatry as one of the primary goals of Halakhah:

Whoever denies idolatry confesses his faith in the whole Torah, in all the prophets and all that the prophets were commanded, from Adam to the end of time. And this is the fundamental principle of all the commandments. (M.T. *Avodah Zarah* II, 4)

In a talmudic discussion of why Mordechai was called *yehudi*, literally a Judahite, although he was from the tribe of Benjamin, R. Johanan says: "He was called *yehudi*, a Jew, because he rejected idolatry. 'For anyone who repudiates idolatry is called a Jew'"(*Megillah* 13a). Now, if our students today are to aspire to become iconoclasts in history, it is important that we educate them to understand the meaning of saying that the *yetzer hara* (evil inclination) toward idolatry is still alive (see Yeshayahu Leibowitz, "Idolatry," in Arthur A. Cohen and Paul Mendes-Flohr, *Contemporary Religious Jewish Thought*).

In his book *The Morality of Law*, Lon L. Fuller asks whether we can know what is bad without knowing the perfectly good. Fuller argues that we can know what is plainly unjust without knowing what perfect justice is. In terms of our concern, we can rephrase his question thus: Is a rejection of idolatry possible without prior faith and knowledge of God? If it is possible for individuals to agree on what they reject without agreeing on what they affirm, then we may be able to create a shared theology of repudiation of idolatry without demanding a clear affirmation of and commitment to belief in God. The believer can share common aspirations with the atheist and the agnostic if they all reject idolatry. This common rejection can be significant if the idolatry that is targeted is luring and serious.

Ephraim Urbach, in his article "The Rabbinical Laws of Idolatry," offers insights that are relevant to our discussion. He notes that although the Talmud records differing approaches to idolatry, "one thing is certain—neither the *Tannaim* of the second century nor the *Amoraim* of the third showed any tendency to compromise or to concede to anything connected with emperor worship." Evidently the worship of idols was not luring to Jews of the period, but emperor worship was a live option that had to be rejected actively. Urbach writes: "According to the Jerusalem Talmud, the *Tannaim* were divided in their opinions about the generality of images, but if it was certain that they were images of kings, all agreed in forbidding them…. In the ancient world there were—on the evidence of Pliny—more gods than human beings…but in that same world, there was only one emperor whose sovereignty and power were felt daily."

The power of Rome, as distinct from pagan idols, impinged on daily community life. It was a felt reality. Emperor worship had to be combated because its attractiveness and power could become a threat to religious commitment. As Urbach develops his thesis he notes that from the time of Antonines onward, the cult of the emperor became "the religion of absolute political power. It was not an individual that was worshipped, but the more than human power of which he was the personification…. Everything connected with this cult was absolutely forbidden [by the sages]."

The idolatry of absolute power has, to this day, not been destroyed. The quest for absolute human control in the twentieth century is a palpable rejection of the sovereignty of God. The demand for total and uncritical allegiance to a political state is idolatrous. Any political figure or party that places itself above criticism has, in an important sense, denied the reality of God. Insisting on criticism, demanding accountability, limiting the dangerous hunger for power, and building political structures to balance competing powers may be our way of implementing the halakhic struggle against idolatry.

The *yetzer hara* of idolatry need not, however, be confined to the political arena but may also be evident in the personal and interpersonal domains. The rabbis use the term "as one who worships idols," *ke'ilu oved avodah zarah*, and other such references to idolatry, with regard to behavior traits and dispositions.

> Rabbi Johanan said in the name of R. Simeon b. Yohai: Every man in whom is haughtiness of spirit is as though he worshipped idols;...R. Johanan himself said: He is as though he had denied the existence of God, as it is said, "Your heart be lifted up and you forget the Lord your God." (*Sotah* 4b)
>
> R. Eleazar also said: Every man in whom is haughtiness of spirit is fit to be hewn down like an *asherah* [an object of idolatrous worship]. (*Sotah* 5a)
>
> R. Hisda said, and according to another version it was Mar Ukba: Every man in whom is haughtiness of spirit, the Holy One blessed be He declares, "I and he cannot both dwell in the world." (*Sotah* 5a)
>
> R. Simeon b. Eleazar said in the name of Halfa b. Agra in R. Johanan b. Nuri's name: He who rends his garments in his anger, he who breaks his vessels in his anger, and he who scatters his money in his anger, regard him as an idolater, because such are the wiles of the Tempter: Today he says to him, "Do this," tomorrow he tells him, "Do that," until he bids him "Go and serve idols" and he goes and serves [them]. R. Abin observed: What verse [intimates this]? "There shall be no strange god in you; neither shall you worship any strange god"; who is the strange god that resides in man himself? Say, that is the Tempter. (*Shabbat* 105b)

One may argue that the evocative language the rabbis use is only meant to be persuasive rhetoric. In order to emphasize the importance of guarding against arrogance and rage, the rabbis used such dramatic metaphors as "I and he cannot both dwell in the world" or "it is as if he had denied the existence of God." I do not deny the plausibility of this interpretation. I suggest, however, that the choice of these terms, with all their associations and overtones, may be *literally* significant and indicative of a more profound understanding of the language of idolatry. Perhaps the rabbis wished to suggest that one might perceive the ugliness of idolatry in a person's character structure. Perhaps they realized that a person who is subject to rage and loss of self-control, or who is swollen with arrogance, manifests character traits that are incompatible with the worship of God.

The capacity for self-transcendence is an essential element in the faith experience. The believer is conscious of human creatureliness and finitude when standing before the Infinite. This awareness should also be manifest in an appreciation of the dignity of others and in a general responsiveness to realities beyond the self. The person who says wholeheartedly "*barukh atah* (Blessed are You)" must be capable of breaking out of the prison of egocentricity. Rage, however, entraps you within your hate. Arrogance imprisons you within your inflated sense of self. Arrogance and rage thus preclude the experience and appreciation of a reality beyond yourself—the existential condition necessary for encountering God.

In this sense, there is an important similarity between these character traits and the obsession with absolute power in the political realm. Hunger for power, arrogance, and rage share a common lack of acknowledgement and appreciation of the dignity of others. Arrogance and the urge for absolute power presuppose states of consciousness in which an individual fails to recognize the implications of being a creature of God.

The translation of idolatry into behavior patterns and character traits is inherent to the spirit of normative Judaism. Halakhah always translates belief into behavior. Just as the rabbis recognized that an acceptance of the kingdom of Heaven is incomplete without the acceptance of the commandments, they also recognized that belief in God is void of significance if it does not shape character.

The importance of practice in Judaism makes the creation of a shared language possible. If faith and dogma were the major focus of this spiritual way of life, then shared discourse between believer and nonbeliever would be far more difficult to achieve.

If our educational system were to emphasize the character traits that emerge from faith in God, and educate toward an appreciation of the contemporary meaning of the struggle against idolatry, we might alleviate the sense of cultural isolation that frequently oppresses the committed student of Halakhah, and begin to create a theological language that would be intelligible to various sectors of the community.

INDIVIDUAL IDENTITY AND COMMUNITY

Mitzvah presupposes the centrality of community within Judaism. Halakhah is the way of life of a community; it builds a collective consciousness within an individual. Systems of thought in which the individual is dominant cannot do justice to a worldview in which law and community are central. Existentialism, with its primary focus on individual self-realization, cannot illuminate the communal aspect of halakhic Judaism. Halakhah can be better understood through the categories of political philosophy, such as law, community, or authority.

Maimonides, the master halakhist, perceived the halakhic system in political terms. For him, the legal category of mitzvah did not exist prior to Moses. Only after the exodus from Egypt, with the formation of community, did Halakhah become the dominant organizing principle. Abraham, says Maimonides, is a philosopher and teacher who persuades through rational argumentation, but Moses, who brings the law, addresses the community in the name of God's legislative authority. Prior to Sinai, human beings served God through reflection on divine power and wisdom revealed in nature. This spiritual way, based on philosophy, is inherently individualistic. The authority of mitzvah becomes central to Judaism only when the collective stands before God at Sinai. Halakhah thus channels the longing for God within the context of community.

According to Maimonides, community and practice remain central concerns even for the Jew who seeks contemplative love of God. In other words, Halakhah can contain an individual's pursuit of self-realization only if the urgency of building a covenantal community remains vital.

Unfortunately, however, rather than serving as a catalyst for building community, Halakhah often becomes an instrument of divisiveness, hostility, and spiritual isolation. Instead of mitzvah awakening the individual to embrace *k'lal yisrael* (the totality of Israel), it is mistakenly used to justify isolation. Jews who understand and value the collective dimension of mitzvah must be pained by the sectarian isolationism prevalent today.

Undeniably, the attempt to build a shared community of value is a lengthy and difficult process, requiring enormous patience and spiritual courage. A sensitive study of Maimonides' approach to revelation would reveal the central importance of the virtue of patience. Process and stages, rather than instantaneous transformations, characterize the educational philosophy of Halakhah. God, the revealer of the law, is the great Teacher who patiently works at bringing about change even over long periods of history. Revelation, as distinct from creation, is anthropocentric. The word of creation expresses the overflowing power of divine sufficiency, but the Word that emanates from Sinai reflects God's loving awareness of the human capacities of His students. In revelation, God, the teacher, listens before speaking. In addressing human beings, God speaks in the language of human beings, *dibrah Torah bil'shon bnei adam*.

The recognition of the importance of process in spiritual growth, the love and acceptance required to speak a language that can be understood and appropriated, must inform a philosophy of education toward Torah. Maimonides claimed that there were three stages in the worship of God: sacrifices, prayer, and contemplative prayer. The highest form is achieved through philosophical knowledge of God revealed in nature. The lowest level, animal sacrifice, reflects the form of worship prevalent in pagan society in Egypt where Jews were enslaved. Given the fact that "a sudden transition from one opposite to another is impossible. And therefore man, according to his nature, is not capable of abandoning suddenly all to which he was accustomed...," God allowed pagan practices to continue with the intention of weaning the community away from them and toward a higher form of worship. Petitional prayer, the next and intermediate stage of worship, leads eventually to love and worship of God through silent meditation.

Worship of God, as understood by Maimonides, expresses the sober passion of a wise teacher who begins a spiritual process from where the students are. A modern teacher should internalize the pedagogic strength reflected in Maimonides' theory of revelation. An educational philosophy in this spirit would develop educators with the ability to listen and respond to another; in other words, to imitate the qualities of God expressed at Sinai.

There are risks in encouraging intellectual openness, in exposing students to views and lifestyles that do not confirm accepted norms and beliefs. This is why we are often warned to be extremely cautious in encouraging our students to confront the modern world. We are told to wait until they are filled with *lehem ubasar* (bread and meat), that is, the knowledge of what is permitted and what is forbidden, before embarking on such a potentially dangerous venture. But how do you know when you are strong enough and learned enough to withstand the challenge of new ideas?

There is an attractive simplicity to the isolationist approach to religious education, but one must also recognize the equally grave risks of waiting for sufficient strength and knowledge. We may discover that when we are finally ready to speak, there is no community capable of or interested in listening.

The opportunity to begin the process of creating a *brit ye'ud*, a covenant of meaning, for our people, does not come often in history. The presence of a living Jewish society in Israel, with its dedication to *brit goral*, a covenant of destiny, constitutes fruitful soil for the creation of a community of meaning. The danger in a separatist religious philosophy of education today is that Judaism may turn into a sect and cease being the way of life of a total community. An educational philosophy that ignores the challenge of present opportunities takes a great risk indeed. Single-minded concern with saving Torah for the select few may entail losing the people as a whole. *This should not be the response of halakhic Jews to history.* The centrality of mitzvah demands that we feel the urgency of concretizing norms within the public domain of *k'lal yisrael*.

There is no authentic life choice that is risk free. All important decisions entail dangers and uncertainties. The choice before us is not between an educational philosophy that is certain of results and one that is fraught with risks, but rather between alternative risks.

Religious education must be informed by a philosophy that enables students to respond responsibly, but also courageously and effectively, to the challenges of our new historical reality. The Zionist revolution created a people willing to accept responsibility for its collective actions within history. The halakhic community must now express a spiritual boldness commensurate with the enormous courage reflected in the establishment of the State of Israel.

6

IN SEARCH OF A GUIDING VISION

FOR JEWISH EDUCATION

THE FOLLOWING ADDRESS was delivered to diaspora educators at
The Melton Center, The Hebrew University, Jerusalem.

> [T]he question was raised: Is study greater or is
> practice greater? Rabbi Tarfon answered and said:
> Practice is greater. Rabbi Akiva answered and said:
> Study is greater. They (those present) all answered and
> said: Study is greater, for study leads to practice.
> (*Kiddushin* 40b)

Talmud shemevi lemaaseh (study that leads to practice) has
been a guiding motif of Jewish education throughout our history.
Learning precedes practice because it gives meaning and purpose to
the nature of practice. The life of practice is thus conditioned and
informed by study. I should like to invert this classical formulation
and argue that today practice—in the deepest sense—is the crucial
condition that must precede and inform Talmud: the life of study.

The teachers of the Gemara, as well as the philosopher John Dewey, understood that learning must be rooted in life. In order to flourish, the intellect requires living situations and living contexts out of which the text can speak.

RECOVERING THE ORAL TRADITION

When we created Akiva School in Montreal, the first serious issue we confronted was whether to give the young students textbooks. "Let's not give them books!" I said. "Let's create the books as we learn. Let's have the children develop the textbooks themselves!" We then had to face the question: What shall we study first?

How you begin can determine the educational "conversation" that will ensue throughout the school year. We wanted to engage the minds of our young students, to focus on something relevant to their lives. I recalled my mother's frustration when time and again I returned home from playing ball in my sneakers. "Duvie, where are your good shoes?" "Ma, I don't know what happened! They were with me on the bus. They just drove away!" I was always losing things.

The world of lost objects is part of the immediate experience of young people. "What should you do when you find a lost article?" is not an abstract theoretical issue for first and second graders. What subject matter could be more relevant to their lives than a discussion of the mitzvah of *hashavat avedah* (returning a lost object)?

The students in our school were thus initiated into the "mysteries" of Torah through the intricate details and considerations involved in *hashavat avedah*. The first biblical text that the students of Akiva School photocopied in creating their own textbooks was this:

If you see your fellow's ox or sheep gone astray, do not ignore it; you must take it back to your fellow. If your fellow does not live near you or you do not know who he is, you shall bring it home and it shall remain with you until your fellow claims it; then you shall give it back to him. You shall do the same with his ass; you shall do the same with his garment; and so too shall you do with anything that your fellow loses and you find: you must not remain indifferent. (Deut. 22:1–3)

For our young students at Akiva School, losing and finding things were familiar everyday experiences. What do you do when you find something? How do you return it to someone you don't know? How do you determine who the owner is? What do you do until you find the rightful owner? These were *their* questions no less than they were the questions of the talmudic teachers who dealt with these issues in tractate *Baba Metzia* of the Babylonian Talmud. In this way, Bible, Mishnah, and Talmud were introduced from within the context of their own living reality. The talmudic concepts of signs of ownership, reliability, and limits of responsibility, and the subtle distinctions that the use of these concepts entail, had become part of the vocabulary and thinking processes of these young students.

Interestingly enough, the meaning and function of *Torah shebeal peh* (the oral discussion) with respect to *Torah shebichtav* (the written law) emerged naturally and spontaneously from the very context of their own debates and analyses. They knew that the biblical text had to be supplemented and expanded for the mitzvah of *hashavat avedah* to be implemented. The idea that the written text—any written text—is inevitably incomplete in the light of both hypothetical and real-life situations evolved almost intuitively in the course of their discussions. There was no need to define the notions of the written and the oral laws in religious or legalistic terms. We had created an existential reality in which the intelligibility and urgency of *Torah shebeal peh* as the necessary outgrowth of a living tradition were clear and obvious.

These seven-year-olds were also experiencing the reality of being part of a traditional discussion. In this case, the participants were Reb Yohanan, Resh Lakish, and their classmates, Billy and Rivka. We encouraged the students to actively join in the discussion of the *Tannaim* and *Amoraim*. There were numerous occasions when the students argued and took issue with the views of Abbaye and Rava. The talmudic text that they later glued into their scrapbooks included the comments of Billy and Rivka alongside those of the talmudic sages.

There were educators in the religious community who objected to this approach, arguing that letting Billy question a great talmudic scholar in his own terms was nothing short of arrogance and irreverence. They were convinced that in creating an educational framework where seven-year-olds felt free to challenge the authoritative giants of the Talmud, I was sowing the seeds of future heresy and disobedience.

Without minimizing the importance of reverence and respect in a traditional culture, this critique ignores one of the most fundamental principles of education. If you cannot disagree with what you read or engage a text critically because of its "sanctity" and authority, then ultimately you will ignore and disregard it.

Condition number one for taking a tradition seriously is being invited to participate in the discussion that is that tradition. Our task as educators is to convince Billy and Rivka that they can take part in the discussion with Rabbi Yohanan and Resh Lakish. They too are members of the community of *lomdei Torah* (students of Torah) who make up the Jewish tradition.

The primary challenge facing Jewish education is how to break through the barriers of time and language in order to bring students into the discussion that spans generations. Whether you sanctify the text by calling it "holy" or the rabbis by ascribing their knowledge to *ruah hakodesh* (the holy spirit), if you don't succeed in making your students part of a common conversation with the past, then no amount of sanctimonious phraseology will save the tradition from the cultural equivalent of a dignified burial.

THE INTERPRETIVE COMMUNITY AND THE DISCUSSION

The first principle of Jewish education is that when you learn Torah you become a part of an interpretive community. The interpretive community is not an independent notion added on to the core idea of Jewish religiosity but is constitutive of what we mean by Torah.

How then do you convince people that being Jewish is being part of an interpretive discussion? How do you introduce the idea that Judaism is not only a religion in the ordinary sense—a faith system, a body of beliefs and practices—but also (and, today, most important) an ongoing discussion of a committed interpretive community?

This, in effect, is the meaning of *Torah shebeal peh* as distinct from *Torah shebichtav*. *Torah shebichtav*—the written law, the Bible—taught independently of *Torah shebeal peh* may convey the idea of a single authoritative voice (God) that defines the content of Torah. Midrash and Talmud add multiple human voices to what is Torah. The initial founding moment of revelation gets absorbed into the discussion of generations. When you bridge *Torah shebichtav* with *Torah shebeal peh*, biblical revelation with the midrashic and halakhic texts of talmudic Judaism, you place the Word of God within the context of a human discussion aimed at appropriating and internalizing the biblical Word into the life of a community.

The crucial point of my using discussion is to emphasize (1) the role of interpretation in appropriating the Divine Word and (2) the continuity and unending nature of the process of unpacking the meaning of the Divine Word. Torah education must internalize the essential notion that *Torah shebeal peh* is a discussion that has not ended. While the biblical canon is contained in twenty-four books, the oral Torah has no final form. It always awaits the creative input of serious and committed students to add their voices to the unending discussion. Another chapter of Torah can be written in classrooms today because the final chapter of *Torah shebeal peh* has not yet been written. This is the deep meaning of the tradition's making the distinction between the written Torah and the oral Torah while insisting on their ultimate unity and integrity.

Unlike Buber and Rosenzweig, I do not believe in the importance of making philosophic sense of Divine speech at Sinai in order to explain and justify the respective roles of revelation and interpretation in Judaism. The issue is not what happened at Sinai but what Jews did with Sinai.

My concern is not with the metaphysics of revelation but with how Jews understood revelation. I do not live by what happened at Sinai; I live by what Jews did with what happened at Sinai. This is the talmudic significance of the expression *Torah lo bashamayim*: Torah is not in Heaven.

CONTEMPORANEITY

I remember the sense of shock and dissonance I felt as a student when people told me they were celebrating the anniversary of Maimonides' death. "What! The Rambam died!" I thought. I couldn't integrate the thought of Maimonides' death with the sense of timelessness and contemporaneity that defined the intellectual ambience of the yeshivah world.

In yeshivot (talmudic academies), the boundaries of history and time evaporate in the heat of debate between scholars and students, past and present. As a yeshivah student I never knew—or cared to know—who lived when. Rashi argued with—and, in this sense, lived at the same time as—Reb Yohanan. Fourth century? Third century? The fundamental concepts of modern historiography, the dates and historical contexts of persons and ideas, were foreign to the ahistorical conceptual framework of talmudic debate. In this sense history doesn't enter the discussion. There is one conversation that embraces Moses, Rabbi Akiva, Maimonides, Rabbi Soloveitchik, and every contemporary student of the text. This is the spirit that my revered teacher, Rabbi Joseph B. Soloveitchik, communicated to his students in his talmudic lectures.

AUTONOMY AND EMPOWERMENT

The rabbis exhibited an autonomy of spirit with respect to history. In their innovative interpretive boldness they evinced a sense of control over the past. This is due, I believe, to the inherent dynamic of being "the people of the book." The text defines your picture of reality. Unless you master it, you will be enslaved by it. You cannot build your future unless you interpret your past. In such a world, learning is empowerment. Discovering new layers of meaning in your sacred texts opens up new possibilities for your future.

In this text-centered world, freedom comes through rigorous analysis and interpretation. The paradigm of freedom is the *talmid chacham* (the Torah scholar) whose interpretive audacity is nothing short of Promethean, especially if judged by fundamentalistic notions of divine revelation (see the fascinating discussion in *Makkot* 23b).

Torah, therefore, has to be reclaimed by the community. Jewish education must empower students to feel part of the interpretive community that constitutes Torah. The empowerment of people to take part in the discussion, to feel intellectually free to become engaged and argue with the tradition, must take precedence over issues of authority and obedience if Jewish education is to renew the discussion that has defined Judaism for the past two thousand years. The paradoxical dialectic of this system is to create the student who is at once totally claimed and totally free.

INTERNALIZATION

How do you create in students the idea that Torah is not a textbook and that its internalization and appropriation by those who study it is crucial for its future?

> How dull-witted are those people who stand up [in deference] to the Scroll of the Torah but do not stand up [in deference] to a great personage, because, while in the Torah Scroll forty lashes are prescribed, the Rabbis come and [by interpretation] reduce them by one. (*Makkot* 22b)

The internalization of Torah was so much a part of talmudic culture that it could even serve as an important consideration in halakhic argument:

> R. Isaac b. Shila said in R. Mattena's name in the name of R. Hisda: If a father renounces the honor due to him, it is renounced; but if a Rabbi renounces his honor, it is not renounced. R. Joseph ruled: Even if a

Rabbi renounces his honor, it is renounced, for it is said, "And the Lord went before them by day" (Exod. 13:21). Said Raba: How compare! There, with respect to the Holy One, blessed be He, the world is His and the Torah is His; [hence] He can forego His honor. But here, is then the Torah his [the Rabbi's]? Subsequently Raba said: Indeed, the Torah is his [the scholar's], for it is written, "and in his Torah he meditates day and night" (Ps. 1:2). (*Kiddushin* 32a-b)

The above text relates to rabbinic scholars in terms of their dignity. Can a rav, a teacher, renounce the public norms of respect associated with his social status as a Torah scholar? For his view that a rav's honor may be waived, Rabbi Joseph brings proof from the biblical account of the pillar of fire that went before the camp in the desert, which shows God's waiving the honor due him by serving as Israel's "tour guide" in the desert.

Raba's response is most interesting and revealing. He challenges Rabbi Joseph's argument on the basis of its analogy between a Torah scholar and God. In one case [God]: the world is His and the Torah is His, therefore, He has the right to renounce His honor. In the case of the Torah scholar, however, is the Torah his? How can he renounce the honor that is his only by virtue of the Torah knowledge he possesses?

Raba then reverses the force of his rhetorical question ("Is the Torah his?") by answering in the affirmative! "Yes. The Torah is his [the teacher's]." Raba's proof text is itself remarkable in its making the one who learns Torah the referent of the possessive pronoun "his" in the expression "his Torah."

In a similar vein, a most powerful and moving analogy is drawn between the scholar who has forgotten his wisdom and the original tablets of the covenant that Moses received at Sinai:

Be careful [to respect] an old man who has forgotten
his knowledge through no fault of his own, for it was
said: Both the whole tablets and the broken fragments
of the tablets were deposited in the Ark. (*Berakot* 8b;
Baba Batra 14b)

The *talmid chacham* who forgets his learning is like the
broken fragments of the tablets of the Ten Commandments. Just as
the fragments of stone were respected because they once contained
the word of God, so too a human being who once contained the
word of God must continue to be respected.

The goal of Torah learning was not detached scholarship but
knowledge as property, as ownership, as internalization of and
identification with the object of learning. The student of Torah
owns the Torah and, in a deep sense, becomes the Torah. In
yeshivot on Simchat Torah, we would dance and embrace our
Rebbe in the same way people embrace and dance with the Torah
scroll. A scroll of parchment has no greater sanctity than a human
being who embodies the Torah in thought and action. The scholar
is free to engage, interpret, and shape the text—for the knower and
the known are one. *Torah shebeal peh* is an integral part of *Torah
shebichtav*.

Unless you study Talmud intensely, you cannot understand
the playful and joyous quality of Torah study. The awesome image
of Torah as the revealed Word of God is transformed into a less
intimidating and more inviting intellectual drama in the hands of
the Torah teacher. He or she is not overwhelmed by the sanctity
and authoritative status of the Divine Word. On the contrary, in
yeshivot you see students swaying rhythmically when they study
Talmud. The voices heard in the *beit midrash* resonate as a
beautiful *nigun* (melody). How to recreate this existential
experience of learning without rejecting the value of Western
thought and culture is the fundamental challenge facing
contemporary religious education.

My plea, therefore, is that we free ourselves from the classic Christian perspective on the Jewish tradition that focused exclusively on the Bible, the "Old Testament," while totally ignoring the rabbinic tradition. Midrash and the whole living interpretative tradition were outside the framework of what Christians understood to be Judaism. Western civilization thus perpetuated the image of Jews as a Bible-centered people.

This myth was later adopted by Ben-Gurion, who believed that he could rebuild Jewish culture in Israel on the basis of the Bible alone. This proved to be a serious mistake, because what the community needed was to regain a sense of the vitality of the tradition. Rather than bypass two thousand years of Jewish history, Israelis needed to know that the tradition had not atrophied in exile but that Judaism was a living culture with the power to grow and change.

WHERE TO START?

How can we recover the sense of vitality and identification with Torah in the modern world? Where do we start?

Abraham Joshua Heschel, one of the great theologians of our age, tried to rehabilitate the souls of Jews by renewing the reality of God as a living possibility. Heschel sought to rehabilitate a religious anthropology by giving meaning to God-talk in the modern world. In *God in Search of Man*, he tried to overcome the modern embarrassment with the realism of prophetic language about God by giving new meaning and vitality to the ideas of divine pathos and intimacy. He therefore spoke a great deal about wonderment, mystery, and awe in order to awaken or create feelings of affinity for the language of the prophets. For Heschel, the key was making sense of a language of personal intimacy with God, of making the God of the tradition into *my* God.

This is my God and I will glorify Him;
The God of my father, and I will exalt Him.
  (Exod. 15:2).

In contrast to Heschel, my position is that you don't begin with "my God" but with "the God of my father." The crucial issue in Jewish education is not whether you can sense the living presence of God but whether you feel a personal, existential identification with the tradition. The challenge of the Jewish educator is to create a living reality where students feel connected to what they study. In contrast to Heschel's theocentric orientation, my concern is with awakening a sense of wonderment and passion to know what the texts of the tradition are about.

As an educator I see my task as not only to impart knowledge but also to create a receptivity and hunger to know. When I was a rabbi (which also means "teacher") people would say to me: "Hartman, why don't you tell people what they're not allowed to do? Tell them about the laws of Shabbat, tell them about *kashrut*, tell them about this and about that...." I understood, however, that "just as one is commanded to say that which will be obeyed, so is one commanded not to say that which will not be obeyed" (*Yebamot* 65b).

Educators must never cease asking themselves, Have we created a receptivity to know? Have we created the conditions for this language to become meaningful and compelling? Heschel believed that this could be done only by rehabilitating the individual's capacity to enter into a relationship with God. While I deeply share Heschel's profound concern and efforts to open our hearts to the living presence of God, in the light of my own experience, I believe you can create a serious engagement with Jewish learning without rehabilitating the sense of the Divine Presence in your life.

REHABILITATING A POST-EXISTENTIALIST
SENSE OF COMMUNITY

In contrast to modern individualistic existential approaches to Judaism, I define Torah first in terms of the categories of political thought. The language of mitzvah is essentially a public, collective language. Despite the religious existentialism of my own teacher, Rabbi Soloveitchik, I maintain that Halakhah is a communal symbolic language. Halakhah is a language that mediates your connection with community—be it your own immediate community or the larger community spanning geography and history.

Like the language of ritual, Halakhah fails without a sense of community and a larger perspective of history. According to Maimonides, Abraham discovered God by virtue of his own philosophic reflections; though he may have reached the pinnacle of religious perfection in his love and knowledge of God, he was without community and hence without mitzvah and Halakhah.

Abraham's individual perfection notwithstanding, mitzvah becomes an important and meaningful feature of Jewish experience only with the inception of community and nation. Abraham, the "lonely man of faith," did not shape his spiritual life in terms of mitzvah and Halakhah. He did not speak to others in the authoritative language of revelation and mitzvah. Moses, the liberator and political leader of a nation, introduced the concept of mitzvah in his public discourse with the people of Israel (see Maimonides, M.T., *H. Avodah Zara*, 1).

In keeping with this conceptual analysis of Jewish spirituality, I maintain that if you wish to rehabilitate the religious experience based on mitzvah and Sinai, you must first rehabilitate the sense of community that gives meaning and purpose to these ideas.

A FAMILY LANGUAGE

As I mentioned at the start of this essay, the problem of Jewish education today is not the absence of books or facilities or access to the right information. The problem is that Jewish education is not preceded by a sense of history and community. The life of study is not informed by the life of practice.

My students at university were often confused by the personal nature of my presentation of Judaism and Jewish philosophy. "Professor Hartman, you speak about Judaism in a way we cannot understand. You speak about your home. You speak about the smells in your house on *erev Shabbat* (Friday evening). You speak about your *rebbe*, your *buba*...."

The underlying idea that I was communicating to them was that the feeling of being part of a family is an inherent feature of this tradition and culture. The language of Judaism is a family language. Judaism is what this family is about—how this family lives, how it thinks, its concerns, its anxieties, its hopes.

This perspective should make us sensitive to one of the important functions of Israel for the future of Jewish education: Israel gives Jews the feeling that there is a larger family and that they are a part of that family. The initial shock that people sometimes feel when they come on aliyah is that suddenly they are no longer marginal. I recall my son's excitement when he went shopping for food in Jerusalem and his joyous remark, "The whole supermarket is kosher!" (This stands in sharp contrast to my experience when I was in Berkeley, California, and I was guided to the supermarket's "ethnic shelf" where Manischewitz products were displayed.) In Israel, your Jewish world need not express a defiant "No!" to your environment. A *chag* (festival) is not something that takes place in the privacy of your home. Suddenly, it is happening all over. The whole country looks different, smells different. Judaism is not your private "Jewish thing."

Israel thus serves Jewish education by enabling the individual to discover a family of Jews, a community of Jews, and a history that shapes this community.

I am not claiming that Israel is a religious country. But, in its very reality, Israel testifies to the fact that the Jewish liturgical calendar shapes the collective identity of the nation. Celebrating Passover in Israel does not express the lonely destiny of the Jew. It resonates in the rich pulsating life of a nation.

Jewish education is failing today because it is cold and lonely. There is nothing resonating "out there" making a person feel: I belong to something larger than my private self and family.

Shabbat has meaning only if there is *erev Shabbat*, (Friday preparation). *Pesach* has meaning only if there is *erev Pesach*. *Rosh Hashanah* has meaning only if there is *Elul* (the month preceding *Rosh Hashanah*). In other words, if there isn't preparation in the community, if Jewish concepts and ideals are not part of your social consciousness and are not woven into the fabric of your social reality, then Jewish education becomes a nearly impossible task.

Ultimately, I believe the Torah can speak only to people who have this feeling of family. Schools today cannot simply be places for transmitting knowledge. They must also be living environments where a person feels connected to the larger drama of the Jewish family.

THE ROAD TO SINAI BEGINS IN EGYPT

Rabbi Soloveitchik (see "The Voice of My Beloved Knocks") understood that Zionism gave meaning and vitality to that part of Jewish consciousness that is essential for making sense of Jewish life and Judaism in the modern world. Judaism doesn't begin with Sinai, with revelation or a leap of faith, but with Egypt, with empathy for a suffering community of slaves. The community of

suffering precedes the community that received the word of God at
Sinai.

Pesach precedes *Shavuot*. *Pesach* is the beginning of the story
that makes Sinai possible. The language of Sinai has to be heard by
a people, by a group of individuals who have become a collective.
Sinaitic revelation is unintelligible to people who have no sense of
history, no sense of empathy for community, no sense of family.

Conversion to Judaism is not a leap of faith or a passionate
embracing of divinity. The potential convert must first profess a
desire to join a people. Ruth's confession of faith and loyalty to
Judaism expresses this very idea:

> ...your people shall be my people, and your God my
> God. (Ruth 1:16)

Maimonides captures this idea in the following halakhic
ruling.

> In what manner are righteous proselytes to be
> received? When a heathen comes forth for the purpose
> of becoming a proselyte, and upon investigation no
> ulterior motive is found, the court should say to him,
> "Why do you come forth to become a proselyte? Do
> you not know that Israel is at present sorely afflicted,
> oppressed, despised, confounded, and beset by
> suffering?" If he answers, "I know, and I am indeed
> unworthy," he should be accepted immediately. He
> should then be made acquainted with the principles of
> faith. (Maimonides, M.T., Book of Holiness, 14:1–2)

Identification with community precedes the moment of faith
because the moment of faith is not a leap of "the alone to the
Alone." The Jew stands at Sinai only after becoming "we." The

primary task of Jewish education is to instill in students a capacity to identify sympathetically with the cultural language of the tradition. One need not make a leap of faith before becoming engaged with Torah texts. One need not make a commitment to Jewish beliefs and practices before entering into a conversation with the sages and students of the tradition.

In an age when Jews have become estranged from the language of Torah, we must seek ways of creating an ability to listen to and appreciate the intellectual and spiritual *nigunim* of prior generations. Whether their words and songs become ours should not define our initial motivation and intellectual quest. Our initial concern is with developing the capacity to hear and to understand the passion of this people, its history, and its covenantal understanding of God.

Before dealing with belief in and commitment to the God of Israel—the God with whom Israel carried on a covenantal dialogue for two thousand years—one must first feel connected to this people and to this family. The condition for understanding the God of your historical family need not be grounded in your personal religious convictions. I often told congregants who felt they lacked the religious faith necessary for genuine prayer that when you read from the *siddur* (prayer book), you are not necessarily giving expression to your own convictions and beliefs. In using traditional prayer language, you have an opportunity to listen to how Jews have passionately expressed their faith in and love for God. You learn to pray by listening to how others have prayed. The language of the past can be appropriated prior to your existential identification with the life of faith.

Heschel understood the alienation and embarrassment that modern Jews experienced in the use of the language of faith. Despite his brilliant attempt at restoring vitality and meaning to the poetry of theological language, I am arguing for an alternative orientation to reviving Jewish education. I am trying to offer a perspective on Torah learning that does not require that a person find God before becoming engaged in the study of Torah and the tradition.

> R. Huna and R. Jeremiah citing R. Hiyya bar Abba said: It is written, "Your fathers have forsaken Me and have not kept my Torah" (Jeremiah 16:11). If only they had kept studying My Torah! Indeed if they forsook even Me all would turn out well provided they kept studying My Torah. If they did forsake Me yet kept on studying My Torah, its inner force, through their engagement with it, would be such as to bring them back to Me.
>
> R. Huna said: Study Torah, even if you not do so for its own sake. For when you study it, even though not for its own sake, finally, because you are engaged in it, you will have a change of heart and study it for its own sake. (*Pesikta de Rav Kahana* 15:5)

Restoring the vibrancy and relevance of the Jewish discussion and the empowerment of being a dignified member of the interpretive community of students of Torah may enable Jews to discover once again that the God of Abraham and Sarah can also be *my* God.

PART III

CELEBRATING RELIGIOUS DIVERSITY

7

CELEBRATING RELIGIOUS DIVERSITY

IN HIS ARTICLE "Confrontation," Rabbi Joseph B. Soloveitchik asserts that it is of the essence of a faith community's commitment to God to believe that history will ultimately justify its own exclusive way and demonstrate the error of all others.

> The axiological awareness of each faith community is an exclusive one, for it believes—and this belief is indispensable to the survival of the community—that its system of dogmas, doctrines and values is best fitted for the attainment of the ultimate good...each faith community is unyielding in its eschatological expectations. It perceives the events at the end of time with exultant certainty, and expects man, by surrender of selfish pettiness and by consecration to the great destiny of life, to embrace the faith that this community has been preaching throughout the millennia. ("Confrontation," *Tradition*, 6,2 [1969])

My presentation of the Judaic approach to other faith communities, however, does not presuppose R. Soloveitchik's claim. Acknowledging the existence and dignity of other faiths need not violate our covenantal faith commitment but, in fact, can enhance our covenantal creature-consciousness. The following exposition emphasizes three themes: (1) the theological tensions between tradition and modernity, (2) how the State of Israel is a catalyst for a new covenantal self-understanding, and (3) how the tradition affirms the dignity of "the other."

There is an inner tension within the spiritual life of those nurtured by a living tradition like Judaism. The tradition provides a total framework for our spiritual self-understanding. It provides the cultural ambiance, the language, the theological categories, the way in which we begin the spiritual life. In contrast to Descartes, we do not find our identity through withdrawing to the isolated self of *cogito ergo sum*. One who lives within the Judaic tradition begins, together with other members of the community, by being claimed by God. Fundamentally, the point of departure for Jewish religious identity is communal and relational. We begin by being situated in the framework of a community of listeners.

> You stand this day, all of you, before the Lord your God—your tribal heads, your elders and your officials, all the men of Israel, your children, your wives, even the stranger within your camp, from woodchopper to water-drawer—to enter into the covenant of the Lord your God, which the Lord your God is concluding with you this day, with its sanctions, to the end that He may establish you this day as His people and be your God, as He promised you and as He swore to your fathers, Abraham, Isaac, and Jacob. I make this covenant, with its sanctions, not with you alone, but with those who are standing here with us this day before the Lord our

God and with those who are not with us here this day.
(Deut. 29:9–14)

Only within community do we hear the commanding word of the living God of Israel. The sin of the wicked son in the Passover Haggadah is his separation from community. Heresy in Judaism is living without empathy for and solidarity with the community of Israel.

> One who separates himself from the community, even if he does not commit a transgression but only holds aloof from the congregation of Israel, does not fulfill religious precepts in common with his people, shows himself indifferent when they are in distress, does not observe their fast, but goes his own way, as if he were one of the Gentiles and did not belong to the Jewish people—such a person has no portion in the world to come. (Maimonides, M.T. *Teshuvah* 3:20)

The community so invades one's identity that it would be correct to claim that one's primary sense of self-consciousness is of a "we." The "I" in Judaism is often so difficult to discover that Spinoza believed that there was no "I" at all. For Spinoza, Judaism must be understood in political-legal categories. Conformism and obedience are the central virtues, which make Halakhah a workable system. Modern critiques of Judaism often focus on the way Halakhah collectivizes religious consciousness and inhibits the development of an autonomous moral personality. Martin Buber, who sought religious immediacy and spontaneity, could not find his way to God through the elaborate framework of the talmudic tradition.

Can you be rooted totally in a community on one level, yet find your own identity as an individual on another level? Must you distance yourself through total rejection in order to discover the meaning of having a self? These are some of the questions that modern individuals pose to the Judaic tradition. How can the tradition respond to these concerns?

The traditional Jew begins not with immediacy but by listening to a story and by participating in the drama of a community standing before God at Sinai. On the other hand, the Midrash says that each Jew standing at Sinai heard the word of God in terms of his or her own individual sensibility. The word of revelation is similar to the manna in the desert: just as each person tasted the manna in accordance with his or her own subjective taste, so each heard God saying: "I am the Lord *your* God" (Exod. 20:1) (*elohecha*—singular, not *eloheichem*—plural). The hearing is individualistic even though the speech is addressed to a collective.

> The Divine Word spoke to each and every person according to his particular capacity. And do not wonder at this. For when manna came down for Israel, each and every person tasted it in keeping with his own capacity—infants in keeping with their capacity, young men in keeping with their capacity and old men in keeping with their capacity.... Now if each and every person was enabled to taste the manna according to his particular capacity, how much more and more was each and every person enabled according to his particular capacity to hear the Divine Word. Thus David said: "The voice of the Lord is in its strength" (Ps. 29:4)— not "The voice of the Lord in His strength" but "The voice of the Lord in its strength"—that is, in its strength to make itself heard and understood according to the capacity of each and every person who listens to the Divine Word. (*Pesikta de Rav Kahana*, 12)

The two aspects of immediacy and of tradition appear also when the election and the covenant are recalled in Deuteronomy:

> It is not because you are the most numerous of peoples that the Lord set His heart on you and chose you—indeed, you are the smallest of people; but it was because the Lord loved you and kept the oath He made to your fathers that the Lord freed you with a mighty hand and rescued you from the house of bondage, from the power of Pharaoh king of Egypt. (Deut. 7:7–8)

To be sure, God had said to Israel, "I chose your ancestors and this is why I am connected with you." It is because of His love for Abraham, Isaac, and Jacob that He feels bound to Israel. On the other hand, the text recalls God saying, "not because you were many, not because you were powerful, but because I loved you." He begins with His love of Israel and then continues, "and because of My oath to your ancestors." There is a direct immediacy to God's love: He loves us not just because Jews are the children of Abraham, Isaac, and Jacob.

The covenant of the ancestors, *brit avot*, has played an essential role in supporting the belief in the eternity of the covenant. The covenant is unconditional because of God's promise to Abraham. Jews are confident God accepts them because of the memory of the covenant with Abraham.

And because traditional Jewish thinkers begin with Abraham's covenant, their interpretive discussion includes both past and present generations. My personal approach to Torah must be one that my grandparents would have been capable of appreciating. In other words, self-assertion and expression are from within the "Jewish family." So much of Jewish philosophy, therefore, takes the form of midrashic exegesis. The self emerges

not only in rebellion but also in the intellectual struggle to unfold and clarify a new interpretation of what my "grandparents" may have intended. Rabbi Akiva, for example, appeals to Moses' authority to defend an interpretation that Moses himself had difficulty comprehending.

> Rav Judah said in the name of Rav: "When Moses ascended on high, he found the Holy One, blessed be He, engaged in affixing coronets to the letters of the Torah. Said Moses, 'Lord of the Universe, who compels You?' He answered, 'There will arise a man, at the end of many generations, Akiva ben Joseph by name, who will spin out of each tittle heaps and heaps of laws.' 'Lord of the Universe,' said Moses, 'permit me to see him.' He replied 'Turn you round.' Moses went and sat down at the end of the eighth row and listened to the discourses upon the Law. Not being able to follow their arguments, he was ill at ease, but when they came to a certain subject and the disciples said to the master, 'Whence do you know it?' and the latter replied, 'It is a law given to Moses at Sinai,' he was comforted." (T.B. *Menahot* 29b)

Even though Moses could not comprehend R. Akiva's lecture, he was comforted by the fact that R. Akiva appealed to Mosaic authority to validate his own interpretation.

The individual "I" surfaces in the collective halakhic framework in two ways: (1) in the experiential appropriation of the mitzvah (how each individual "tastes" it) and (2) in the intellectual reinterpretation of the tradition.

The Judaic tradition's openness to novelty finds expression in the moment of God's encounter with Moses at the burning bush. God gave Moses two messages for the children of Israel:

> Moses said to God, "When I come to the Israelites and say to them, 'The God of your fathers has sent me to you,' and they ask me, 'What is His name?' what shall I say to them?" And God said to Moses, "*Ehyeh–Asher–Ehyeh* sent me to you." And God said further to Moses, "Thus shall you speak to the Israelites: 'The Lord, the God of your fathers, the God of Abraham, the God of Isaac, and the God of Jacob, has sent me to you.' This shall be My name forever, This My appellation for all eternity." (Exod. 3:13–16)

I take *Ehyeh-Asher-Ehyeh* to mean "I will be—I will be manifest in new ways." God is understood in two ways: as the God of Abraham, Isaac, and Jacob and as the God who says that radical novelty and surprise are possible. The past does not exhaust our understanding of the plenitude of the divine reality. We can build our spiritual lives with two perspectives: with a sense of surprise, wonderment, and openness to new possibilities, and, at the same time, with a sense of being totally claimed by our ancestral past.

Nowhere is the tension between tradition and modernity felt more strongly today than in the State of Israel, and above all in Jerusalem. One senses in the tradition-bound eternal city of Jerusalem that something radically new is being demanded of the Judaic spirit. While it may be hard to articulate it clearly, a Jew can feel the exciting beginnings of a new reality in the Ingathering of the Exiles.

On one level, Jews have come home from everywhere. No longer do we meet our people in history only through praying for the Ingathering of the Exiles. Yet, it is precisely in the home to which we have returned that we find ourselves so divided. Here we may even wonder: "Have we really always been a family?" The UJA slogan "We are one" sounds hollow when Jew meets Jew only to realize how little each understands the other. "Can chronic divisiveness, such as the growing polarization between observant and nonobservant Jews, turn into civil war?" is not an abstract question in Israel.

The polarization of the religious and the secular is increasing. Some of the major issues in local newspapers concern not only security but also whether a cable car will run on the Sabbath in Haifa or whether a Petah Tikvah cinema will show films on Friday night. The chief rabbi of that town, locked in jail for leading a violent illegal demonstration against the cinema's opening, claimed he was speaking in the name of God and therefore above the law of the state. Four hundred policemen could not spend the Sabbath with their families because they had to prevent Jews from clashing with one another. Religious controversy breeds anger, cynicism, and distrust among brothers and sisters who have come home after praying for so long:

> Sound the great Shofar for our freedom; lift up the banner to bring our exiles together, and assemble us from the four corners of the earth. Blessed are you, O Lord, who gathers the dispersed of Your people Israel. (Daily Prayer Book)

Not only do members of the same faith community meet as strangers, but, in our encounter and struggle with the Palestinians, we also meet the stranger, the different one, the "radically other." We Jews came home believing that we would finally fulfill our age-old dreams of returning to the promised land of our ancestors, only to discover that there were Arabs who also claimed to be deeply rooted in the land we called home.

In this land, we are confronted with many others who are connected to the land in such different ways. When Mormons start to build a university in Jerusalem, religious zealots try to stop them, claiming that it is a missionary plot. The *muezzin* calls thousands of Muslims to their mosques as thousands of hasidim go to the Western Wall. Believers of different faiths rub shoulders in the narrow alleys of the Old City as the musics of different faiths ring out simultaneously.

We have come home, yet to a home that does not offer us security and serenity but forces us to interact with "the other." Usually, when you come home, you expect to be free of the need to integrate all the dissonance you encounter outside. Paradoxically, it was easier to do that in the diaspora, where we could build ghettos. A ghetto is not only a physically bound area but also a framework that allows Jews to define themselves in their own terms and language, without having to confront "otherness." It is a social and cultural opportunity for self-definition, where our immediate surroundings confirm our internal communal language, making cultural monism a real possibility. In coming home to Jerusalem, however, we are invaded by multiple experiences of radical diversity. Here, in our home, "the other" invades our self-definition.

As I look at the teeming diversity of faith experiences in Jerusalem, I believe that the God of the Exodus drama, Who answered "I will be," is now calling upon us to respond in a different manner. Something new is happening when "the other," the stranger, the different one, impinges on our self-definition. The return of the Jewish people to Israel challenges us to rethink the long tradition of messianic triumphalism. Our return was meant to provide us not only with a haven from anti-Semitism but also with a new way of integrating "the other," the different one, into our covenantal consciousness. In the full flowering of Jewish particularity in Jerusalem, the people who taught the world to strive for the unity of humankind through belief in God are now being called on to present a different understanding of the universal vision of God's kingdom in history. In the city that nurtured holy wars, we must now bear witness to the dignity of particularity, to the redemptive significance of celebrating the partial and the incomplete.

What new religious sensibility is now required to meet this challenge? The Gnostics could not understand the world as the expression of a loving God. Human suffering, death, tragedy, evil, pain, loving a child and watching him or her die—these could not be reconciled with a just and loving God. The very experience of the world, they thought, contradicted the idea of God as love, which therefore had to be anchored in a different drama. One must escape the world in order to discover the true God.

Judaism, however, affirmed that creation "is good" in the eyes of God, as it is said repeatedly in the first chapter of Genesis. God affirms our humanity in its otherness, in its diversity, in its finitude. Although we are fragile, corporeal creatures, who are here today and gone tomorrow, who experience pain, tragedy, and loss, the human reality is not sin. "And God saw all that He had made, and found it very good" (Gen. 1:31). Creation thus introduces a new value in the mind of divinity: finitude. The human being as creature has ontological worth, as the midrash says: "'And found it very good' and behold death (*mavet*) was good" (*Midrash Rabbah* Genesis, IX, 5). We do not have to transcend human finitude in order to feel dignified. We do not have to go beyond the concrete and the temporal in order to live an authentic life.

The affirmation of human beings, with all their human limitations, is the soul of the covenantal message. The covenant is not God's desire for humanity to escape from history but God's gracious love, which accepts humanity in its finite, temporal condition. In the covenant, God seeks to enter the temporal; God does not ask that the temporal be absorbed in eternity. It is in this sense that the covenant—as Martin Buber and R. Joseph B. Soloveitchik argued—is contrary to the mystical, to the quest to lose individual consciousness by being absorbed into the One.

The amazing message of the biblical story of the manna is that God enters into a relationship with a people who cannot live with uncertainty. The story would have been nice and uplifting if Israel had gathered just enough manna for one day and said, "God, we trust you." Instead, the story relates that Israel gathered more than enough manna for one day, hoarding away extra, which invariably rotted. God, as it were, had asked them: "Can you not spend one night sleeping with uncertainty?" But they responded: "No. We do not have the strength to trust!"

History is dramatically different from the creation story in Genesis. In the beginning, God creates human beings in His image and has great dreams of what they can become. When, however, they do not turn out as He expected, His love turns to rage and violence. Great expectations can turn into great hatred if they are not grounded in an appreciation of human limitations. This is what happens in the biblical flood story.

> The Lord saw how great was man's wickedness on earth, and how every plan devised by his mind was nothing but evil all the time. And the Lord regretted that He had made man on earth, and His heart was saddened. The Lord said, "I will blot out from the earth the men whom I created—men together with beasts, creeping things, and birds of the sky; for I regret that I made them." But Noah found favor with the Lord. (Gen. 6:5–8)

If you love the dream too much, you may destroy the reality on its account. Earnest revolutionaries, in the name of their love of humanity, can become haters of human beings if theirs is the love of an abstract dream rather than an appreciation of concrete people.

In contrast to the flood, the covenant with God in the desert reveals a God who has given up His fantasies about humanity. God began to accept the meaning of human limitations only after Noah left the ark.

> Then Noah built an altar to the Lord and, taking of every clean animal and of every clean bird, he offered burnt offerings on the altar. The Lord smelled the pleasing odor, and the Lord said to Himself: "Never again will I doom the earth because of man, since the devisings of man's mind are evil from his youth; nor will I ever again destroy every living being, as I have done." (Gen. 8:20–21)

Israel in its limitations is accepted by God, as is Israel who builds a golden calf and Israel who wants to return to Egypt every time water or food is in short supply. Israel in sin and rebellion is still loved because God's covenant is based on what human beings really are. If it were based on unrealistic divine expectations, I would be frightened of accepting the Sinai covenant. But because of the frank descriptions of Israel's failures, I know that the divine demand (mitzvah) is grounded in reality. The divine commandments (mitzvot) are given to vulnerable, fragile human beings. When I put on *tefillin* (phylacteries) and pray in the morning, it is not human grandeur that is being acknowledged but rather human vulnerability and imperfection. I can love God and sense God's acceptance of me as a weak, finite human being. I am a "commanded one" within the context of human limitations.

The covenant thus signifies the restored dignity of the concrete and the finite. It expresses the ability to love in spite of human limitations, to build meaning in the face of death, to act today without certainty about tomorrow. George Steiner is mistaken when he claims that "tragedy is alien to the Judaic sense of the world." One has only to read the Book of Job to realize that Job's problem was never resolved. God does not answer Job's questions at the end of the story, but, as Maimonides understood, Job gained a new perception of history and God. People may think the Book of Job has a happy ending, but anyone who has experienced the death of a child knows how painful it is to love after undergoing such a tragic loss. Yet, Job had the courage to start a new family in spite of the tragic uncertainty of life.

Death invades our lives, often making our dreams and aspirations into a joke. Yet, knowing that we are frail and vulnerable, we still love and build families. We know our weaknesses, yet we take our lives very seriously. Can we live with that kind of tension? For many people, this is impossible unless they can believe in a total and final resolution to human suffering through eternity, through redemption, through the ultimate liberation from death. It is difficult to argue with people who have that need. I am convinced that this longing to defeat death through religious faith also creates the need for certainty. The yearning for this kind of salvation can be so profound that you begin to doubt the validity of your way whenever you see other people choosing a different path. As a result, people choose to be deaf to each other's music in order to feel certain they are among the chosen ones blessed with eternal salvation.

The fear of death is, in an important sense, similar to the fear many people have of religious diversity. The consciousness of death creates fear, uncertainty, and a sense of a lack of control. Similar reactions can arise in pluralistic societies where "the other" cannot be absorbed into your own particular categories of living. Radical differences unsettle your sense of certainty. Can you live with uncertainty, or must you have absolute, ironclad truths whereby God discloses to you: "This is My way; follow it and you are saved;

deviate from it and you are lost"? Do we need absolute certainty in order to build a spiritual way of life? Must I believe that ultimately "the other" is an instrument for my own redemption, and that at the end of history God will reveal who was right?

Must I believe in Maimonides' explanation of the instrumental relationship between Judaism and its main monotheistic rivals?

> But it is beyond the human mind to fathom the designs of the Creator; for our ways are not His ways, neither are our thoughts His thoughts. All these matters relating to Jesus of Nazareth and the Ishmaelite [Mohammed] who came after him, only served to clear the way for King Messiah, to prepare the whole world to worship God with one accord, as it is written "For then will I turn to the peoples a pure language, that they may all call upon the name of the Lord to serve Him with one consent" (Zeph. 3:9). Thus the messianic hope, the Torah, and the commandments have become familiar topics—topics of conversation [among the inhabitants] of the far isles and many peoples, uncircumcised of heart and flesh. They are discussing these matters and the commandments of the Torah. Some say, "Those commandments were true, but have lost their validity and are no longer binding"; others declare that they had an esoteric meaning and were not intended to be taken literally; that the Messiah has already come and revealed their occult significance. But when the true King Messiah will appear and succeed, be exalted and lifted up, they will forthwith recant and realize that they have inherited naught but lies from their fathers, that their prophets

and forbears led them astray. (Book of Judges, Book XIV, uncensored version)

There is an alternative religious sensibility not driven by the need for cognitive certainty, which I associate with the famous passage in the Babylonian Talmud (*Eruvin* 13b). The rival schools of Hillel and Shammai were in such disagreement that the Torah was on the verge of being divided into two Torahs. The Talmud relates that a certain dispute ended when a heavenly voice was heard, saying: "These and these are the words of the living God, but the Halakhah is according to Hillel." Now, if both points of view are acceptable, why then did God declare the law to be like Hillel? The Talmud answers that whenever Hillel presented his position in the house of learning, he would always mention Shammai's position first. He was so "considerate and modest" that when addressing students, he would begin by discussing the alternative opinion to his own, and only after showing its plausibility would he defend his own opinion. He never taught Torah under the pretense of possessing the sole truth; he was aware that two opposing opinions might both be plausible and meaningful.

Although the law is decided in accordance with the majority, the minority point of view was never dismissed or regarded as devoid of cognitive or religious significance. A return to the minority opinion was always a possibility.

And why do they record the opinion of the individual against that of the majority, whereas the Halakhah may be only according to the opinion of the majority? That if a court approves the opinion of the individual it may rely upon him, since a court cannot annul the opinion of another court unless it exceeds it both in wisdom and in number; if it exceeded it in wisdom but not in number, or in number but not in wisdom, it cannot annul its opinion; but only if it exceeds it both in wisdom and in number. (Mishnah *Eduyyot* 1:5)

To the person of faith, living according to the majority opinion is significantly different from accepting the one and only authoritative option. If your tradition is based on learning, interpretation, and disagreements among scholars, rather than on the absolute word of prophetic revelation, you cannot escape the haunting uncertainty of knowing that alternative ways are religiously viable and authentic

Judaism was able to accomplish the transition from the biblical tradition, based on revelation, to the talmudic tradition, based on reasoned argumentation. Despite the radical difference between prophet and rabbinic sage, Judaic teachers were able to convince the community that the oral and the written traditions together form a religious unity. This achievement may shed light on the way we ourselves can structure a spiritual communal life that does not require absolute, dogmatic certainty. Let us therefore include ourselves among those teachers who taught a commitment to Judaism and a love of God while accepting the unsettling idea that "these and these are the words of the living God."

In the rabbinic tradition, no school of thought exhausts the wisdom and intention of God. Rabbinic Jews do not leave their human skins when they mediate and interpret the word of God. From a Maimonidean perspective, even revelation does not transcend the context of a particular historical frame of reference. The rabbinic and Maimonidean traditions should lead us to understand the meaning of being claimed by a revealed Divine Word, which is filtered through the arguments and decisions of finite human beings who apply Torah in daily life.

To the contemporary Jew, God's word at Sinai is part of a two-thousand-year-old human discussion. If one cannot accept a spiritual way of life mediated by limited, finite human beings, then one cannot live within an Orthodox halakhic tradition.

Israel's election at Sinai and the renaissance of a third Jewish commonwealth are deeply informed by an appreciation of human finitude and particularity. The presence of diversity in Israeli society in terms of the dignity of "the other," be it the Christian, Muslim, or Palestinian "other," makes us conscious of the fact that no one person or community exhausts all spiritual possibilities.

The Bible speaks of two important concepts of love: love of the neighbor and love of the stranger. In our neighbor, we meet a person with whom we share common values, familial ties, and communal solidarity. "Love your neighbor" extends the self to others through community solidarity. "Love the stranger" asks me to meet the other with whom I do not share a common history and memory, the different one, the person who cannot be assimilated within my communal frame of reference. In this respect, the Bible frequently recalls our own historical experience of suffering under a totalitarian system where we lacked dignity because of our otherness. We were abused because differences were a source of fear and intolerance. This experience of Egypt, says the Bible, must teach us to empathize with, rather than feel threatened by, those who are other. "And you shall love the stranger because you were strangers in the land of Egypt."

The Jewish community suffered many different Egypts throughout history because we embodied the scandal of particularity. We became the permanent strangers in history, the stumbling block to those who attempted to impose a monolithic religious and political order.

We who have returned to build the third Jewish commonwealth, where we are the majority culture and where the national, social, and political frameworks support our collective dignity, must also realize that the Egypts of our history must teach us to appreciate and celebrate the dignity of the stranger in our midst. Loyalty to our historical roots demands that we learn from history not to reenact the trauma of the victim, who lives with fear and suspicion. Instead, the memory of our suffering and our profound isolation in history must be transformed into new sources of values and energies empowering the stranger to flourish with dignity in the midst of our own national community.

8

REVELATION AND CREATION

The Particular and the
Universal in Judaism

IT HAS OFTEN been claimed that belief in revelation and divine election is incompatible with religious pluralism. Belief in the biblical Lord of history Who reveals Himself to His chosen people seems to reduce the faith commitment to one central issue. Given the competing claims of Judaism, Christianity, and Islam to being the true heir to Abraham's legacy, the crucial concern of faith must be: Which faith community mediates God's vision for history? From such a viewpoint, religious tolerance and openness to other faith communities undermine uncompromising commitment to the true faith God has revealed.

The Bible is often noted for its zealous and passionate intolerance to idolatry, not for its liberalism or respect for other ways of worship. The prophetic, as opposed to the philosophic, pathos (Jerusalem vs. Athens) is held responsible for the religious wars of zealots claiming to possess the keys to the Kingdom. (The spatial claustrophobia of the religious sites in the Old City of Jerusalem is impressive.)

REVELATION AND CHOSENNESS

Traditionally, Christian theology regarded the Jews as those who blindly persisted in living according to a superseded divine dispensation. Islam treated both the Jewish and the Christian scriptural traditions as distortions of the truth proclaimed in the Koran. Responding on behalf of Judaism, Maimonides portrayed Christianity and Islam as aberrations, and argued that their adherents would repent of their folly when Jews returned to their ancient homeland and the Messiah reestablished the Jewish polity (M.T. *H. Melachim*, Judges 11). Are divine love and election subject to a scarcity principle that limits the authenticity of the faith experience to one and only one religious tradition? Must believing Jews view Christian pilgrims coming to Israel as earnest devotees ultimately misguided in their spiritual quest? Need their persistent advocacy of Christianity be an embarrassment and a threat to a Jew's faith commitment, and vice versa?

The locus of the problem is not the belief in one God but the belief in divine revelation and election. Theologies in the spirit of Aristotle, which recognize a monotheistic principle but without the notions of election and divine intervention in history, are compatible with religious pluralism. Divine worship where God is primarily a principle of perfection, eliciting adoration and religious fervor, can easily make room for multiple faith communities (see Yehuda Halevi, *The Kuzari*, I, 1–4). Similarly, eighteenth-century deism was a philosophically attractive alternative to biblical religion because it neutralized revelation and history, thereby allowing for religious tolerance and pluralism. The God who is above history is also above particular communities.

Those committed to the biblical tradition, however, cannot follow the deistic route to accommodate religious pluralism. They do not worship the "ground of being" but a God who is very much involved in human history. The biblical drama is concerned essentially with history rather than nature. As Leo Strauss correctly emphasized in *Athens and Jerusalem*, it is the human being and not nature that is fashioned in God's image.

History and revelation mediate a divine reality that seeks to be embodied in the social and political structures of the faith community. But this raises the inevitable question: To whom is the word of God addressed? Even if world history as a whole is the framework within which the Divine Presence operates, the principle of election implies an exclusive providential relationship to a single community (see Ramban's commentary to Lev. 18:25).

Biblical revelation asserted God's involvement in human history. Because God has a stake in history, the divine–human encounter answers both divine and human interests. However scandalous it may sound to the metaphysician, the biblical tradition maintains that God does not execute His designs for history without the cooperation of at least some part of humankind. Revelation to a particular person or people thus becomes essential to the aims of the biblical Lord of history.

The notion of revelation implies that the human way to God must conform with the revealed word of God. If the faith experience were a matter of human beings seeking to express their awe and love for divinity—that is, if it were a one-directional movement of the human toward the divine—then the criterion of legitimate faith expressions would be subjective, allowing for a variety of religious attitudes and approaches. Kierkegaard's dictum "truth is subjectivity" could be used to justify multiple faith postures, each channeling the worshipper's feelings toward God. But in revelatory faiths where there is reciprocity between human beings and God, the will of God plays an essential role in determining the nature of religious life. It is not sufficient to express my own will and feelings. I must also ask: "What does God ask of me?" Revelation draws us into a dialogic relationship with God; natural theology, deism, and the worship of the "ground of being" religions are ultimately monologues. Unlike the latter, revelatory systems require some source of knowledge of what God wants and how God responds to our religious practices. The individual's sincerity alone is not religiously self-validating; he or she must wait for God's response in order to determine the validity of his or her religious way of life.

Since God has such a stake in the divine–human relationship, the content of revelation is a vital component of biblical religion. A spouse may choose a gift for the beloved with infinite passion, yet the beloved may derive no pleasure from the gift itself. A gesture may be noble and expressive of deep emotion, yet its content may be unappealing. Revelation entails our asking whether God is prepared to sit down with us at the table we have prepared with passion and sincerity. As the book of Leviticus describes so graphically, questions of correct cultic practice and ritual are vital in a revelatory framework.

Herein lies the importance for biblical religion of knowing who has access to the revealed Word. The Torah and the New Testament disagree about forms of worship. Why did God accept Abel's offering and reject Cain's? Centuries of rivalry and conflict, when faith communities responded to one another according to the model of Cain and Abel, bear witness to the moral urgency of the dilemma of pluralism and biblical theology.

AN ALTERNATIVE APPROACH TO BIBLICAL THEOLOGY

The biblical drama is marked by a dialectical interaction between the themes of creation and revelation. The Torah begins with God acting in freedom to create the universe. One's very existence as a creature implies a relationship to God. This relationship, however, does not involve concepts of election or history. All things created, animate as well as inanimate, are affirmed as manifestations of God's will. "And God saw all that He had made, and found it very good" (Gen. 1:31). The experience that grows from human awareness of creation may be termed an "ontological relationship" to God. In the context of this relationship, all beings are equal creations of one God. By thus becoming conscious of the self, a human being becomes aware of the interconnectedness of all beings bound together by the divine, all-embracing love and power expressed in creation.

The Jewish prayer book speaks of God as "who in His goodness renews the act of creation continually each and every day," implying that divine creation is an abiding feature of reality and not merely a foundational moment. All things share an enduring ontological relationship with God. The joys of hearing a bird sing, of viewing a sunset, of being caressed by an evening breeze are all occasions for celebrating the gift of creation. All of life is sacred, because it mirrors the loving affirmation of the God of creation.

Creation, however, also contains the seeds of a dialectical movement to history, since the first human being was created endowed with freedom. Human freedom gives rise to human rebellion and sin, thus beginning a process leading to divine revelation and election. Freedom allows humankind to become separated and estranged from God. Sin and estrangement introduce the principles of divine judgment and divine responsiveness.

The God of creation can remain nondiscriminating: all of existence equally reflects the overflowing power of God. The early chapters of Genesis narrate God's repeated attempts to overcome the estrangement caused by human sin and rebellion. Humankind's unrelenting opposition to God's will, however, repeatedly frustrates these efforts. A new solution begins to emerge with the story of Abraham, which introduces the principle of *election*.

Through election, God seeks to create a community that will restore the primal relationship of being, not through creature consciousness but through commitment and choice.

The relationship between human beings and God is now mediated by human freedom. God no longer simply speaks and produces results automatically, as in the creation ("And God said...and there was"). With revelation and election, the arena of the God–human encounter shifts from nature to history. Because of the unpredictability of human history, the biblical story now becomes truly dramatic. God agrees, as it were, to share the stage with humanity, to limit His own freedom and power so as to sustain human freedom and responsibility.

> Now the Lord had said, "Shall I hide from Abraham what I am about to do, since Abraham is to become a great and populous nation and all the nations of the earth are to bless themselves by him? For I have singled him out, that he may instruct his children and his posterity to keep the way of the Lord by doing what is just and right, in order that the Lord may bring about for Abraham what He has promised him." (Gen. 18:17–19)

Before punishing the people of Sodom, God, as it were, consults with Abraham, His covenantal partner.

REVELATION AND COMMUNITY

In contrast to Martin Buber, who understands revelation and election in terms of radical spontaneity, classical Judaism interpreted Sinai in terms of the revelation of law to community. If the aim of revelation is to build community, then spontaneity must be superseded or at least balanced by categories of structure and order. Divine involvement in history must not be limited to radical spontaneity and singular moments of surprise. The classic Jewish view stressed that the Sinai revelation established a community through mitzvot, which provide the structure of a permanent relationship with God.

Revelation expresses God's willingness to meet human beings in their finitude, in their particular historical and social situation, and to speak to them in their own language. All these constraints prevent one from universalizing the significance of a particular revelation. Revelation in history, therefore, is always fragmentary and incomplete. Divine–human encounters cannot ever exhaust the divine plenitude. New human situations demand reinterpretation of the content of revelation. That is why interpretation of and commentary on the content of revelation are continuous activities. While the commentator does not create an original, independent work, he or she plays a creative role in determining the normative content of revelation.

The Greek Neoplatonists believed that human reason could ascend to the level of divine thought and thus liberate the individual from the limits of human finitude. When Christian, Islamic, and Jewish theologians adopted this Greek concept of participation, they abandoned an essential feature of biblical religion, namely, creature consciousness. Subsequently, medieval philosophers went to great lengths to justify the need for revelation, given the belief that human beings could participate in the divine mind through reason.

Revelation need not be understood as a source of absolute, eternal, and transcendent truth. Rather, it is God's speaking to human beings within the limited framework of human language and history. Reason and revelation are not rival sources of knowledge. Revelation is not unique by virtue of its cognitive content. The Bible does not compete with Plato or Aristotle. Revelation is an expression of God's love and confirmation of human beings in terms of their finitude and creatureliness; it is God's speaking to human beings for their own sake and not in order to reveal the mysteries of the Divine mind.

In Judaism, human beings become susceptible to the sin of idolatry when they believe they can transcend the limits of the human condition. There is nothing more efficacious for restoring humility to the human spirit than confronting people who do not share your "self-evident" truths. Because Buddhism, Hinduism, Christianity, Islam, and Judaism are distinct spiritual paths, they bear witness to the complexity and fullness of the Divine reality. The lack of unity within Christianity and Judaism testifies to the radical diversity within human consciousness and to the rich mosaic of views and practices inspired by the quest for God in human history. Consciousness of the existence of multiple faith commitments can be spiritually redemptive. It can help you realize that your own faith commitment does not exhaust the full range of spiritual options.

When the particularity of revelation is recognized, biblical faith does not have to seek to universalize itself. We may be living in a redemptive period of history precisely because religious pluralism has acquired legitimacy in the eyes of so many. Even though ecumenism is often driven by political considerations, the very fact that people feel the need to appear tolerant and committed to pluralism, whatever their inner convictions, indicates how deeply pluralism has become ingrained in the spirit of the age. In modern societies, people have little patience with exclusive, doctrinaire religious attitudes. Notwithstanding its problems and limitations, secular liberal society has created conditions for the emergence of religious humility by constraining the human propensity to universalize the particular.

CREATION AND MESSIANISM

Creation can be viewed as a metahistorical category. The creation story in Genesis can serve as a corrective to the possible distortions of God's revelation in history by conveying the idea that human beings must recognize the universal sanctify of life, since all of life was given through the creative power of God. A mishnah in *Sanhedrin* explains the significance of the creation of a single human being as follows:

> Therefore humankind was created singly, to teach you that whoever destroys a single soul, Scripture accounts it as if he/she destroyed a full world; and whoever saves one soul, Scripture accounts it as if he/she saves a full world. And for the sake of peace among people, that one should not say to his fellow, "My father is greater than yours"; and that heretics should not say, "There are many powers in Heaven." Again, to declare the greatness of the Holy One, blessed be He, for a human being stamps out many coins with one die, and they are all alike, but the King, the King of Kings, the Holy One, blessed be He, stamped each human being with the seal of Adam, and not one of them is like another. Therefore each and every person is obliged to say, "For my sake the world was created." (IV, 5)

The Babylonian Talmud adds that God collected elements from the four corners of the earth to form the first human being. These two statements imply that the principle of the sanctity of life must not be limited by considerations of race, color, nationality, or creed. The principle of creation universalizes the sanctity of life, thereby extending it beyond the confines of any particular revelation.

An ethic based on the sanctity of life would satisfy Kant's condition of universalizability, since creation is prior to both revelation and election. Micah's vision of the end of days reflects the messianic significance of the creation theme:

> In the days to come,
> The Mount of the Lord's House shall stand
> Firm above the mountains;
> And it shall tower above the hills.
> The peoples shall gaze on it with joy,
> And the many nations shall go and shall say:
> "Come,
> Let us go up to the Mount of the Lord,
> To the House of the God of Jacob;
> That He may instruct us in His ways,
> And that we may walk in His paths."
> For instruction shall come forth from Zion,
> The word of the Lord from Jerusalem.
> Thus He will judge among the many peoples,
> And arbitrate for the multitude of nations,
> However distant;
> And they shall beat their swords into plowshares
> And their spears into pruning hooks.
> Nations shall not take up
> Sword against nation;
> They shall never again know war;
> But every man shall sit
> Under his grapevine or fig tree
> With no one to disturb him.
> For it was the Lord of Hosts who spoke.
> Though all the peoples walk
> Each in the names of its gods,
> We will walk

In the name of the Lord our God
Forever and ever. (Micah 4:1–5)

Our task today is to characterize messianism in terms of the universal ethical conception derived from creation. Faith commitments based on revelation may contain a universal thrust, not in order to universalize their particular understanding of revelation, but rather in order to universalize the ethical consciousness implied in the story of creation. No particular community can fully realize itself if the ethical fails to become embedded in human consciousness. As long as violence and brutality are dominant anywhere in the world, no particular community can fully realize its unique spiritual way of life because it must act to counter the threat posed by such violence and brutality. Historical redemption is impossible as long as Eichmanns and Himmlers walk the earth.

Herein lies the proper universal dimension of messianic aspirations. The messianic dream must be of a world in which all human beings realize that they were created in the image of God, that they owe their existence to God, and that therefore all of life is sacred. Only then will the God of creation reign in history.

Revelation implies that God accepts humanity with its limitations and recognizes that people realize their human potential within particular communities. To the committed Jew, Judaism means loving one's people's memories and one's parents' songs, loving Rabbi Akiva and Maimonides, living in a particular city and being a citizen of a particular country. The belief that space can become holy to God means that God allows the finite and particular to contain Him symbolically. This was God's message to Solomon at the dedication of the Temple. And this is the meaning of the Promised Land: God allowed Himself to be mirrored for a particular people in a particular land.

Nevertheless, the Jew lives out Judaism with great anticipation that one day all human beings will give up war and acknowledge the sacredness of life. Until there is universal triumph of the ethical, history will remain a fragile and inhospitable home for every human being. Does this mean that all humankind must embrace the Jew's history or recognize its superiority? No. Messianism may aspire to universal redemption through a universal acknowledgement of the Creator God, that is, through the principle of the sanctity of all life. The knowledge of God that will fill the earth on "that day" will be the knowledge derived from "creation" over and above "revelation."

The understanding of revelation and election just outlined can make room for religious pluralism. The key concept is the particularity of revelation. Revelation is not addressed to humanity in general, but to a particular individual or community. And because of this inherent particularity, it need not invalidate the faith experience of other religious communities.

Election represents a particularization of God's relationship to humankind by virtue of divine involvement in history, without the implication that there is only one exclusive mediator of the divine message. Consequently, theologians who claim that worshipping the universal God is incompatible with election are making a "category mistake." The universal God is the God of creation. But it is God as the Lord of history who enters into specific relationships with human beings and who is therefore loved in a particularistic manner. All intimate love relationships claim exclusivity by their very nature.

The distinction between creation and history enables biblical faith to admit the possibility of religious pluralism without neutralizing its passionate commitment to the biblical Lord of history. Revelation and election belong to the domain of history, where particular communities serve God in ways that mediate their particular memories.

The radical particularization of history eliminates the need for faith communities to regard one another as rivals. Competition between faith traditions arises when universality is ascribed to particular historical revelations. When revelation is understood as the concretization of the universal, then "*whose* truth is *the* truth?" becomes the paramount religious question, and pluralism becomes a vacuous religious ideal. If, however, revelation can be separated from the claim of universality, and if a community of faith can regain an appreciation of the particularity of the divine–human encounter, then pluralism can become a meaningful part of biblical faith experiences.

The dream of a universal community under the kingdom of God should be divorced from history. When it is the historical goal of a particular faith community, it can become, as it has been, a terribly dangerous idea. The fact that there are real differences among faith communities means that those who aspire to universality will often have to resort to a universalism of the sword. On the other hand, the concept of creation, not the concepts of community and history, must nurture the dream of a universal ethical awakening of human consciousness. The Jew, the Christian, and the Muslim are all one, insofar as they are creatures of God. One thus acknowledges the sacredness of life common to all human beings irrespective of their ways of life and modes of worship. Any person who takes a human life mars the image of God in all of us.

The Jewish people suffered for centuries from other peoples' misplaced emphasis on history as the domain in which to establish universal religious truth. The Jewish people had the opportunity to learn this lesson long before the twentieth century. Time and again it suffered for its stubbornness in resisting visions of universalization. As an expression of particularity in history, its very existence was often treated as a scandal. Thus, although the tendency toward universalization may have existed in Judaism itself during the late biblical and early rabbinic periods, the lived history of the Jewish people subsequently became a testimony to the evil that results from universalizing the particular.

Jews express loyalty to their tradition not only by their allegiance to the Bible and to rabbinic texts but also by recognizing the implications of the lived experience of their people: "And I shall be sanctified in the midst of the children of Israel" (Lev. 22:32). We can respond halakhically to our past suffering by striving to discover in the contemporary world how the presence of "the other" can be spiritually redemptive. Thus the attempt to establish a secure framework for religious pluralism and tolerance in the State of Israel is not tangential to our national rebirth. Our return to independent political existence affords us the opportunity to become the first biblical religion to acknowledge that revelation can never exhaust the plenitude of creation. One bears witness to the God of creation by rejoicing in the limits of one's own finitude.

Our return to normalcy can become an assertion of the religious significance of particularity. We have returned not to a universal, heavenly Jerusalem but to a particular, earthly Jerusalem. The dream of history should not be the victory of one faith community. Each faith community should walk before God in its own way while remembering that no community can exhaust the universal God of creation.

The conception of home, which our particular historical memories have nurtured, must be integrated with the theme of creation that proclaims the dignity of every human being. Exclusive reliance on revelation would make it impossible for us to share our home with the Palestinian people. If, however, our consciousness of revelation were to become infused with creation, then we could learn to celebrate our coming home even if it were not be realized fully and completely.

The rabbinic tradition taught us to say grace even over incomplete meals, for it realized that God does not always offer us finished and complete frameworks of meaning. The rabbis in the Talmud understood this when they related the story of the ministering angels questioning God for "showing favoritism to Israel."

> Sovereign of the Universe, it is written in Your Law, "Who lifts not up the countenance [shows no favor] and takes no bribe" (Deut. 10:17), but do You not regard the person of Israel, as it is written, "The Lord lift up His countenance [bestow His favor] upon you" (Num. 6:26)? He replied to them: And shall I not lift up My countenance for Israel, seeing that I wrote for them in the Torah, "And you shall eat and be satisfied and bless the Lord your God" (Deut. 8:10) but they are particular [to say grace] even if the quantity is but an olive or an egg! (B.T. *Berachot* 20b)

I understand this midrash to mean that although, in the Torah, God enjoined Israel to say grace after a full and satisfying meal, Israel developed the capacity to say grace even over small, incomplete meals. The rabbis thus taught us to experience religious gratitude for the incomplete and the partial satisfaction of our desires.

I can understand the pain that many Israelis feel at the prospect of sharing their home with "an other." In doing so, however, they would bear witness to Judaism's ability to combine "Beloved is Israel" with "Beloved is every human being created in the image of God."

9

ABRAHAM JOSHUA HESCHEL

A Heroic Witness to Religious Pluralism

ABRAHAM JOSHUA HESCHEL was a man of thought and action. His models were the Hebrew prophets, who were outraged by social injustice and by the brutalization of the human spirit. He felt the urgency of the moment, and the need to correct the moral failures and mediocrity of religious institutions and bear witness to how a devoted Jew can participate in the universal struggle for human rights and justice.

Heschel's masterful and impassioned use of evocative images and metaphors were never substitutes for concrete action. In deed, as in word, he personified the spiritual and moral implications of his religious perception of life, of his prophetic sense of "divine pathos." His intense love for his own people and tradition did not blind him to others. His tireless efforts against the Vietnam War and his public support of Martin Luther King, Jr. and the struggle for civil rights in America expressed the same spiritual and moral sensibility as his pleas for Russian Jewry and the security and well-being of Israel.

In keeping with his view that Judaism affirmed the sanctity of time over space, he was quick to respond to the major historical events of his time. There was always some event or historical situation that impelled Heschel to write. In response to Israel's political isolation, Heschel tried to correct the view that the rebirth of the State and the Jewish people's love and concern for Jerusalem were modern expressions of "biblical tribalism." He argued passionately and relentlessly that loyalty to Israel, which the modern world often perceived exclusively as an expression of Jewish tribalism, contained a universal message of hope and concern for all of humanity.

> The ultimate meaning of the State of Israel must be seen in terms of the vision of the prophets: the redemption of all men. The religious duty of the Jew is to participate in the process of continuous redemption, in seeing that justice prevails over power, that awareness of God penetrates human understanding. (*Israel: An Echo of Eternity*, p. 225)
>
> The modern world, haunted by the bleak perspective of the twentieth century, has been given a concrete symbol of hope by the return of this people to its land. Pagans have idols, Israel has a promise. We have no image; all we have is hope. Israel reborn is a verification of the promise. The promise of redemption of all people involves the presence of this people in this land. (p. 101)

Although Zionism and Israeli society were predominantly secular, Heschel described these modern phenomena in the light of his understanding of biblical spirituality.

> Israel reborn is an answer to the Lord of History who demands hope as well as action.... It is a land where the Bible is at home....
>
> What is holy about the Holy Land? It is not only because its space is filled with frozen echoes of a voice heard in the past. Israel is a prelude, an anticipation....
>
> The State of Israel is not only a place of refuge for the survivors of the holocaust, but also a tabernacle for the rebirth of faith and justice, for the renewal of souls, for the cultivation of knowledge of the words of the divine. (pp. 118–122)

Heschel wrote *The Earth Is the Lord's* in response to the Holocaust, trying to recapture the spirit and values of a unique civilization that had been decimated. Although some may find fault with Heschel's selective, idealized picture of Eastern European Jewry, one should read his essay in the light of his passionate concern with rescuing contemporary Jewry from cultural and national assimilation.

Heschel felt the burden of generations on his shoulders; his task was to revitalize and renew interest in Jewish thought and practice. Unlike nineteenth-century *Wissenschaft* writers, whose treatment of Judaism has been described as a way of providing for its "dignified burial," Heschel attempted to breathe new life and vitality into Jewish culture and religion.

> In this hour we, the living, are "the people of Israel." The tasks begun by the patriarchs and prophets and continued by their descendants are now entrusted to us. We are either the last Jews or those who will hand over the entire past to generations to come. We will either forfeit or enrich the legacy of ages. (*The Earth Is the Lord's*, p. 107)

THE WRITTEN WORD AND MUSIC

Unless one is attuned to the lyrical-poetic style of Heschel's prose, one may mistake his impassioned style for superficiality. To fully appreciate Heschel's thought, one must read him as if one were listening to a moving *nigun* (melody)—slowly, thoughtfully, allowing the depth of his insights to take root in one's soul.

> Listening to great music is a shattering experience, throwing the soul into an encounter with an aspect of reality to which the mind can never relate itself adequately. Such experiences undermine conceit and complacency and may even induce the sense of contrition and a readiness for repentance. I am neither a musician nor an expert on music. But the shattering experience of music has been the challenge to my thinking on ultimate issues. I spend my life working with thoughts. And one problem that gives me no rest is: do these thoughts ever rise to the heights reached by authentic music? (*The Insecurity of Freedom*, p. 76)

Heschel lived in a world that was crumbling. His one hope was to captivate his readers with a stirring "melody" that could arouse and inspire. Rather than try to persuade by clever argumentation, Heschel chose to enchant by the great line or the powerful image that would haunt the soul of the sensitive reader. He did not write as a formal theologian embellishing esoteric arguments with lengthy footnotes. Instead, he argued simultaneously on different levels, drawing on multiple traditions and sources, combining a wide variety of themes and "melodies" into a sweeping concert of ideas that he hoped would "rise to the heights reached by authentic music."

THEOLOGY AND METAPHOR

Heschel was convinced that Jewish philanthropic, communal, and religious institutions would not withstand the powerful forces of assimilation in Western society unless individuals were to appreciate and to personally identify with the spiritual worldview of Judaism.

> Judaism is a personal problem.... Jews attend Jewish meetings, belong to Jewish organizations, and contribute to communal and national funds. But when left alone, or retired in our homes—they are poor in religious spirit....
> If the individual is lost to Judaism in his privacy, the people are in danger of becoming a phantom.... Unless a person knows how to pray alone, he is incapable of praying within the congregation. (*The Insecurity of Freedom*, pp. 191, 215)

Heschel was less concerned with collective Jewish frameworks than with family and individual life. Like his contemporary, Rabbi Joseph B. Soloveitchik, he had little respect for theologians and rabbis who marketed religion in terms of peace of mind or who neutralized the centrality of God in the name of ethical humanism.

True prophets differed from modern social reformers and revolutionaries because of the "divine pathos" that informed their perspective on life in general and on human society in particular. Unlike their secular counterparts, the prophets' sense of moral outrage mirrored their identification with God's outrage at human injustice and mediocrity. Heschel attempted to restore this theocentric perspective to contemporary Jewish life by showing that human relations and social realities take on new meaning when seen through the eyes of God—that is, with divine rather than human pathos.

The God to whom Heschel refers in his philosophy of sympathetic divine identification is not the transcendent, impersonal deity of the mystics but the more "human" God of the Bible. Heschel's phenomenological analysis of the prophetic experience of divine pathos differs from mystical accounts of ecstasy and union in that the relationships between God and Israel and God and prophet do not obliterate the individuality or personalities of the parties to the relationships. The prophet's emphatic identification with God was made possible by the realism of biblical theology, by the vivid and vital characterizations of God as a living character in the biblical drama.

Heschel, therefore, unlike Maimonides, was not reticent about attributing human emotions and qualities to God. Maimonides tried to capture the conceptual purity and uniqueness of the transcendent divine reality, whereas Heschel was less concerned with abstract conceptual consistency than with allowing God to become a living reality for modern Jews often embarrassed by religious language and culture. Heschel's writings are thus full of graphic, anthropomorphic depictions of God. He preferred the experiential intensity of religious narrative to the intellectualism of dogmatic theology.

HALAKHAH AND AGGADAH

Heschel stands in sharp contrast to modern Jewish thinkers who treat Jewish law, Halakhah, as the essence of Judaism. The danger of emphasizing the obligations and prohibitions of halakhic practice to the exclusion of aggadic motifs in Judaism is the risk of losing God at the center of religious life.

Out of sheer punctiliousness in observing the law, one
may come to be oblivious to the living presence of the
Lord. (*The Earth Is the Lord's*, p. 83)

The vastness and specificity of Halakhah can blind a person
to the *telos* of Judaism, to the covenantal relationship between God
and Israel. One can, for example, become so immersed in the
myriad details of the Sabbath laws that one becomes oblivious to
the significance of the Sabbath as a symbolic celebration of divine
creation. It was crucial, therefore, for Heschel, to establish the
importance of Aggadah, the nonlegal, narrative sections of rabbinic
literature, as a legitimate and religiously vital component of
halakhic Judaism.

Yeshayahu Leibowitz, by contrast, claimed that Halakhah
per se, not theology, constitutes the essence of Judaism. He argued
that classic Judaism prescribed explicit rules of behavior without
formulating an official dogma or theology. Halakhah, he
concluded, was the single common denominator underlying the
variety of religious orientations and sensibilities in the classical
Jewish tradition. Traditional Judaism was shaped essentially by
talmudic rabbis and not by biblical prophets. Talmudic teachers
extrapolating and elaborating a comprehensive structure of
normative behavior—rather than God-intoxicated visionaries—
changed the Jewish community's way of life and ensured its
continued existence throughout history.

In contrast to Leibowitz, Heschel believed that the secret to
reviving Judaism in the modern world lay in joining a theocentric
passion with halakhic commitment. He attempted to guide Jews
back to Halakhah by way of the prophets, by restoring the
prophetic sense of divine concern for individual human behavior.

From a rationalist's point of view it does not seem plausible to assume that the infinite, ultimate supreme Being is concerned with my putting on tefillin every day. It is, indeed, strange to believe that God should care whether a particular individual would eat leavened or unleavened bread during a particular season of the year. However, it is that paradox, namely, that the infinite God is intimately concerned with finite man and his finite deeds; that nothing is trite or irrelevant in the eyes of God, which is the very essence of the prophetic faith....

If we are ready to believe that God requires of me "to do justice," is it more difficult for us to believe that God requires of us to be holy? If we are ready to believe that it is God who requires us "to love kindness," is it more difficult to believe that God requires us to hallow the Sabbath and not to violate its sanctity? (*Man's Quest for God: Studies in Prayer and Symbolism*, pp. 102–103)

In these remarks to an audience of Reform rabbis who were estranged from traditional halakhic practice, Heschel tried to show that the same theological metaphors of divine concern and obligation that apply to the moral norms of religious life apply equally to the symbolic ritualistic norms of Judaism. The dramatic theological background is no less anthropomorphic in the case of doing justice as it is in sanctifying the Sabbath.

When addressing a halakhically committed audience, however, Heschel would often shift intellectual gears and challenge "religious behaviorism" as a degenerative form of halakhic Judaism. He would argue against the traditionalist's dismissal of Aggadah as being religiously inferior to the "hard" discipline of pure legal exegesis. He tried to reverse the strict legalistic attitude prevalent in some Orthodox circles by cultivating an approach to Halakhah that mediated, rather than mitigated, the God-intoxicated passion of the prophets.

> The modern Jew cannot accept the way of static obedience as a short cut to the mystery of the divine will. His religious situation is not conducive to an attitude of intellectual or spiritual surrender. He is not ready to sacrifice his liberty on the altar of loyalty to the spirit of his ancestors.... His primary difficulty is not in his inability to comprehend the *Divine origin* of the law; his essential difficult is in his inability to sense *the presence of Divine meaning* in the fulfillment of the law.

Heschel's book *The Sabbath* exemplifies his unique approach to Halakhah. In contrast to standard works on the Sabbath that offer exhaustive accounts of the thirty-nine categories (and subcategories) of work prohibited on the Sabbath, Heschel's book is based on the insight that modern Jews need to discover a compelling Aggadah of the Sabbath before they can relate to it as Halakhah. When one begins to understand the meaning of being enveloped by a sacred day and the meaning of sacred time, only then can one appreciate the religious significance of the halakhic rules and regulations of the Sabbath.

According to Heschel, the Sabbath ushers in a new reality mediated by the practices, rituals, and restrictions of Sabbath observance. *The Sabbath* introduces the reader to the poetry of this special day. Heschel speaks of "eternity in time"; the additional soul (*neshamah yeteirah*) that was said to enter a person on the Sabbath; the positive spiritual dimensions of *menuhah* (rest); the significance of stillness and declaring a truce between oneself and the world; the architecture of time and the art of rest. The seventh day is an armistice in the struggle for economic and social survival, a day of peace with nature and with all of being, a way of being in the world without control or manipulation, a day of true independence, of freedom from the distractions of technological society.

Heschel's way of talking about the Sabbath, in particular, and about halakhic observance, in general, has a unique and refined quality that gives the potentially dry and formal details of legal behavior an added dimension of religious, aggadic meaning, shaping it into a path leading toward spiritual intensity.

The doctrines of the divine origin of Torah from Sinai or the "thirteen principles of faith" are often used to categorize Jewish thinkers, but differences of emphasis within the same framework of beliefs and practices can make very real differences in one's religious life and experience. The religious world one inhabits is often determined less by the "ontological furniture" provided by official dogma and Law than by the human qualities and sensibilities that rearrange the same furniture into vastly different living areas. Heschel recognized that the character, not necessarily the stated ideology, of the religious person is often the best explanation of that person's religious worldview.

Heschel believed that the "poetry" of a spiritual way of life must precede and inform its "prose." In light of this imagery, I would say that if the "rhythm" of Heschel's description of living by the mitzvot is "poetry," then Yeshayahu Leibowitz's philosophy of Judaism is decidedly "prose." To Leibowitz, living according to Halakhah requires, and must consciously express, decision and discipline; to Heschel, one cannot pray without the sensibility of the poetic imagination, without a sense of wonderment and surprise. To Leibowitz, prayer is paradigmatic of the heroic act of will and self-surrender that informs halakhic practice; personal spiritual sensibilities must be sacrificed on the altar of halakhic regularity, *tfilat keva* (fixed institutionalized prayer). While Heschel also recognized the centrality of regularity and discipline in halakhic life, his explanation of its importance is predicated on the poetic, aggadic sensibility that he cultivated.

Prayer becomes trivial when ceasing to be an act in the soul. The essence of prayer is Aggadah, *inwardness*. Yet it would be a tragic failure not to appreciate what the spirit of Halakhah does for it, raising it from the level of an individual act to that of an eternal intercourse between the people Israel and God; from the level of an occasional experience to that of a permanent covenant. It is through Halakhah that we belong to God not occasionally, intermittently, but essentially, continually. Regularity of prayer is an expression of my belonging to an order, to the covenant between God and Israel, which remains valid regardless of whether I am conscious of it or not. (*Man's Quest for God*, p. 68)

To Leibowitz, prayer has no unique status or experiential quality, and he therefore subsumes it under his singular, comprehensive category of mitzvah. The same intentional attitude of acting out of duty that informs all mitzvot applies equally to prayer. Prayer is simply an instance of mitzvah. To Heschel, however, prayer is *the* orienting framework for understanding mitzvah.

What is a mitzvah, a sacred act? A prayer in the form of a deed. (*Man's Quest for God*, p. 69)

Heschel also believed that the study of Judaic texts was insufficient to revitalize the Jewish soul in the modern world. In keeping with his theocentric diagnosis of the problematic state of modern Jewish life, he measured the quality of Jewish learning by its impact on the prayer experience.

This is the way of finding out whether we serve God, or an idea of God—through prayer. It is the test of all we are doing. What is the difference between Torah and *Wissenschaft des Judentums*? If an idea we have clarified, a concept we have evolved, turns into a prayer, it is Torah. If it proves to be an aid to praying with greater *kavannah*, it is Torah; otherwise it is *Wissenschaft*. (*Man's Quest for God*, p. 69)

JUDAISM AND CHRISTIANITY: INTERFAITH DIALOGUE

Heschel, no less than R. Soloveitchik or Prof. Leibowitz, was a halakhic Jew committed to the authority of Halakhah and rabbinic Judaism. With regard to interfaith dialogue, however, there were great differences among them stemming from the deeper differences of their respective philosophies of Judaism.[1]

To Soloveitchik, the concept of Halakhah is the dominant, constitutive idea underlying Jewish life and experience. The emphasis on Halakhah as the essential focus of religious consciousness (see his book *Halakhic Man*) draws attention to the unique features of Judaism relative to other religions. If the soul of Judaic spiritual life revolves predominantly around the normative practices of religious life, its distinctive symbolic rituals, prayers, and texts, then the differences between Christianity and Judaism become magnified into enormous, insurmountable obstacles to mutual understanding in matters of faith.

In other words, if you conceive of religious consciousness as derivative from—and therefore secondary to—the primary behavioral framework of religious life, then you can easily conclude that Christianity and Judaism are essentially incompatible. Whereas the former faith is nurtured by the passion of Jesus' resurrection, which informs its liturgy and symbolic practices, the latter is the product of Sabbath observance, Torah study, and all the other distinctive features of Halakhah.

Yeshayahu Leibowitz focused on the primacy of Halakhah to the exclusion of any other form of religious expression. Halakhah is both necessary and sufficient for defining Jewish religiosity; it is *sui generis* and cannot be explained by or subsumed under more general religious concepts, such as "sensibility" or "characterology." His ideal Jew accepts Halakhah as the quintessential form of divine worship, independent of and untainted by ulterior notions of purpose or utility. By contrast, Joseph Soloveitchik suggests that the commandments shape and develop a religious personality. While the concept of "religious experience" has an important place in Soloveitchik's writings, to Leibowitz the term is meaningless. Leibowitz acknowledges only one spiritual act: to proclaim that God, and only God, is the center of the universe. Simply stated, Halakhah is service of God.

To Leibowitz, Jewish–Christian dialogue is impossible because there are no shared religious experiences, sensibilities, or character types on which to base a discussion. Leibowitz also maintained that there was a fundamental disparity between the religious worldviews of Christianity and Judaism. By announcing redemption from sin for humankind, as symbolized by the crucifixion, Christianity adopted an anthropocentric (and therefore idolatrous) religious outlook that contrasted with the Jewish paradigm of faith, the *akedah* (binding of Isaac), which symbolized Abraham's readiness to sacrifice his son to fulfill God's command. Here, a human being sacrifices everything for God, whereas in Christianity, God sacrifices Himself for the sake of humanity.

In contrast to the Christian's preoccupation with the redemption of humanity, Leibowitz's Jew emulates Abraham at the *akedah* by affirming a total, unquestioning commitment to Halakhah. To Leibowitz, offering anthropocentric reasons for mitzvot undermines the heroic posture of unconditional surrender to God's will, subverts the idea of the centrality of God, and empties religion of its essence and profundity. Mitzvot should not be interpreted in terms of human significance, not even as means to developing humility or other desirable character traits, for their very meaning as religious entities consists in their leading us to transcend the human.

There is a similarity between the positions of Leibowitz and Soloveitchik on interfaith dialogue in terms of the historical background of past suffering that informs their views. They both carried the burden of the past—the bitter memory of exile and of Judaism's humiliating subservience to its dominant religious rival—into the present. Behind their theological and philosophical arguments, one senses the voice of the injured victim affirming the dignity of the Jewish people.

Leibowitz discovered Jewish dignity in political Zionism, whereas Soloveitchik focused on the diaspora, where Jews could affirm commitment to Judaism without apology, that is—without reducing their commitment and individuality to that great cultural leveler, universal intelligibility. For Soloveitchik, unconditional commitment to mitzvot that could not be assimilated into the majority's concepts of rationality or utility was vital for maintaining Jewish pride and self-respect in the modern world.

In his article "Confrontation," he warned Jews against "trading favors" with the majority religion and of compromising the essential "loneliness" of faith. He viewed Jewish pleas for changes in the Catholic liturgy as demeaning symptoms of the neurotic Jewish need for public confirmation by the non-Jewish majority. Past indignities had produced an obsession with gaining acceptance into Western culture and society, and therefore Soloveitchik was worried that Jewish leaders lacked the necessary wisdom and self-respect to refrain from negotiating Jewish dignity with their Christian counterparts. For this reason, too, he opposed Heschel's going to Rome to meet with the Pope.

Whereas Leibowitz ruled out interfaith dialogue altogether, Soloveitchik emphasized a radical form of uniqueness that precluded theological "bargaining" but that allowed for the cooperation of different religious communities in remedying social evils and in promoting shared social, cultural, and technological efforts to enhance human dignity and well-being.

Although totally committed to normative Judaism, Heschel was not the paradigmatic "halakhic man" in Soloveitchik's sense. For one thing, he was claimed primarily by Aggadah, which, he believed, expressed the teleology of Halakhah. In contrast to Soloveitchik's Lithuanian roots, his background and sensibilities were informed by the Hasidic tradition, wherein the quest for God and for the inner spiritual meaning of external forms remains a constant, driving motif of religious life. Because he conceived of Judaism from the perspective of Aggadah—i.e., from the inner devotional thrust behind halakhic forms—Heschel was able to discover common grounds for interfaith discussion and understanding within the faith experience itself.

Of the three attitudes to Jewish–Christian dialogue, Heschel's stands apart from the others in terms of its independence from historically conditioned conceptions and attitudes. Although a proud East European Jew, a "brand plucked out of the fire" who witnessed the destruction of a society and culture he loved and respected, Heschel overcame the bitter and angry memories of Jewish suffering in formulating his attitude to Christian dialogue. In *No Religion Is an Island*, he was able to put aside anger and resentment for past injustices and formulate an argument—a theology—with a broader, more universal appeal that could "speak to" Christians and other faith communities.

Generally speaking, the specific nature of Heschel's intended audience is a crucial factor determining the structure and content of his writing. In *No Religion Is an Island*, he was concerned with the Christian mission to the Jews and tried, as did Soloveitchik in "Confrontation," to awaken among Christians a sense of our shared humanity and common concerns and tasks as human beings.

Heschel, however, went further than Soloveitchik by incorporating the Christian perspective into his arguments. Given the fact that the Bible is an important framework for Christian self-understanding, Heschel presented arguments that used the Bible as premise and point of reference. Unlike traditional apologetic writers, he related seriously to the spiritual worldview of his audience, adapting his arguments to the latter's concepts and values, not only his own.

Heschel pursued his arguments for the legitimacy of a shared spiritual language between Jews and Christians on two levels: (1) the specific theological and cultural beliefs and values of these two traditions and (2) the universal spiritual concerns that transcend and unite all genuine faith experiences.

According to Heschel, something went wrong in Christianity when Christians rejected the Jewish people and Judaism. One of his central assumptions—recurring throughout his writings and characteristic of his personal approach to Judaism and theology—is that the Bible mirrors the God of Israel to such an extent that the reality of God is, as it were, a function of the reality of the Bible. And since the reality of the Bible is in turn linked to the reality and vitality of the people of Israel, Christians must realize that they cannot relate fully to the biblical God without relating to the people of Israel.

To Heschel, the presence of God is most vividly and concretely conveyed in the words and images of the Bible, a book that is intimately bound up with the historical community of Israel. Jews, therefore, are a vital part of the Christian experience. Heschel thus returned the discussion to one of the original questions of early Christianity: Inasmuch as the Christian experience is tied to the God of Abraham, to what extent is Scripture, as understood by the Jews, central to Christian self-understanding?

Unlike Soloveitchik and Leibowitz, Heschel was not reluctant to invoke a shared Judeo-Christian tradition. He repeatedly called on Christians to notice the continuity of their worldview with the Jewish experience and the continuity of the link between Jews and the God of Israel. He turned to Catholic theologians and asked rhetorically whether it would really be *ad majorem Dei gloriam* to have a world without Jews, whether their concept of the triumph of God required that Torah scrolls no longer be held and read in synagogues, that the ancient Hebrew prayers in which Jesus himself worshipped cease being recited, and that the Sabbath, the festivals, and the whole law of Moses no longer be observed by Jews. Putting the issue bluntly, he asked Christians: Would your spiritual life be enriched if Jews stopped being loyal to their tradition, a tradition so deeply bound up with your heritage?

Heschel did not ignore the particular religious traditions of the faith communities in question, nor did he skirt the sensitive issue of differing beliefs by shifting the focus of interfaith dialogue to religiously neutral social and humanitarian concerns. Not only did he address Christians from the "safety" of universal humanism, but, in direct contrast to Soloveitchik's "Confrontation," he appealed to their own religious convictions and sensibilities by arguing that in order to have access to the God of Israel, they must appreciate the religious significance of the living community of Israel. Their mission to the Jews was religiously misguided from a *Christian* point of view inasmuch as their own spiritual experience depended on Jews' remaining living witnesses to the Scripture they both shared.

Heschel also wrote about the spiritual service to humanity that Christians performed for Jews. It is our duty to remember, he claimed, that it was the Church that brought the knowledge of the God of Abraham to the Gentiles by making Hebrew Scripture available to humanity. Also, many Jewish works, from Philo to Ibn Gabirol, were preserved only in monasteries. Had it not been for Christian scholarship, Jews would know nothing about Josephus.

By raising these seemingly minor points, Heschel patiently but systematically argued for a new Jewish perspective on its relationship with other faiths. In contrast to many traditional Jewish views of Judaism's place among the nations and religions of the world, Heschel believed that a viable isolated faith experience could no longer be built in a world of interdependency. You could not hope to sustain Jewish culture if the "significant" world in which you lived was thoroughly secular and if the language of religion was dead.

Heschel understood that Christianity had created a religious universe in which Judaism could flourish.[2] He understood that self-sufficiency was an illusion in contemporary society. While most people would agree with regard to politics and economics, many still believe that religion is essentially a private experience. They refuse to recognize the fundamental change that modern secularity has brought about in the overall context of our lives. Rivalry and exclusivity are self-defeating religious attitudes in the light of our need for one another to help create a religious universe where the life of faith will not become an anomaly.

According to Heschel, Jews must recognize that Judaism has a stake in Christianity's success. When you weaken Christianity, you thereby weaken the cultural importance of the Bible in Western society, and thus you also undermine the viability of the Jewish people insofar as the future of the Jewish people depends on the Bible's being a central category in Western self-understanding.

This argument was further developed in *Israel: An Echo of Eternity*, where Heschel tried to explain the meaning of Israel to the Christian world after the Six-Day War. Again, he claimed that the Christian world needed a living people of Israel if they wanted a living God of Israel, if they wanted the Bible to be alive to them. This, then, was the crux of his "biblical" appeal for interfaith understanding. The Jewish people's fate in history is tied to the Bible's becoming a central category for human self-understanding.

In addition to addressing the unique spiritual bond connecting the Jewish and Christian traditions, Heschel also pointed to a dimension of religious life that he believed all persons of faith shared regardless of their particular traditions or spiritual ways of life. Heschel addressed Jews and Christians alike from his theocentric perspective. The supreme issue facing all religious persons today, he wrote, was not Halakhah, not law, normative practice, official dogma. The problem was not that people did not observe the Sabbath or attend church, but that God was not alive in people's hearts, that the passion of the faith experience was a dead issue for so many people.

In all his writings, Heschel tried to reawaken and reenliven the concept of God independent of particular traditions or loyalties. He was one of the few modern Jewish theologians who could convey a sense of the living reality of God beyond the particular doctrinal and normative traditions of specific faith communities. By taking the mystic sense of divine ineffability and unknowability seriously, he was able to relativize religious dogma and norms by pointing to the inherent particular, culture-bound nature of all religious traditions. Whereas for Soloveitchik the ineffability of the faith experience was what separated members of different faiths, for Heschel it was what united them.

Heschel struggled to make us cognizant of the inescapable phenomenological limits of the language of religious thought and practice. His goal was not to attack the validity of particular religious traditions but to awaken people to theological and religious dimensions beyond their own traditions. With respect to Jews, he could appeal to Maimonides' ideas about negative theology and the epistemological limits to knowledge of God as strong countervailing arguments against the kind of absolutist cognitive claims often made by revelatory systems. His goal was to loosen the grip of religious absolutism by shifting attention to the absolute nature of God, thereby showing that equation of religion and God to be a form of idolatry.

> Does not the all-inclusiveness of God contradict the exclusiveness of any particular religion?...
> The ultimate truth is not capable of being fully and adequately expressed in concepts and words. (*No Religion Is an Island*, pp. 13–15)

Heschel thus hoped to make us realize that "no word is God's last word, no word is God's ultimate word" (p. 16).

There is, of course, a danger, as Heschel well knew, of undermining legitimate differences among religious traditions in the name of an eighteenth-century-like deism or a philosophic religion that reduces conventional religion to social convention.[3] Heschel tried to avoid slipping into a kind of abstract spiritual universalism that delegitimized individual loyalties and traditions because "we are all basically the same; we all worship the same God." His was a concrete universalism, a universalism that tried to limit—rather than destroy—particular religious passions and commitments. His aim was to maintain a creative tension between the universal and the particular so that (1) no abstract universal would vitiate the individuality of the religious experience and (2) no particular tradition would claim the fullness and comprehensiveness of the universal.

Heschel would have taken issue with the prevalent assumption that religious faith is, by nature, exclusive and absolute.[4] He challenged this widespread assumption by asking: How can a human being transcend the limits of particularity? You cannot escape having a particular history and biography; the rituals, symbols, and traditions of a particular community always mediate your religious life and beliefs. So, rather than make dubious claims to universality that explicitly or implicitly overstep the boundaries separating finite humanity from infinite divinity, Heschel used the concept of divine infinitude negatively, as an argument for spiritual humility. Divine infinitude forces you to face the dilemma: How do I ensure that my particular religious experience will not block me from the larger spiritual dimension that transcends my local tradition and faith system?

Heschel therefore asked Jews, in an aggadic rather than halakhic mode: What is the most important aspect of the life of faith? Are we not sometimes struck by the experience of encountering a truly spiritual person, even if he or she is from a totally different tradition than our own? Do we not share religious sensibilities beyond the doctrines, symbols, and rituals of our respective traditions?

Some may argue that if this is what Heschel believed, why did he not go all the way and relativize revelation in history entirely? Why not recommend an epistemology of revelation that precludes absolutist truth claims a priori? Why is it legitimate to postpone the quest for absolute religious certainty to an eschatological future—the deus ex machina of religious uncertainty? If the all-inclusiveness of God contradicts the exclusivity of particular religious claims, why should "the prospect of all men embracing one form of religion remain an eschatological hope" (p. 14) or the judgment that the "diversity of religions is the will of God" be restricted to "this aeon" (p. 14)? Is the "blasphemy" of stating "I alone have all the truth and the grace, and all those who differ live in darkness and are abandoned by the grace of God" (p. 14) limited to a specific time and place? If the obsession with religious uniformity is vulgar and misguided today, then why condone the belief that uniformity could replace pluralism in the future?

Heschel's method of addressing communities estranged from one another was first to listen and then to speak to them "in their own language." He realized that he was dealing with religious traditions wherein notions of truth played a central role, wherein revealed truth and absolute certainty were practically correlative notions, wherein people lived with eschatological beliefs in the inevitable triumph of their respective faith traditions. Yet, without changing the vocabulary of their basic beliefs and convictions, Heschel tried to work "from within" to explain and justify a form of radical religious pluralism "in this aeon."

The fact that Heschel did not carry the implications of his ideas further than he did was not a sign of his intellectual timidity but rather of his being a concerned and caring religious thinker whose primary goals were to teach, to persuade, and to affect the present behavior of human beings.

Heschel was aware of the interdependency of ideas and actions, of the relationship between absolutist cognitive claims and moral arrogance and conceit. He understood that beliefs about possessing the exclusive key to truth and redemption had brutalized religious consciousness and practice throughout history. Nevertheless, he refused to suggest a radical relativization of all religious truth claims—a move that would have placed him outside traditional theological modes of discourse altogether. Instead, he explored possibilities within traditional religious systems of loosening the rigid grip of exclusivity and of making room for a genuine appreciation of other faiths and theological perspectives.

Abraham Joshua Heschel had a dramatic impact on the nature of the discussion in which Jews try to make sense of their history and tradition. Although he himself did not always follow his arguments to their ultimate conclusions, he set ideas into motion that expanded the range of religious options for Jews in the modern world.

Heschel's writings abound with exciting but often unrealized implications. In *No Religion Is an Island*, he leads up to, but not quite to, the point where religious pluralism becomes a permanent feature of revelatory faith systems. Similarly, Heschel's teleological approach to Judaism has serious implications for traditional normative practice insofar as his approach is more than a rhetorical, midrashic spin on halakhic practice aimed at bringing Jews into the fold. If you take Heschel's idea of the primacy of Aggadah seriously, you will soon find yourself rethinking the idea of Halakhah as a formal, legalistic religious system. Halakhic authority and discipline, as traditionally understood, may not be able to sustain the polarity between Aggadah and Halakhah.

Those of us who take Heschel's thought seriously must be prepared to take his ideas further by asking: What is the meaning of halakhic practice in the light of the teleological refinement he taught us to appreciate? How should we understand revelatory claims in the light of the skeptical implications of his theological and epistemological analyses?

In reading Heschel, we must concentrate not only on what he said but also on what he suggested and intimated. Contemporary theology must carry his arguments beyond the point to which he himself was prepared to go. We must be true to the spirit of his words and to the essence of his insights if we are to do justice to the rich implications of his thought.

---

1. Many of Heschel's arguments regarding interfaith dialogue would apply to Eastern religions as well as to Christianity and Islam. Nevertheless, his main concern was with healing the hatred and suffering that resulted from the Judaic–Christianen counter in history.

2. This type of argument is reminiscent of Yehuda Halevi's *The Kuzari*, where the king initially invited only teachers of Christianity and Islam in his quest for the true religion. He had no interest in consulting

representatives of the despised and marginal religion of Judaism until he realized that both Christians and Moslems traced their spiritual origins to Abraham, Moses, and the whole biblical tradition. In other words, Christianity and Islam shared a universe where it was important to talk to Jews. The king could not ignore Judaism because of the importance of Christianity and Islam as religious options. Had he lived in India or China, he would not have felt it necessary to talk to Jews before choosing a spiritual way of life.

3. See Yehuda Halevi, *The Kuzari*.

4. In "Confrontation," Soloveitchik remarks, as a kind of obvious observation, that all religionists believe in the ultimate vindication of their faith systems, if only in the eschatological future. It is thus axiomatic and religiously necessary that religious faith claims absolute certainty, exclusivity, and the hope for its ultimate triumph over all other faiths.

10

AN OPEN LETTER TO A REFORM RABBI

Jerusalem, August 1989

Dear Sam,

Thank you for your comments on my talk to the Central Conference of Reform Rabbis. As you know, although I disagree with the Reform movement's approach to Halakhah, I am nevertheless deeply disturbed by the lack of tolerance and respect for Reform Judaism in Israel.

The Reform rabbinate has been exposed to a great deal of abuse here in Israel. Reform rabbis, who command the respect of their congregations and communities abroad, are either ignored or delegitimized by the Orthodox establishment in this country. Israel, which has opened its gates to Jews from all corners of the world, has not yet learned to appreciate the heterogeneous approaches to Jewish identity, history, and spirituality that have developed over the last two hundred years.

One ultra-Orthodox rabbi recently remarked that just as the government of the state refuses to speak to the PLO, so should it refuse to speak to Reform rabbis. Any sitting together or mutual discussion implies recognition, and any recognition of the Reform or Conservative movements would endanger the security and well-being of Judaism.

It is outrageous that you should be compared to the PLO, which seeks the destruction of the Jewish State. The pain and humiliation that you are experiencing must be understood as part of the difficult process of rebuilding the Jewish nation in the midst of the enormous ideological diversity within the Jewish people.

I regard the Law of Return, which welcomes Jews from all over the world to make Israel their home, regardless of their ideological views, as the most profound expression of Zionism's Jewish soul. As a religious Zionist who is committed to the aspiration embodied in that law, I cannot say to Reform Jews, "Your bodies are welcome, but not your value systems."

Israel must be a place where diverse Jewish groups, with their own perceptions and values, can engage in serious discussion with one another. Respect for religious pluralism is a vital necessity if Israel is to serve as the spiritual and physical home of the entire Jewish people. One cannot embrace Zionism and the Law of Return, yet delegitimize Reform and Conservative rabbis throughout the world. One cannot say, "All are welcome because we share a common destiny," yet deny them religious freedom and dignity because of their nontraditional belief systems.

In the diaspora, Jews are not forced to live intimately together. The neutral public space of the non-Jewish world in Europe and North America allows for a psychological distancing of Jews from one another, which in turn diminishes their hostility and aggressiveness. Israel, by contrast, focuses the disagreements within the family and does not allow us to enjoy the type of space that the diaspora gives to Jewish life. Politically, economically, and socially we are thrown together into a common life; we must face each other and learn what it means to be a family whose members disagree about the heritage of our parents and grandparents.

The violently aggressive language used by certain Israeli circles toward the Reform and Conservative movements, which offer different interpretations of our Jewish heritage, is a direct result of the fact that we have come home. When one comes home after a long absence, one expects that all the members of the family will fit one's own conception of what the family and the community should be. In coming home, one relaxes, but one also allows oneself to manifest the type of hostility found among members of a family. One can expect hostility of this kind when members of a family discover how different they are from one another, how deeply they disagree about the family's past, present, and future.

You may ask: Why should we expose ourselves to this type of humiliation? Why participate in a political environment that treats us with such animosity and abuse? Shouldn't we reformulate our vision in such a way that the State of Israel becomes less important? Why not divorce ourselves from Zionism and the State of Israel?

I believe that your refusal to divorce yourself from the State of Israel is based on a profound appreciation of the connection between peoplehood and convenant in Judaism. Judaism begins not with an individual leap of faith, but with a leap of solidarity with the Jewish community. The Jewish child learns the essence of Jewish identity at the Passover Seder in saying, "We were slaves to Pharaoh in Egypt." The emphasis is on "We"—that is, each generation must see itself as if it has come out of Egypt.

One cannot appropriate Judaism's language of faith without identifying with the Jewish people's struggle for political and social liberation. One cannot enter a covenantal relationship with God outside the collective framework of the Jewish people.

Regardless of how one interprets the concepts of revelation and election, it is clear in Judaism that God elects a people, not single individuals. Peoplehood and nationhood are the central frameworks for building spiritual meaning in our daily life. Israel prevents us from identifying faith as "the leap of the alone to the Alone."

Israel is not just another Jewish community. To understand the concern for Israel among Jews in the diaspora, we must appreciate how Israel has succeeded in mediating the Jewish nation's visibility in the world. A Jew's sense of connection with the people of Israel, his or her historical and collective identity, is shaped by the State of Israel.

The Jewish people is not just a faith community; it is not merely a collection of individuals, each longing to connect himself or herself spiritually with God. Rather, Judaism is a way of life of a people chosen by God to be a medium of His vision of holiness and justice. In a religious sense, therefore, Jewish life in the diaspora would be impoverished if your congregations were disconnected from the drama of Israeli society.

One of the great men of faith in the twentieth century, Rabbi Joseph Soloveitchik, taught me how to understand the deep connection between the renewal of convenantal Judaism and the commitment to the State of Israel. For Soloveitchik, the shared suffering and common historical fate of the Jewish people represent what he calls a *brit goral*, a "covenant of destiny," which is the foundation of the halakhic category of collective responsibility (*arevut*).

In contrast to Soloveitchik, a small minority of the Jewish people see no religious significance in the establishment of the State of Israel. They believe that the Jews were meant to live as a powerless people until the coming of the messianic age. For them, any assertion of political power, any manifestation of the will to national self-determination, distorts what was meant to be Israel's historical destiny. The very meaning of being a holy, covenantal nation is to submit to the rule of the Gentiles until God, through His gracious love, brings about the messianic redemption of Israel.

The majority of the Jewish people have repudiated this understanding of Jewish history; they see the effort of the Zionist revolutionaries to establish a national home for the Jewish people as a legitimate expression of our historical destiny. As you know, there are many different ways of interpreting the covenantal significance of Israel. The mystic Rabbi Kook, for example, believed that God's redemptive design for history was being enacted through the secular Zionist drama. Alternatively, for Soloveitchik, the religious significance of the state lies in the fact that Israel has galvanized the Jewish people's will to manifest their identity publicly in Western civilization. Israel has given Jews the courage to be an activist community rather than to live permanently as Marranos.

Although the Reform movement's interpretation of the covenant of mitzvah is very different from that of Soloveitchik, you clearly share his appreciation of the "covenant of destiny." Because of your loyalty to the covenantal community of Israel, you are exposed to a humiliating and painful dilemma. On one hand, you cannot build your spiritual self-understanding independently of Israel; on the other hand, by allowing Israel into your consciousness, you suffer the indignation of being delegitimized. Indeed, you are even told that you are enemies of that very covenantal faith experience which connects you with the people of Israel. How can you sustain your commitment to the covenant of destiny if Israeli law prevents you from being an active participant in the effort to renew the covenant of Sinai? This is the profound burden that the Reform and Conservative movements are forced to bear today.

Paradoxically, if you were total secularists who had abandoned your covenantal loyalty to Torah, you would be welcome in Israel. The State of Israel knows how to welcome secular Jews but has not yet learned how to accept radically different orientations within the life of faith.

You are subjected to abuse because you are people of faith who proclaim that the Sinai covenant can be appropriated differently from the way it has been interpreted within traditional halakhic Judaism. Your determination to remain loyal to your understanding of Judaism should be understood by your own Reform movement as an act of spiritual heroism. The extent and duration of your humiliation will depend on how quickly Jews throughout the world come to understand the religious significance and far-reaching implications of the "Who is a Jew?" issue.

As you know, this issue does not merely concern a handful of Reform converts who wish to immigrate to Israel. The real question is how to build a people and a nation in the midst of radical ideological diversity.

We have built a country; we must now learn to build a nation. The pioneers who built this land endured malaria, abuse, and poverty. The soldiers who defended this country paid a high price for its security. Many died in order to make Israel a viable national home for the Jewish people. Nothing was ever achieved in this country without great pain. Your own suffering is the price you must pay in order to bring the Jewish people to a new level of spiritual dignity, which can embrace the value of religious pluralism. Your refusal to abandon Israel, despite your humiliation, is a testimony to your willingness to fight the war for the moral well-being of this nation.

The indignation that you are forced to undergo is the sacrifice you must make for loving a people that does not yet understand how its members can live together in radical spiritual disagreement. I believe that your profound spiritual mission is to continue to struggle until we have discovered new foundations of pluralism within our religious heritage.

Modern Israel has taught us that the Ingathering of the Exiles is not as uplifting and redeeming as we had thought. It is one thing to pray for the Ingathering of the Exiles. It is quite another challenge to live together afterwards amidst our differences. The liberal notion that religious faith should express the individual's free choice is not easily understood by Jews who have lived in totalitarian political environments or traditional ghettos.

In Israel, pluralists are often labeled as relativists lacking any serious convictions. It is feared that acknowledging the dignity of the "other," of the person who offers an alternative meaning structure, leads inevitably to anarchy or to the loss of society's central values. Many religious Jews therefore find it easier to deal with secularists than with Reform and Conservative Jews. No Judaism is preferable to a Judaism that is different from what one believes to be the essential will of God.

It is important that we learn that respect for other points of view does not imply relativism. One can simultaneously maintain that the way one lives reflects the truest interpretation of Judaism and yet respectfully recognize that this position is not held by all Jews.

The fight for pluralism in Israel does not require Orthodox, Reform, or Conservative Jews to compromise their appreciation of Halakhah and Torah. It *does* mean that no group may use the instruments of the state to impose its own interpretation of Judaism on the entire society.

Please appreciate how far we are from understanding that intense religious commitment is compatible with respect and appreciation for those who differ with us. Your suffering and constant exposure to abuse from religious circles in Israel indicate how far we are from appreciating the meaning of civilized disagreement. We have not yet learned how to build a society in which communities holding different religious convictions can flourish without asking the state to enforce their position.

So far I have tried to explain why it is important that you continue your struggle to validate your spiritual integrity within the public space of Israeli society. I should also like to share with you my perception of how your movement's covenantal commitment can enrich Israel's religious life. I referred earlier to two moments in the faith experience: solidarity with the people's struggle for national liberation, and commitment to the covenantal framework of mitzvot. The covenant of mitzvot presupposes empathy and solidarity with the whole community, irrespective of its moral and religious quality.

However, it is important to remember that solidarity does not imply agreement with whatever the community does; it does not mean that whatever policy the Israeli government pursues must be accepted unconditionally. Unconditional loyalty to a nation or a state is tantamount to idolatry. Many modern Jews mistakenly believe that peoplehood is the necessary and sufficient condition of Jewish identity. The Reform movement must help correct this one-sided view of Jewish identity. It must struggle against the tendency to make loyalty to the nation the exclusive framework for organizing Jewish life.

The Reform movement's covenantal perspective can serve as a prism through which one can properly define the value of solidarity with the community. In other words, you must remind the Jewish community that the covenantal moment is constitutive of Jewish identity.

The Reform movement was not quick to embrace Zionist nationalism. Initially it defined itself as a faith community rather than a national and political movement. Although Reform leaders eventually recognized the importance of peoplehood and solidarity with the State of Israel, their initial reluctance can still be utilized to remind us that Jewish identity goes beyond empathy with the suffering condition of Jews. Solidarity with the suffering of the Jews in Egypt is only a preparation for the covenantal experience of Sinai.

It would be a tragic mistake for Reform Jews to identify themselves with secular Zionism in Israel. Your repudiation of the religious Zionist establishment in Israel must not lead you to choose the secular option. The Reform movement is a religious movement, and its appreciation of Israel must be expressed in religious categories. You are a religious community, and in participating in Israeli society, you must be loyal to your religious perspective.

It is important that Jews rediscover the old talmudic principle "He who rejects idolatry is as if he accepts the entire Torah." In order for faith in God to possess any vitality, we must understand what it negates. By clearly denouncing the new forms of idolatry, you will help Jews discover ways in which faith can be a vital option in the modern world.

You can contribute to the effort to free Jews from their embarrassment in talking about God and the passion of the faith experience. How often have I heard it said that Christians talk about God, while Jews talk about Halakhah. You can help to correct this distortion because of your ease in celebrating the covenantal moment of faith at Sinai.

In addition to your contribution to the battle against idolatry, and to the rehabilitation of covenantal faith, you can also help articulate the human values and characteristics implicit in the life of mitzvot. Even though you do not speak the language of Halakhah, you can contribute to the realm of Aggadah. For example, although you reject the halakhic interpretation of "You shall not work on the Sabbath," you can embrace the idea that the Sabbath celebrates God's creation and human finitude. Articulate how the Sabbath develops the characteristic of gratitude, the sense that life is a gift, and the need to give up the longing for absolute power. By focusing on the human characteristics implicit in a life of mitzvot, you may clarify how Israel's calling to be a holy people should affect our perception of power.

By contrast, the Conservative movement does understand itself as a halakhic movement. Therefore, its task in Israel is not only to rehabilitate covenantal consciousness but also to show the wide range of interpretative possibilities allowed for by Halakhah. To be true to its claim to be a halakhic movement, Conservative Judaism must show that its halakhic positions can be validated by the interpretative power of Halakhah. In this way, the Conservative movement can show the Jewish world that "the four cubits of Halakhah" are wider than we ever imagined, and that the Jewish tradition has always contained the resources to meet new situations and appreciate new values. Conservative Judaism bears the burden of legitimizing its present actions in relation to the authority of the past. The Reform movement, however, is not burdened by a concern for halakhic continuity; it is burdened by the claim of God upon human life, by its receptiveness to the covenantal moment, and by its rejection of nationhood as the exclusive value defining Jewishness.

Your expansion of covenantal consciousness must be welcome within the Israeli context. What a rich Jewish community we would have, both in the diaspora and in Israel, if members of different synagogues—those who build their lives around the covenantal focus and those who build their lives around Halakhah—were to gather in each other's homes to discuss Torah and the different ways their respective rabbis are interpreting the tradition!

Such a dialogue would ensure that Jewish faith would be based on conviction rather than habit. Theological diversity within the Jewish community would encourage the development of communities founded on conviction, knowledge, and choice.

Orthodoxy, both in Israel and abroad, would thrive on vibrant Conservative and Reform movements. The presence of alternative options would challenge its membership to build conviction out of understanding. Intense concern with the details of the Law would then grow from a perspective of joy and love, rather than from an authoritarian mode of being, in which the Conservative and Reform movements are delegitimized. I have no objection to rabbis, whether Orthodox, Conservative, or Reform, who try to persuade through argumentation that their way is the correct expression of Judaism in the modern world, but nothing is more destructive of the religious life than enforcing one's point of view through violent demonstrations or coercive legislation.

America has founded a great civilization on the principle of "live and let live." Freedom actually facilitates conviction. Political coercion is ultimately self-defeating because it prevents the individual from seeing his or her collective belief as an expression of personal dignity. Living a Judaic way of life can become an expression of personal conviction when the Jewish people are given the opportunity to choose between alternative spiritual options.

The Talmud says that any argument for the sake of heaven must endure. I believe that our discussions and disagreements are for the sake of heaven. To be sure, I have tried in my writings to clarify why I cannot accept your celebration of autonomy at the expense of halakhic authority. Indeed, there are many issues that divide us. But I am grateful that you came to Israel and enabled me to witness your religious passion. Your presence contributed to my own quest to serve God with joy and love. In conclusion, I can only express my hope that the Reform movement will not understand the covenant of mitzvah in such a way that it burns the bridges to communal solidarity. It is important that you reconsider your approach to halakhic issues, such as your controversial claim that the Jewish identity should be defined by both matrilinear and patrilinear descent, which threaten our shared covenant of destiny.

All the movements in Judaism must find the way in which our common covenant of destiny controls our interpretation of the covenant of mitzvah and the Halakhah.

Sincerely,
David Hartman

II

ISRAEL'S RESPONSIBILITY

FOR WORLD JEWRY

Reflections on the Debate

about the Conversion Law

AS A DIASPORA Jew who has taken up residence in Israel, I am deeply struck by the lack of understanding in Israel and abroad of the *hok hamara* (conversion law) issue—one of the more important issues confronting Israel since its inception.

Neither diaspora Jews nor (and especially) Israelis seem to grasp what is really going on. ("How many converts are there anyway?" said one member of Knesset—as if expecting someone to answer: "No problem! We Israelis can easily smuggle them in illegally!") The Israeli government sets up commissions, and everybody is in on the "secret" that when the proposed legislation comes to a vote, there will be a delay and then a further delay (the best way for the Knesset to deal with a very deep spiritual crisis!).

The fact is that this issue has serious implications for the future of Israel and the diaspora. The underlying question is not "Who is a Jew?" or "Who is a rabbi?" but "How should Israel respond to the presence of religious diversity within the Jewish world?" or "Why is having an official Orthodox Chief Rabbinate that defines and controls what counts as legitimate Jewish spirituality such a mistaken religious approach for the Jewish people?"

MODERN HISTORY AND THE CRISIS OF DISCONTINUITY

The Six-Day War was one of those rare moments in Jewish history when Jews were united. The thought of another possible *hurban* (destruction) brought Jewish life to a complete standstill. One concern, one fear, gripped the whole Jewish world, which held its breath as one in anxious anticipation. This unique moment of solidarity and existential oneness with the Israeli reality brought home the idea to many people like myself that Israel was not just another Jewish community.

The significance of Israel for world Jewry can be understood in terms of two features of modernity that could have threatened Jewish continuity: (1) radical individualism and (2) radical evil.

Modern consciousness reflects the overriding influence of a liberal ideology committed intellectually, culturally, and socially to the values of autonomy and individualism. In addition to this distinctively modern preoccupation with individual self-realization independent of and apart from community and peoplehood, Jewish existence was placed in jeopardy by the profound cynicism and despair that could have shaped Jewish consciousness following the Holocaust.

As a result of the Holocaust, Jews as a people could have chosen "invisibility": living a life of hiding, of being faceless, of avoiding public exposure. The stereotypical picture of *galut* (diaspora) Jews walking in public is of a person moving quickly, quietly, and on the side of the street where you were least noticed. There is safety in not being noticed. Visibility means danger. As one of my older congregants in Montreal used to tell me: "Why do Jews need to build big homes in Hampstead? They will be the first victims of future pogroms." If God hides in history, then Jews must also hide in history.

This desire to be invisible, to leave history as an identifiable community, was reinforced by the bitter disappointment of Jews in the one country they had revered as the best and most perfect expression of Western culture and humanism. If the homeland of Lessing, Kant, Goethe, and Beethoven could produce such barbarism and hate, then Western culture and humanism were bankrupt and fraudulent. There was nothing to learn from Western civilization. There was nothing to trust or believe in.

The pervasive cultural influence of radical individualism and the traumatic impact of the Holocaust in the modern world threatened the very foundations of Jewish existence. The Jewish people could have succumbed to a national ethos of cynicism and withdrawal, of giving up their public Jewish identity, of choosing to become invisible in history.

ISRAEL AND THE CHOICE OF VISIBILITY

Israel represents the alternative response, of a people returning to history and community without necessarily being fully conscious of or able to articulate the significance of Israel from this perspective. When someone once asked me, "Why did you come on aliyah?" I answered half-jokingly, "Because Israel is too important to be left to the Israelis." What I meant was that the importance of this reality often eludes the immediate awareness of those most responsible for its existence.

The people who created this reality—the pioneers, the *kibbutznikim*, the farmers, the soldiers—set in motion a momentous historical process by restoring Jewish visibility in history. Israel said, "No more hiding." Israel restored our sense of community, of "we," of our sense of the distinctive Jewish integration of personal identity within the larger context of community.

Against the background of despair and cynicism following the Holocaust and the modern *zeitgeist* of radical self-realization, it said: "We will not choose invisibility. We will 'go public' despite the vulnerability of such exposure." Israel thus became the most important visible, public framework in which the collective life of the Jewish people is acted out in world history.

VISIBILITY AS A JEWISH IMPERATIVE

The theological and human significance of covenantal election can be interpreted in terms of the burden of being visible in history. One of the distinctive features of biblical theology is God's presence in the life of community. Aristotle's God had no such ambitions. Israel's God wanted to be mirrored within the collective life of human nations, to "be sanctified in the midst of the children of Israel."

The collective, as opposed to the individual, nature of biblical election means that despite the radical evil present in the world, you don't leave history. And the call to Israel to bear witness to the Spirit means that a successful export economy and high-tech industries are not the long-awaited answer to Jewish prayers. Human beings will never be fully satisfied by economics alone. They need to be touched by a vision that nurtures their souls.

Israel must bear witness to the human spiritual need for something larger, for a larger dream, for a larger purpose in life. As a historical people, Israel must continue to believe in and bear witness to the idea of possibility—the possibilities of what human communities can become.

"I will be" is the name of God. Idolatry is the fixation of God into one form, one moment. The imageless God of the Bible, the God whose name is *ehyeh* ("I will be") is the basis of the hope of what human history can become—and of the pain of the nonrealization of this dream.

The rebirth of Israel has kept this dream alive by serving as an antidote to individualism, to the loss of community, to the loss of memory and of history, and to the cynicism that could have paralyzed us as a result of the radical evil of the Holocaust. Israel thus speaks to the very soul of the Jewish people. It is a living testimony to the Jewish people's loyalty to their foundational covenantal memory.

ISRAEL: A FAILURE OF SELF-UNDERSTANDING

When Israeli government officials expressed surprise and bewilderment at the uproar created in the diaspora by the proposed conversion law, I said to the Prime Minister: "You must realize that as the Prime Minister of this people you have two constituencies, one that relates to you politically—that votes in the elections, that expects social and economic leadership, that forces you to compromise, to form coalitions, etc.—and another that relates to you out of spiritual need and concern. The latter feel connected to the government of Israel because their lives as Jews are nurtured by this reality. Their war of survival as Jews is with assimilation. They don't know whether Jewish life will continue, whether their grandchildren will be Jewish."

I wonder whether Israeli politicians understand the implications of saying to half of the Jewish world that their synagogues and their rabbis are not authentic because they do not reflect "Judaism" and that therefore theirs is a fraudulent Jewish reality. All too many Knesset members do not understand that

Israel is needed by the Jewish people not as a political haven but as the most important expression of Jewish memory, history, and visibility. To tell the majority of diaspora Jewry that their Jewish way of life does not count in Israel betrays a total lack of understanding of the important meaning of Israel in their lives.

The Israeli politicians' defensive excuse regarding the trivial and inconsequential nature of the proposed legislation suggests either deep naiveté or deep cynicism. How can delegitimizing Conservative and Reform rabbis in Israel imply nothing about these forms of Judaism in the diaspora? "If you believe I am *treif* in Jerusalem, how can you believe I am kosher in New York or Chicago?" (Unless, of course, you believe that *treif* is affected by the presence of UJA support!) What naiveté! What cynicism!

If you say Conservative and Reform rabbis are *treif* here, then you are saying that Conservative and Reform rabbis are *treif* anywhere. And the number of Jews affected is irrelevant. Is there no appreciation of the soul of this country or of the Jewish people? Shouldn't the government feel responsibility for the whole Jewish people? Do we Israelis cynically measure the significance of Israel for world Jewry solely in terms of financial and political support, or do we want them to feel that Israel is vital to their spiritual identities?

And how can Israel be vital for them when they are told that their Judaic way of life is not welcome in this, their spiritual home? How can Israel remain important to them if their only leverage is the threat of withholding contributions? Israeli newspapers and "enlightened" politicians say: "We are going to lose American support!" But no one says: "What are we doing to the Jewish people's *yiddishkeit*? What are we doing to their sense of history and memory and hope and the dream of 'Next Year in Jerusalem'?" Israel cannot sever itself from responsibility for the moral and spiritual renaissance of the Jewish people without losing its *raison d'être* for much of the Jewish world.

The core of the issue is not conversion per se but the consigning of religious ownership of Israel to the Orthodox establishment. As my teacher, Rabbi Joseph Ber Soloveitchik, feared, the possibility of Orthodox Judaism's becoming a sect within the Jewish people is gaining ground as the centrality of *klal yisrael* gradually recedes from consciousness. When the Jewish people worshipped the golden calf at the foot of Mt. Sinai, God said to Moses: "Go down," which the midrash interprets metaphorically as meaning, "Go down from the heights of your spiritual greatness, because all that I have given you was only for the sake of Israel. Now that they have sinned, I have no need for you."

You don't stand at Sinai as a singular person before God. Your spiritual consciousness is historical and collective. To be a Jew requires a leap of solidarity with a people even if they worship pagan gods. Making the State of Israel the spiritual possession of one segment of the Jewish people undermines the most important instrument for building Jewish collective consciousness today.

THE DIASPORA:
HELPING ISRAELIS UNDERSTAND THEMSELVES

The climate of discussion in Israel today has made American Jews bolder in expressing their threats. While their decision to "play hardball" may prove effective politically, the main thrust of American Jewry's case should emphasize their deep desire to be Jews and to safeguard their *yiddishkeit*. By so doing they would help Israelis understand themselves, for they seem to have little or no understanding of their importance to Jewish spiritual identity throughout the world.

In other words, bring your spiritual hungers—not only your economic and political influence—here. Let Israel understand your spiritual bond with this reality. Help Israel understand its Jewish mission. Israelis see the diaspora as a *gan eden*—a paradise of material affluence and well-being. They do not grasp the needs of the Jewish soul, of the unsatisfied spiritual hungers present in the Jewish world.

They have little appreciation of the problem of Jewish continuity in the diaspora and of the overwhelming problem of assimilation in a modern pluralistic society. We must emphasize the obvious—but often overlooked—point that the Reform and Conservative movements did not invent secularism. They are not responsible for the modern world. (They may have done a lot of good things, but not that!)

The Reform and Conservative movements did not create the alternative family lifestyles that compete with traditional forms. These reflect the sexual revolution of modernity, in which gender identities and sexual preferences are constantly being revised. The abundance of social and cultural options and the ascendance of liberalism and pluralism are what modernity is about. They are not *Jewish* creations!

Reform and Conservative rabbis are involved with these issues not because they brought them into being but because of the exposure and vulnerability of their congregants to these social and cultural phenomena. It is important for Jews in Israel to understand and appreciate the situation of a Jewish leadership having to compete with the attractions of pluralism, secularism, and whatever else the modern world has to offer. Perhaps then they would be willing to concede that when these religious leaders make mistakes, it is with the intention of saving Jews and not in order to destroy Torah. I understand the pressures these rabbis are under. Here in Israel, I don't have the same pressures. I don't have to decide how to respond to intermarriage so as to salvage something Jewish from an otherwise hopeless situation.

The Israeli response to diaspora leaders should be: How can we help you in your battle with modernism and secularism? Rather than isolate and delegitimize them, we should strengthen and encourage them. But above all, they should be made to feel our understanding and empathic identification with their uphill struggle.

A MISPLACED CONCERN WITH AUTHORITY

Their (and our) problem is not one of authority. As a young rabbi just out of the rabbinical academy, I experienced frustration at realizing that the problem of serving as a rabbi was not that I lacked the knowledge or the status to render halakhic decisions, but that no one had questions to ask me! I had the authority to issue judgments, but no one felt the need for judgments. I soon realized that the main religious issue facing Judaism in the modern world was not the authority of Halakhah. The role of the rabbi in America today is not to be an authority figure or a judge. What are missing are not answers but questions! The rabbi has to instill a desire to ask questions, to be bothered by Judaism, to feel that Judaism is important enough to want to ask about it.

There are no burning halakhic issues today because the Jewish people do not see themselves as a people of Torah. You must first make contact with Torah, with mitzvah, in order to be concerned about Halakhah. First you have to know who you are, that the God of Israel has a stake in your life, that Judaism may have something to say to your life.

The answer is not the dogma of *Torah min ha-shamayim*— whether you believe that every word of the Torah was divinely given—but whether you find significance in it. Too many people are zealous about saving the dogmatic and halakhic principles of

Judaism at the expense of the majority of Jews. They want to guard the purity of traditional Judaism without having the patience to lead people through a spiritual process, to allow people to grow, to fall in love with *yiddishkeit* through example.

Orthodox Judaism's intensity and passionate concern for Halakhah and Jewish education can serve as important catalysts to other movements in Judaism. Isolating itself from world Jewry by delegitimizing other forms of Judaism only undermines its vital importance and mission as a living example for world Jewry.

I am convinced beyond doubt that the burning issues facing Judaism today are not halakhic authority or even halakhic mistakes. The real issue is *pekuah nefesh* (saving a life)—whether this people is going to disappear. This is not the time for Israel to issue messages to the world about halakhic authority, about whose conversion is genuinely halakhic. If Israel were to face the issue honestly, it would say: "Israel declares war on the disappearance of Jews, on Jewish alienation from their spiritual heritage."

At this moment in history we must embrace all Jews. We must strengthen all Jews fighting to keep the idea of Torah alive. I say this not because of my commitment to liberalism and pluralism but because of my commitment to Torah and to God, and because I believe that the future of the Jewish people is too important to be left to Israeli politicians or the religious establishment.

No matter what future legislation will be passed in the Knesset, diaspora Jews must never turn their backs on Israel. We are in the early stages of nation building. Thus far, we have reclaimed the land and have built a home for all Jews. The history of the homeless, wandering Jew is over.

We are now in the process of building the moral and spiritual foundations of our society. This is a momentous historical period. All Jews throughout the world must participate in the process. Their spiritual and communal needs must be understood in Israel so that a message of Torah that is inclusive and morally compelling can emanate from Jerusalem to the whole Jewish world.

PART IV

RELIGIOUS PERSPECTIVES ON
THE FUTURE OF ISRAEL

12

ZIONISM AND THE
CONTINUITY OF JUDAISM

IN AN INTERVIEW on his views of Zionism, Gershom Scholem said:

> Zionism has never really known itself completely—
> whether it is a movement of continuation and
> continuity, or a movement of rebellion. From the very
> beginning of its realization, Zionism has contained two
> utterly contradictory trends. So long as Zionism was
> not consummated in practice, these two trends could
> dwell peaceably together, like two books containing
> contradictory views, standing together on the same
> bookshelf....
>
> In my opinion it is manifestly obvious that these two
> trends have determined the essence of Zionism as a
> living thing with a dialectic of its own, and have also
> determined all the troubles we are confronted with
> today. Is Zionism a movement that seeks a
> continuation of what has been the Jewish tradition

throughout the generations, or has it come to introduce a change into the historic phenomenon called Judaism?

...the conflict between continuity and rebellion is a determining factor in the destiny of Zionism....

Judaism is a living thing that is not amenable to a dogmatic definition. Innovation cannot be defined in advance. Because innovation arises, not from denying one's tradition, but from a dialectic, a metamorphosis of tradition. And these two trends have not yet run their course. (*Unease in Zion*, ed. Ehud ben Ezer, pp. 273, 275)

Zionism may be viewed as a continuation of the Jewish tradition. But unlike those who equate Zionism with messianism, I share Scholem's view of Zionism as "a movement that asserts that we must accept the decree of history without a Utopian cover." Zionism expresses a rejection of the posture of waiting for the Messiah and of acting as a nation in history only when one is convinced of the imminent realization of historical redemption.

JUDAISM VS. THE GREEK WORLDVIEW

The biblical worldview has often been contrasted with the classic Greek philosophic tradition. Judaism and Greek culture, Jerusalem and Athens, typify two comprehensive outlooks.

The Jewish tradition commences with an account of creation. The idea of *creatio ex nihilo* (creation out of nothing) is the ultimate starting point of a worldview founded on the notion of Divine Will. In contrast, the Greek philosophical tradition can be characterized by the notion of the eternity of the universe. Unlike the active God of the Bible, Aristotle's God is fixed in an eternal state of self-contemplation. Since the most perfect activity was believed to be thinking, and since thought about anything less than perfection implied imperfection, God must think about what is absolutely perfect, namely, Himself.

When the eternal self-contemplating God of Aristotle is held up against the "human" biblical God who is involved in history and is often frustrated and enraged by human failures, the contrast is "scandalous" and perhaps even ludicrous.

Though the biblical account of creation portrays the unlimited power of God to create a universe, the scenario changes abruptly with the creation of human beings who begin challenging divine plans and commands. In the Bible, the human species symbolizes the frustration of divine power, God's inability to shape the world entirely according to His will. Human freedom to oppose divine will and power is the ultimate rationale for the Sinai covenant. The biblical narrative portrays the shift from a reality characterized by the unencumbered creativity of an omnipotent being whose will is automatically realized ("Let there be...and there was...") to a covenantal history, where the recalcitrance of human beings convinces God to share the destiny of history with human partners. The story of Adam's and Eve's disobedience in the garden, together with the descriptions of human sinfulness and rebellion in chapters 3 to 12 of Genesis, are the dramatic prologue to the covenant with Abraham and later with the people of Israel at Sinai. A human being who instinctively does the good does not require a Torah. A God who cannot be disobeyed does not enter a covenantal relationship.

My concern with the biblical account of God who interacts with human beings is not strictly theological, but rather anthropological. For my purposes, whether the biblical account of God is true literally or metaphorically is less important than its possible anthropological implications. In understanding a people's concept of God, we gain access to their conception of life and to the significance of their personal and communal forms of living.

Leo Strauss correctly indicated the absence of a concept of messianism in the Greek philosophical tradition. In *Jerusalem and Athens*, Strauss related the concepts of a "new creation," a "new man," and a "new history" to the doctrines of creation and Divine will. The Greek tradition of eternal necessity encourages human beings to acquire the wisdom to accept what is necessary and inevitable. Belief in a world as the creation of a personal God serves as the ground for living with hope, wonder, radical innovation, messianism, and *tikkun ha-olam* (restructuring of the world).

Spinoza, like the Stoics, attempted to uncover regularity and necessity and to accept what could not be otherwise. The one release the Stoics offered from the grip of the tragedies and suffering of history was a kind of "contemplative transcendence," as opposed to the "active transcendence" that emerges from the biblical tradition. One transcends the painful features of daily life through withdrawal and "apathy" and by not demanding that reality embody one's moral and spiritual aspirations. The individual transcends the tragic dimensions of life by discovering sources of meaning and independence within the self. Perfection becomes a personal inner quest in defiance of an imperfect, unalterable external world. The locus of human transcendence is the individual human soul; it is there one discovers liberation.

Individualistic transcendence contrasts with the Jewish challenge "to perfect the world under the reign of the Almighty." Jewish spirituality demands an activism that attempts to alter the external reality. Not content to rest within the privacy of the individual soul, this activism demands that reality be remolded in the light of the prophetic vision of history. The Judaic principle of will, in the concepts of creation, miracle, and revelation, creates a human restlessness with the imperfections of society.

Mitzvah and Halakhah are based on a covenant between God and Israel that demands that the Jewish people become a mature, responsible partner in the covenantal relationship.

Consequently, exclusive reliance on Divine Grace, quietism, and fatalistic resignation do not characterize typical Judaic responses to everyday life. The halakhic response to illness was to encourage human initiative in medical treatment. The various welfare institutions and the emphasis on the commandment of *tzedakah* (charity) that typify traditional Jewish communities reflect this activist thrust.

Although these forms of activism were present in traditional Jewish societies, it would be a distortion to ignore the pervasive influence of a belief in supernatural messianic redemption, which created the traditional passive response to the Jewish people's collective suffering in exile. The Zionist secular revolution was a rejection of this traditional messianic posture, which was, I maintain, antithetical to the full realization of the covenantal ideal.

Zionism can be characterized as a continuation and perhaps even a crystallization of an essential thrust of the Jewish worldview. Zionism gives expression to a people's refusal to define what is possible solely on the basis of what is given; it reflects the concept of "will" implicit in the doctrine of creation. Zionism encourages the development of a person who cannot rest while historical conditions remain unaltered. "Let there be..." expresses the rejection of the eternity of the universe because it captures the essential principle of a worldview predicated on belief in the possibility of change and novelty.

To see the living reality of the State of Israel in its cities, its agriculture, its hospitals, and its social welfare and immigrant absorption programs is to witness the translation of the belief in a creator God into the living history of a people. The strength of the Zionist revolution emerged from its capacity to restructure reality on the basis of Jewish hopes and aspirations. Empirically oriented critics in the twentieth century argued, and continue to argue, against the feasibility of a Jewish state in the Middle East. But Israel bears witness to the notion of a creator God Who proclaims,

"Where there was chaos, let there be order." Israel thus embodies an anthropology that emerges from a theology of creation, which proclaims the possibility of radical novelty by negating eternal necessity.

MITZVAH AND ZIONISM

Another concept that dominates traditional Jewish religious experience is mitzvah (divine commandment). The concept of will implicit in the doctrine of creation provides for the logical possibility of revelation (see Maimonides, *Guide*, II, 25). Revelation of Torah, however, adds the new dimension of normative demand. The paradigmatic moment of encounter between God and human beings is characterized not by mystic enlightenment or contemplative spirituality, but by the revelation of law to a people. At Sinai, a people meet a God who commands; the content of revelation is not cognitive information but rather normative expectation. Revelation in Judaism does not satisfy a cognitive quest for metaphysical knowledge; it demands an active human response in the form of the implementation of the divine command.

Aristotle ends the *Nicomachean Ethics* with a discussion of the highest perfection a human being may achieve: intellectual contemplation. Maimonides, by contrast, ends *The Guide of the Perplexed* (III, 54) by incorporating moral excellence into his description of the perfection of the intellectual love of God.

The Jewish tradition questioned the value of intellectual achievement if it made no difference in practice. One could justifiably be critical of scholars on the basis of their conduct. In the dispute between R. Tarfon and R. Akiba about "which is greater in importance—learning or practice?" the conclusion was *talmud gadol* (learning is greater) but with a significant qualification: learning is greater because ultimately it leads to practice.

This tradition continued in the ethos of Zionism, which embodied the spirit of the active, practical orientation of traditional Judaism. While Zionism was not anti-intellectual, it rejected the approach to talmudic study that legitimized the development of a parasitical learning class unwilling to take an active role in nationbuilding. Zionism condemned the tradition of a learned aristocracy that isolated the intellectual from the practical affairs of life. It revolted against the image of the East European yeshivah (talmudic academy) student.

Torah study becomes distorted when it shrinks to a mere fascination with legal detail. As in all disciplines involving research and learning, whether secular or religious, intellectual activity has an inherent attraction. The danger of theoretical learning is that the beauty of intellectual rigor may lead one to treat learning as an end in itself.

Zionism continued the normative orientation of Judaism by challenging the intellect to make a difference in practice. If learning does not manifest itself in creating greater responsibility for human affairs, its achievement distorts the true spirit and purpose of Torah. Jews were not meant to live permanently in the Sinai desert. They were charged with the task of embodying Torah in the concrete structures of a people living in its own land.

Zionism categorically rejected the approach to Torah study articulated by R. Simon ben Yohai:

> Should God not all the more have brought them in [to the land] by the straight road? But God said: "If I bring Israel into the land now, every one of them will immediately take hold of his field or vineyard and neglect the Torah. But I will make them go round about through the desert forty years, so that, having the manna to eat and the water of the well to drink, they will absorb the Torah." On the basis of this

interpretation, R. Simon the son of Yohai said: "Only to those who eat manna is it given really to study the Torah. Like them are those who eat *trumah.*" (*Mekhilta de-Rabbi Ishmael, Beshallah,* p. 171)

Our Rabbis taught: "And you shall gather in your corn" (Deut. 11:14). What is to be learned from these words? Since it says "This book of the law shall not depart out of your mouth" (Joshua 1:8), I might think that this injunction is to be taken literally. Therefore it says, "And you shall gather in your corn," which implies that you are to combine the study of them [the words of the Torah] with a worldly occupation. This is the view of R. Ishmael. R. Simeon b. Yohai says: Is that possible? If a man ploughs in the ploughing season, and he sows in the sowing season, and reaps in the reaping season, and threshes in the threshing season, and winnows in the season of the wind, what is to become of the Torah? No; but when Israel perform the will of the Omnipresent, their work is performed by others, as it says, "And strangers shall stand and feed your flocks, etc.," and when Israel do not perform the will of the Omnipresent, their work is done by them, as it says, "And you shall gather in your corn." (B.T. *Berakhoth* 35b)

According to Simon b. Yohai, involvement with the problems and demands of everyday life is incompatible with intellectual excellence. The Torah scholar can, therefore, develop either capacity only in a condition of total grace, as symbolized by the desert, or in a utopian messianic society. The challenge of secular Zionism is to integrate the life of the intellect with the practical concerns of maintaining an autonomous, nonmessianic

Jewish state. Zionism forces the culture of the *beit ha-midrash* (academy of learning) to recognize that the revelation of the Torah in the desert was a preparation for entering into a land where manna would not fall.

Many Jews in the diaspora are apprehensive about living in Israel because of the nature and scope of the responsibilities required in building a total Jewish society. Unlike living elsewhere as an alienated poet or religious enthusiast, living in Israel demands a "talmudic" concern with details. If you ignore or are sloppy with particulars, you ultimately destroy the spirituality of this country. Plumbing, electric wiring, telephones, safe roads, politeness, patience, reliability in ordinary social interactions—all fall within the scope of responsibilities of a person committing to the spiritual character of an entire society.

The involvement with details that characterizes Jewish legal texts such as the Talmud reflects the conviction that the greater your knowledge, the greater the scope of your responsibilities. If knowledge and erudition do not make a difference in the marketplace and in community, then they are closer to Aristotle's ideal of human perfection through contemplation than to the Jewish conviction that "greater is learning for it leads to practice." If you cannot tolerate the complexity of social and political life and the demanding concern with detail, you will find an earthly Jerusalem unbearable.

ZIONISM AND "PRIMITIVE" JEWISH PARTICULARISM

Jewish particularism is a recurring issue that receives prominence whenever Judaism is defended or attacked. The centrality of peoplehood confounds attempts at defining Judaism as a "religion" or as a universal ethical framework. Spinoza distinguished Judaism from Christianity in terms of the former's national-political character:

> Though many moral precepts besides ceremonies are contained in these five books [the Pentateuch], they appear not as moral doctrines universal to all men, but as commands especially adapted to the understanding and character of the Hebrew people, and as having reference only to the welfare of the kingdom.... Christ, as I have said, was sent into the world, not to preserve the state nor to lay down laws, but solely to teach the universal moral law.... His sole care was to teach moral doctrines, and to distinguish them from the laws of the state; for the Pharisees, in their ignorance, thought that the observance of the state law and the Mosaic law was the sum total of morality; whereas such laws merely had reference to the public welfare. (*A Theological-Political Treatise*, pp. 70–71)

Kant also focused on the legalistic aspect of Judaism as a definitive characteristic of the Jewish faith:

> The *Jewish faith* was, in its original form, a collection of mere statutory laws upon which was established a political organization; for whatever moral additions were then or later *appended* to it in no way whatever belong to Judaism as such. Judaism is really not a religion at all but merely a union of a number of people who, since they belonged to a particular stock, formed themselves into a commonwealth under purely political laws, and not into a church; nay, it was *intended* to be merely an earthly state. (*Religion within the Limits of Reason Alone*, p. 116)

The inadequacy of such analyses of Judaism notwithstanding, it is evident that Zionism did not invent the idea of the centrality of peoplehood. Though some Jews have agonized over defending Judaism against the slur of narrow parochialism, the relationship between Judaism and a particular national entity goes back to biblical sources.

The Midrash states (in *Sifre*, Deut., *Piska* 43) that mitzvot were given for Jews to perform in the Land of Israel. In its discussion of the meaning of fulfilling the commandments in the diaspora, the Midrash argues that performing mitzvot in exile trains and prepares Jews for performing these norms in their proper context, which is the Land of Israel.

> "And you will soon perish from the good land that the Lord is giving you. Therefore impress these My words upon your very heart: bind them as a sign on your hand and let them serve as a symbol on your forehead" (Deut. 11:17–18). Even though I am about to exile you from the Land [of Israel] to a foreign land, you must continue to be marked [as distinctive] there by the commandments, so that when you return they will not be new to you. A parable: A king of flesh and blood grew angry with his wife and sent her back to her father's house, saying to her, "Be sure to continue wearing your jewelry, so that whenever you return, it will not be new to you." Thus also the Holy One, blessed be He, said to Israel, "My children, you must continue to be marked by the commandments, so that when you return, they will not be new to you." (*Sifre*, *Piska* 43)

In exile, Jews are, as it were, in "spring training"; the "regular season" begins only officially when they return to the Land of Israel.

Our Rabbis taught: One should always live in the Land of Israel, even in a town most of whose inhabitants are idolaters, but let no one live outside the Land, even in a town most of whose inhabitants are Israelites; for whoever lives in the Land of Israel may be considered to have a God, but whoever lives outside the Land may be regarded as one who has no God. For it is said in Scripture, "to give you the Land of Canaan, to be your God" (Lev. 25:38). Has he, then, who does not live in the Land, no God? But [this is what the text intended] to tell you, that whoever lives outside the Land may be regarded as one who worships idols. Similarly it was said in Scripture in [the story of] David, "For they have driven me out this day that I should not cleave to the inheritance of the Lord, saying: Go, serve other gods" (I Sam. 26:19). Now, who ever said to David, "Serve other gods"? But [the text intended] to tell you that whoever lives outside the Land may be regarded as one who worships idols. (Tosefta A.Z.V.) (B.T. *Ketubbot* 110b)

Modern Jews have often been embarrassed by the ethical implications of the primitive tribal images evoked by such language. Consequently, they often presented the Bible in a developmental perspective: from early tribalism to the prophetic universalism of "on that day the Lord will be One and His Name One" (Zech. 14:9). Isaiah's visions of the end of days signal the beginning of a universalism that will emancipate future generations from primitive biblical tribalism. To the dismay of enlightened German Jews, such as Hermann Cohen and Julius Guttmann, Spinoza and Kant had identified Judaism as being thoroughly particularistic and hence devoid of moral and spiritual significance. In reaction to the charge that Judaism was nothing but the way of life of a nation-state with a particular political structure, some Jewish thinkers identified Judaism with ethics, arguing that Judaism was, in fact, the most universal of religions.

In contrast to modern Jewish apologetics that denied the national "family" features of Judaism, Zionism restored Jewish peoplehood to its original biblical significance. In its struggle to win the hearts of Jews, it often found itself competing against the universalistic sentiments of international socialism, which promised to solve the "Jewish problem" once and for all by abolishing national differences. Zionism rekindled the passion of "primitive" Judaism and, in so doing, created the basis for a renaissance of Judaism based on the centrality of peoplehood.

In order to avoid misunderstanding, it is vital to distinguish between exclusive and pluralistic orientations to nationalism. Particularism is rightly feared when it undermines universal ethical principles, that is, when it denies the dignity of all human beings or the universal human rights that theories of "natural law" have attempted to formulate.

Particularism, however, need not always be guilty of ghettoizing its own way of life but may acknowledge the legitimacy and value of other traditions and loyalties. One must be alert to the danger of claiming that the history of the Jewish people is the only spiritually significant history. The commitment to the development and intensification of a particularistic mode of life is, to me, inseparable from commitment to a pluralistic universe of cultures and traditions.

Universalism was discredited in the modern era because (1) it showed itself to be little more than the tyranny of one particular ideology over other ideologies, thus exposing the true chauvinist and tribal nature of its alleged universality and (2) it replaced loyalty to actual people and cultures with loyalty to reified verbal abstractions. Religious life loses its vitality when it becomes identified solely with abstract ethical doctrines. By establishing a dichotomy between the historical-political domain and the religious-spiritual domain, religion eventually becomes irrelevant to the serious concerns of human society. By relegating religion to the private domain of the solitary individual, the secular city reflects the demise of religion. Religion becomes harmless and impotent when the concept of the holy is removed from the matrix of a collective, political reality.

Zionism enabled Jews to stand Spinoza and Kant on their heads by proclaiming that true spirituality must be related to national-political frameworks. Zionism created the conditions for proving that universal tolerance and respect for the dignity of all human beings can be achieved not by abolishing human differences but rather by fostering particular loyalties. The Zionist revolution enabled Jews to perceive Judaism as the story of a particular people and a God who "dwells" in the Land of Israel and is sanctified by the moral quality of the total framework of society.

Zionism restored legitimacy to "biblical tribalism" and, ironically, indicated a way of withstanding the destructive consequences of misguided universalisms. It enabled Jews to proclaim their loyalty to the God of Israel and to a particular land without shame. Mitzvot take on significance when performed by individuals who are not embarrassed by their loyalties to family and community.

In light of the above analysis, it is understandable why, as Gershom Scholem says, Zionism is a movement both of continuation and of rebellion. It is a continuation of a worldview that affirms belief in novelty and radical change in history, but it refuses to restrict itself to the interpersonal nonpolitical domain. It continues the talmudic emphasis on the unity of thought and practice, but it rejects making the *beit midrash* a substitute for the marketplace. It continues the particularistic thrust of Jewish spirituality but rejects indifference to the significance of other religious traditions.

Because of the Zionist rebellion, Judaism is challenged to discover new ways of balancing the various tendencies within the tradition. Zionism offers Jews the opportunity of fully realizing the universal thrust of the prophetic ethical vision without abandoning the intense particularism that rabbinic Judaism made possible.

13

WIDENING THE SCOPE OF

COVENANTAL CONSCIOUSNESS

FORWARD-LOOKING TECHNOLOGICAL consciousness can never fully define Jewish identity in Israel, since the very geography of the country brings the forward-moving thrust into confrontation with the historical aspirations and memories of the Jewish people. Jerusalem has always been the vehicle through which Jewish hopes and dreams were expressed. Israel invites powerful ideological passions, since it connects a Jew to the larger historical memories of Jewish experience. One cannot avoid meeting the prophetic social vision of Isaiah when living and working in Israel.

It is thus understandable that urgent practical questions of security and the economy do not exhaust what preoccupies Israelis. They get excited about spiritual and religious issues that seem strange to the outsider who sees Israel as a besieged country fighting for its survival. Governments fall in Israel over questions of religious principle, such as alleged violations of the Sabbath and "Who is a Jew" legislation. The disturbing questions that perplex Israeli society reflect a need to clarify how to apply the Jewish tradition in a modern society.

In Israel, in contrast to the diaspora, the synagogue and Jewish family life cannot sufficiently generate the spiritual religious vitality needed to make Judaism a viable option for modern Israelis. It is not accidental that the national literature of the country is the Bible. This does not mean, however, that at present a biblical religious passion infuses the country, but only that the parameters of Judaic spirituality in Israel mirror the larger historical and political perspective of the biblical outlook. We find many people identifying with biblical heroic types and with prophetic moral and messianic aspirations, even though they lack an appreciation of the theological foundations of the biblical worldview.

INTIMACY AND ACTION

One can distinguish several modes of relational intimacy between God and Israel deriving from the Sinai covenant. One very powerful symbol of intimacy between God and His people is the Temple: "Let them make Me a sanctuary that I may dwell among them" (Exod. 25:8). The sacrifices expressed the ongoing relationship between God and Israel, as well as the attempt to restore it whenever it was disrupted by sinful behavior.

A second mode of intimacy with God, as developed by the tradition, was the three great pilgrimage festivals of *Pesah* (Passover), *Shavuot* (Weeks), and *Sukkot* (Tabernacles). Whereas the sacrifices and prayer express the feeling that God is directly involved in one's personal life, the festivals express the relationship of the historical community of Israel (*K'nesset yisrael*) with its God. In every generation, the Exodus, the receiving of the Torah, and the sojourn in the desert are appropriated by the community as its own experiences.

Another very powerful expression of covenantal intimacy is the Sabbath.

The Israelite people shall keep the Sabbath, observing the Sabbath throughout the ages as a covenant for all time: it shall be a sign for all time between Me and the people of Israel. (Exod. 31:16–17)

Thus far, covenantal Judaism has been described in terms of direct relational intimacy with God. There is, however, another aspect of the covenant that is vital today, despite its having been overshadowed by the symbolic and ritualistic modes of relational intimacy. Besides the *covenant of intimacy* there is also a *covenant of social and political action*. In the Bible, God gave not only ritualistic commandments but also commandments related to how to build social, economic, and political structures that mirror the Divine Presence in the world. The covenantal drama is not limited to moments of participation in symbolic holy time; it also extends to *hol*, mundane everyday life.

In Leviticus 19, the concept of a holy community includes a vast range of activities not only related to symbolic times and rituals. "You shall be holy" (Lev. 19:2) implies not merely observing the Sabbath, abhorring idolatry, and eating sacrificial food (19:3–8) but also making provision for the poor, outlawing theft and fraud, and pursuing justice (19:9–15) as well as many other demands, both ritual and social. The religious impulse that infuses this chapter expresses God's demand to be present in the totality of human activities.

Leviticus 19 and 25 act as correctives to any attempt at identifying holiness with separation from the everyday rhythms of life. Holiness has to be embodied in the political framework of the community. It is not an invitation to single individuals to pursue their own private spiritual quests.

The covenantal experience can thus be divided between moments when the reality of divinity is felt in a direct, personal way (holy time, prayer) and situations when God-awareness lacks the immediacy and intensity of religious worship.

LEARNING AND PRAYER

When the last king of Judah and the leaders of the people were exiled to Babylon, Jeremiah prophesied a return within seventy years. And they did return, but not in the way envisaged by Jeremiah and Ezekiel. The contrast to the triumphal entry of Joshua is even more striking. After the exile, there were no conquering armies, no collapsing walls of Jericho. Instead of twelve tribes, only a small band of individuals returned to Jerusalem. A new Temple was built, but it was a modest structure instead of the grand building with its institutions described in detail by Ezekiel.

Faced with repeatedly disappointed or only partially fulfilled expectations, the covenantal community could have reacted in various ways. It could have lost faith in the plausibility and effectiveness of the covenantal promises. Or it could have postponed all its expectations to some "great day of the Lord" when God would redeem the world. The way chosen by Ezra and Nehemiah was to seize the limited opportunities offered by an imperial ruler friendly to his Jewish subjects (compare Nehemiah 2 and Ezra 7).

Rabbinic Judaism continued in the spirit of Ezra when it gave the community new ways of expressing their covenantal identity under difficult historical conditions. The rabbinic period saw an expansion of collective experiences, such as prayer and the public reading of the Torah, which reinforced covenantal consciousness. Through liturgical celebrations, Jews reminded one another that their memories were not illusions. The synagogue and communal prayer became a framework for sensing the presence of God within community. After the Temple was destroyed and the sacrifices ceased, any ten Jews who gathered together in prayer bore witness to the ever-present sanctifying power of God in their midst.

The community, wherever it found itself, now became the active carrier of God's presence in history. God became portable, as it were, through having become embodied in the halakhic life of the community. Sanctification of God was manifested not only by the grand historical drama of Ezekiel or by heroic acts of martyrdom but also by the personal lives of pious Jews whose actions made God beloved by their fellows. As the Mishnah, the Talmud, and the subsequent halakhic literature emerged, Jews became increasingly a community of learning as well as a community of prayer. God was present not only when Jews engaged in prayer but equally when they engaged in Torah study.

Although the creation of the State of Israel created the social and political conditions for restoring the full scope of covenantal Judaism (in terms both of relational intimacy and social, political action), nevertheless, as a result of centuries of exile we developed a rabbinic leadership skilled at guiding Jews only within the framework of the covenant of intimacy.

Many contemporary talmudic scholars are highly competent in dealing with halakhic minutiae that express the passion of the covenant of intimacy. But they are often silent or reticent before the larger demands of the covenant of social and political action. Their covenantal consciousness is directed toward religious celebration within the confines of the family, the school, and the synagogue but not within the larger social and political realms. The challenge to articulate a Judaism that can be mirrored in the total life of a nation is postponed to the messianic era. Many religious leaders believe that our task today is to expand on those covenantal symbolic and ritualistic mitzvot that reinforce our unique identity and separation from the surrounding nations and religions. The biblical demand that we become "a holy nation" is reduced to mitzvot dealing with marital relationships, sexual modesty, dietary laws, Sabbath and festival observance, and so on.

MITZVAH AND HALAKHAH

In order to cope effectively with the new, enormous challenges to traditional Judaism that surface in Israeli society, it is important to rethink the relationship between Halakhah and the revelatory framework of mitzvah and, above all, how to combine respect for tradition with the need for radical innovation. The revelatory category of mitzvah precedes halakhic specification. Halakhah is the material concretization of mitzvah, by the community and its leadership, for specific times and situations. Halakhah takes the mitzvot heard through revelation and gives them a particular form suited to the situations encountered by the listener.

Although the distinction between mitzvah and Halakhah is clear in principle, it is not always clear where to draw the line between them. Is the Bible mitzvah? Is the Talmud Halakhah? Are only the Ten Commandments mitzvah and the rest of the Bible Halakhah?

In interpreting Torah today, do we listen only to our canonical texts, or does the interpretive tradition mediate how we listen to these foundational texts? Since Jewish spiritual life has been nurtured by an interpretive tradition for the past two thousand years, we cannot maintain continuity with our tradition while ignoring how earlier listeners understood the Sinai revelation. Who, therefore, are the authoritative voices to whom we must answer and justify our new interpretations? To the *tannaim* and *amoraim* of the talmudic era? To Maimonides (twelfth century), Joseph Karo (sixteenth century), Moshe Isserlis (sixteenth century), the Hafetz Haim (twentieth century), or Moshe Feinstein or Rabbi Joseph B. Soloveitchik (twentieth century)?

Traditional halakhic thinking is often conservative because of its fundamental need to demonstrate its essential continuity with the legal rulings of the past. Precedent and reinterpretation are the forms through which new legal decisions are normally introduced. The continuity of the interpretive tradition is essential for legal continuity. But what should we do when we meet new situations that we cannot in good conscience cover and justify by legal precedents?

DEVELOPING LAW IN THE ABSENCE OF PRECEDENTS

The confused reaction of the Israeli rabbinate to the influx of Ethiopian Jews is a conspicuous example of new situations that emerge in Israeli society—situations that cannot be dealt with easily by conventional principles of halakhic decision making. The Ethiopian Jewish community was totally cut off from the ongoing interpretive discussion of the Law for as long as two millennia. How could they be welcomed into a framework defined completely by the teachings of halakhic thinkers of the talmudic and gaonic periods?

The Ethiopian Jewish community defined its religious self-awareness by the Bible. Its members had a lively sense of mitzvah, as shown by their strict observance of the laws of family purity. They stood valiantly in opposition to all forms of idolatry, proudly proclaiming before a hostile world the unity of the image-less God of Judaism. Now, what weight should a contemporary halakhic jurist give to their rejection of idolatry? Is their unconditional and heroic commitment to the Torah sufficient to qualify them for immediate entry into a Jewish community informed by the ongoing talmudic halakhic tradition? Is the commitment to mitzvah—independent of rabbinic interpretation—sufficient, or is traditional rabbinic halakhic practice constitutive of the meaning of Torah and mitzvot?

Yeshayahu Leibowitz called for a new way of doing Halakhah that was not necessarily bound by concepts of precedence and reinterpretation. He was frustrated by the inability of contemporary rabbinic leaders to respond effectively to new situations that called for bold and innovative halakhic decisions. He therefore appealed to the religious Zionist community to act independently of its rabbinic leadership by creating new Halakhah through the practice of community.

Leibowitz understood that Zionism and the establishment of the State of Israel must create new patterns of thought for developing Halakhah. We must find ways to conduct a modern State on the Sabbath without relying on nonobservant Jews or non-Jews to act as "*Shabbat goyim.*" Religious Jews cannot expect to build a viable Jewish state that is parasitical on the existence of nonobservant Jews. Religious Zionists must establish a religious society for all Jews. You cannot fill your police and fire departments with nonobservant Jews and call yourselves a Torah society. Leibowitz's work was an important example of how a committed halakhic thinker struggles to make sense of the commitment to serve God through mitzvah, together with the decision to create a new Jewish political reality.

THE SPIRIT OF THE LAW

When one enters a totally new frame of reference, such as the State of Israel, no adequate solutions for the development of Halakhah can be found without regaining an awareness of the wide range of values that inspired the development of this legal tradition. What may unite our own halakhic response with the practice of the Jewish tradition is not necessarily identical halakhic forms, but the seriousness with which we respond to the mitzvot and our commitment to continuing our covenantal identity. What we need to learn from the past is not so much how previous generations solved particular problems, or the particular forms of their halakhic frameworks, but rather the underlying spirit and teleology that infuses Halakhah. It is not only to legal norms that we owe our allegiance, but also to the values and the human character that these laws attempt to realize.

In modern Israel, we cannot go back to the agrarian framework of biblical society. The Bible reflects the connection of family and tribe to fixed geographical areas, the lack of a money economy, and other conditions incompatible with modern modes of economic organization. If, therefore, we want to treat the State of Israel as an opportunity to reinstitute the laws of the Sabbatical and Jubilee years, we must try to uncover the spirit and goals of these mitzvot. We must consider how the concerns with distributive justice, with social equality, and with preventing permanent economic helplessness that infuse the biblical laws of the Sabbatical and Jubilee years can find expression in modern Israel. The prophetic warning that exile is due to the nonobservance of the Sabbatical and Jubilee laws should stimulate our halakhic leadership to recommend ways of avoiding such problems as long-term indebtedness, the economic exploitation of local and foreign workers, and unjust labor–management relations. Reducing the Sabbatical year to dietary food laws and the rabbinic solution of "selling" the land of Israel to an Arab so that we can eat its produce testifies to a total failure of halakhic imagination and courage.

Similarly, traditional Halakhah includes a considerable amount of legislation relating to the king and the hereditary monarchy. There is a great gap between those laws and modern parliamentary democratic sensibilities. Yet, we can learn a great deal from the spirit of those laws as described by Maimonides in the *Mishneh Torah*.

> Just as Scripture accords great honor to the king and bids all pay him honor, so it bids him cultivate a humble

and lowly spirit.... He must not exercise his authority in a supercilious manner.... He should deal graciously and compassionately with the small and the great, conduct their affairs in their best interests, be wary of the honor of even the lowliest. When he addresses the public collectively, he shall use gentle language.... At all times, his conduct should be marked by a spirit of great humility. (Judges, Kings and Wars, 2:6)

Many laws of the monarchy deal with the temptations and corruption of power. In modern terms, this implies that those who hold political power and authority must be imbued with a higher normative and moral consciousness.

Halakhic thinking must also be applied to minimizing the abuse of power in general. How do our hospitals and patient care reflect the dignity and sanctity of human life taught in the halakhic tradition? How do the norms of *tzedakah* (charity) in rabbinic Judaism offer us guidance in organizing our welfare institutions? How does the talmudic understanding of family life relate to the abuse of children and wives? How should divorce laws be restructured so as to minimize the demeaning abuse of power in divorce proceedings? If the teleology of Halakhah is to mirror "ways of pleasantness and peace" and "beloved are human beings created in the image of God," what type of hadakhic practices must be introduced into our society?

In dealing effectively with such issues, we will restore the moral power of our covenantal destiny.

INSULATION AND INTEGRATION

Never before in Jewish history has there been a concentration in one political framework of such intense, yet diverse, ideological points of view regarding the meaning of our spiritual legacy. In a situation of such ambiguity and complexity, it is understandable why we are witnessing such extreme polarization between the religious and the nonobservant communities. The repudiation of the quest for integration and dialogue with other cultures by a large segment of the Orthodox community is symptomatic of the unease this community feels with the new challenges Israel forces us to confront. The level of intolerance and anxiety in our debates and discussions is indicative of how threatened is our political and religious leadership by the challenges of modernity.

Different human values and sensibilities have entered the daily life and the self-understanding of the modern Jew. The rabbinic tradition responded with creative intellectual boldness to the challenges that the destruction of the Temple and exile brought into Jewish history. Rabbinic Judaism taught us how to perpetuate Judaism in an alien and often hostile world. Modern religious leadership must learn from the innovative spirit of the talmudic tradition. Our covenantal conscience must not be nurtured only by a vision of Halakhah that exclusively emphasizes symbolic rituals and mitzvot that separate us from others and create a passionate life of religious worship and halakhic intensity.

The rabbinic tradition taught us how to develop a spiritual culture in isolation from the world. Our task is to develop a sense of covenantal holiness reflecting Judaism as the total way of life of a politically independent nation, but without fueling Jewish identity by appealing to Balam's dubious blessing: "There is a people that dwells apart / Not reckoned among the nations" (Num. 23:9).

14

ALIYAH

THE TRANSFORMATION AND
RENEWAL OF AN IDEAL

THE CALL TO aliyah today often creates feelings of estrangement and hostility among diaspora Jewry. At a recent gathering of leaders of world Jewry, the president of Israel called for aliyah as the obvious solution to the diaspora's concern with Jewish continuity. After all, assimilation would cease and their continuity would be assured if Jews would only leave the "fleshpots" of the diaspora and join the historic renaissance of the Jewish people in its homeland.

The president's speech was misunderstood as patronizing and humiliating, ignoring the efforts of world Jewry to build their own viable educational and religious frameworks. They were turning to Israel for partnership, not salvation.

Is this encounter symptomatic of a deep cultural schism within the Jewish people? Must Israeli leaders be silent about aliyah—the central motif of the modern Zionist revolution—in order to maintain meaningful dialogue with the diaspora?

In the following essay I shall argue that the concept of aliyah must undergo a radical transformation if it is not to become extinct and irrelevant. But before continuing, I shall discuss a feature of Jewish law that informs my position.

THE LANGUAGES OF
MIRRORING AND ASPIRATION

Jewish law can be understood in terms of the distinction between mirroring and aspiration, that is, between norms that reflect the moral sensibilities of the community and those that point to new moral and spiritual values.

One function of law is to provide political stability, order, and continuity by incorporating and mediating existing standards and values. A law that ignores what the majority of people can appreciate and appropriate in everyday life is in danger of losing its normative credibility. Law thus mirrors where people "are at."

Another function of law is to awaken the community to strive to higher goals and ideals. From this perspective, law educates rather than mirrors. Its goal is to challenge and inspire the community to aspire to new spiritual heights. Maimonides' interpretation of the different forms of worship—sacrifices, petitional prayer, and contemplation—is an excellent model for understanding the educative, leading function of Jewish law (see *The Guide of the Perplexed*, III, 32, 51).

In the final analysis, law must balance the conservative need for stability against the progressive pull to educate and change. A law that mirrors the moral and spiritual status quo without awakening higher possibilities becomes lifeless and banal; a law that speaks the language of aspiration without recognizing what people are really like ceases being a workable framework because of its utopian, dreamlike quality.

This distinction can shed light on the problematic meaning of the concept of aliyah in contemporary Jewish life.

THE CONTEMPORARY PROBLEM
OF ALIYAH LANGUAGE

In the past, aliyah was a response to political crises that threatened the existence of Jews. Massive aliyah to Israel was directly related to persecution and anti-Semitism. Jews "escaped" to Israel. Aliyah was more often a "running away from" than a "striving for something higher" (as the word *aliyah* itself suggests).

The North American experience, however, differs radically from this paradigm. In America, Jews are very comfortable. Even when experiencing a sense of marginality, Jews basically feel safe and at home. Although American Jewry appreciates the need for a Jewish homeland as a refuge for Jews in distress, they personally do not experience any threat to their physical survival, which might drive them to consider aliyah as a serious option.

This is the crux of the dilemma: We can no longer talk an aliyah language that is nurtured by fear and physical crisis. The overriding threat to the future of North American Jewry is assimilation, not anti-Semitism or marginality.

No matter how serious a threat assimilation is, it is not experienced as a life-threatening crisis. Although caring committed Jews do consider assimilation a real crisis, those who assimilate view their behavior as free and uncoerced. They are not reacting to an external threat. Some might even recommend assimilation as a liberating alternative to the burdensome guilt of feeling responsible for Jewish history and culture.

Ironically, assimilation can be understood as a Jewish longing for normalcy—the very same idea that traditionally inspired many Zionists. If our aliyah pitch is to live a "normal" life, we expose ourselves to the response that intermarriage, assimilation, and California living are perfectly good ways of achieving normalcy.

The limited range of human lifestyles of the Eastern European ghetto is not the social reality that Jews experience in Toronto or Los Angeles. For many Jews living in pluralistic democracies that offer an unlimited range of opportunities for personal self-fulfillment, the Zionist dream of normalcy has already been realized. For them, the promise of aliyah has been fulfilled!

We must understand this new historical reality and, instead of hunting for signs of anti-Semitism in order to reignite the cause of aliyah, we must face the fact that North American Jewry is not a community in crisis.

A CONCEPTUAL TRANSFORMATION
OF ALIYAH LANGUAGE

However difficult it is for the Zionist movement to admit it, the community of crisis that formerly fueled interest in aliyah by making it alive and relevant for Jews no longer exists. The traditional survival- and normalcy-oriented appeals of aliyah no longer resonate in the hearts of Jews today. If Israelis are to avoid the frustration of issuing endless aliyah proclamations that fall on deaf ears, they must understand that you cannot speak about aliyah to people who do not appreciate the significance of living an intense Jewish life.

The quality of daily Jewish life in the diaspora is the necessary groundwork for turning aliyah into a relevant live option. If you enjoy living as a Jew in Dallas, then one day you may want to realize your Jewish self in Israel. But if Jewish living in Dallas has no vital moral and spiritual significance, then living as a Jew in Jerusalem is a dead option.

The "safe haven" and "normalcy" appeals that gave vitality to the language of aliyah in the past must be replaced by an aliyah language that conveys the spiritual and moral excitement that Israeli life makes possible. Before worrying about the future of diaspora Jewry, Israeli leaders concerned about aliyah should first address themselves to the problematic moral and spiritual quality of Jewish life in Tel Aviv, Haifa, and Jerusalem.

Receptivity to the language of aliyah is a function of the sense of Jewishness that permeates a person's daily life. For my father, being Jewish and living as a committed Torah Jew was natural and self-evident. His instinctive answer to my asking him about the meaning of Jewish observance was, "This is how my father lived and how his father lived!" To him, my questions were irrelevant because of the inherent power of the past that informed his present identity and practice. He could only sing a Jewish *nigun*.

While this was true of my father's world, for me and my generation these were no longer pointless questions. The importance of the tradition and of being Jewish had ceased to be self-evident. Knowledge and personal conviction were necessary now if the tradition was to be a live option in my life. In some very important sense, I chose—and I must continuously choose—to live a committed Jewish life.

Although I know that my family, my teachers, and my early yeshivah education shaped my identity profoundly (leaving the Jewish people is not, and never was, a real option for me), I nevertheless realize that in contrast to my father's Jewish experience, my commitment to continue my father's and grandfather's way of life has to be reappropriated through knowledge and personal conviction. Living in dynamic pluralistic societies challenges me continually to confront and reclaim the spiritual vision of my ancestors.

Leaving Montreal, where I had built a synagogue and worked tirelessly to further Jewish institutions and university studies, wasn't simple. It was not an easy decision to leave a productive rabbinic and university career and to uproot my family from a normal and comfortable way of life.

I often say to people who ask me what inspired me to make aliyah: "I was among the few members of my congregation who listened to my sermons! I was so inspired by the rhetoric of aspiration that I forgot what Israel was really like."

After making aliyah, I soon realized that Israel was not exactly what my sermons were about. It took me several years to bridge the gap between the Israel of my *drashot* (sermons) and dreams and the manic-depressive quality of daily life in Israel.

Without the powerful and inspiring image of a Jewish national spiritual renaissance—of what I innocently believed Israel to be like—I would not have had the strength to uproot my family or to persevere in facing the strains and tensions of Israeli life.

I have come to understand from my own experiences that the language of aspiration is both a catalyst for change and an important counterweight to the feelings of futility and despair that can undermine serious attempts at effecting change. The rhetoric of hope and the belief in future possibilities is not a regressive escape into childish fantasy. It is essential for sustaining the vitality of a broader perception of what human life can be. In this sense, I am happy and grateful that I listened to my sermons!

Articulating a new vision of aliyah and of what Israel could be—or rather, of what "Israel really is about"—is not a form of escape or a denial of the vulgar parts of Israeli political life but is necessary for reinvigorating the Zionist ideal of aliyah. Focusing exclusively on the Holocaust and the possibility of future anti-Semitism will not move Jews to leave the comforts of Los Angeles for Israel. We must let go the crutches of anti-Semitism and alienation in order to create and sustain conviction—in order to move aliyah from "mirroring" to "aspiration."

INDIVIDUALISM, HISTORY, AND
NATIONAL CONSCIOUSNESS

How do you make the language of aliyah resonate in people's souls without sounding anachronistic or pointless? How do you move the focus of "aliyah language" from crisis response to personal conviction?

Jews in Israel and throughout the world must understand the significance of our dream to return to Israel and Jerusalem. The themes of Jerusalem and of the ingathering of the exiles are central themes of our daily prayers.

Why did the tradition make our return to the land, to Jerusalem, an essential feature of Jewish identity? Why did land and nation become constitutive elements of Jewish spiritual self-understanding? What makes Jewish nationalism distinct from other forms of nationalism? Serious Jewish leaders must offer intelligent answers to all these questions.

To be a Jew is to be claimed by three thousand years of history. The individual is the carrier of a legacy, of a covenantal promise of the Jewish people to become a holy nation. The Jewish family, therefore, was always imbued with a national purpose: to mediate the founding memories of the Jewish people for the next generation.

> And make them known to your children and to your children's children: The day you stood before the Lord your God at Horeb, when the Lord said to me, "Gather the people to Me that I may let them hear My words, in order that they may learn to revere Me as long as they live on earth and may so teach their children." (Deut. 4:9–10)

Traditionally, the central concern of the Jewish family was to cultivate a sense of being claimed and an appreciation of the ultimate significance to human behavior in the eyes of God. Families mediated the language of mitzvot.

In contrast to this notion of the family, the modern Jewish family often understands itself in psychological terms. Individual happiness and social adjustment are central parental concerns. The family is essentially future-oriented. History and memory are peripheral, if not totally irrelevant, to the overriding preoccupation with the child's psychic and economic well being.

Aliyah is predicated on the premise that the "I," the individual, can shape and be shaped by the "we," the nation. The drama of community informs the drama of self-fulfillment. For aliyah to become a serious option, the notion of the individual self must become more relational and community-oriented. Notions of shared history and memory must inform individual self-realization. Unless we overcome the ethos of self-sufficiency, aliyah language will have little chance of being heard.

The power of community and family must be among the most important Israeli exports to the diaspora. The new Zionist dream for Israel must be infused with the belief that the liberal concern with individual rights and dignity can flourish together with a deep commitment to history and community.

ISRAEL: THE PUBLIC FACE OF THE JEWISH PEOPLE

Aliyah must regain the inherent force of aliyah. The word itself implies "going up," aspiring to, striving for something higher. It must become a concept that challenges, that points to new possibilities and alternatives, that disturbs complacency and self-satisfied acceptance of the status quo.

The message of aliyah should convey the idea of privilege—the privilege of bringing up children with a sense of history and community. This must become the central thrust of aliyah as a language of aspiration.

As a Jew who lives in and loves Jerusalem, who feels privileged to have brought his family here, I can testify to the excitement and authenticity of living in a nation still involved with shaping its future identity.

In contrast to my religious life in the diaspora, my celebration of the Sabbath and Jewish festivals does not place my identity in opposition to my environment. On Yom Kippur, the streets of Jerusalem mirror the awe and sanctity of the day. Here, my public-self talks to my private-self; my outer-world shapes, and is shaped by, my inner-world.

Even though I feel anger and frustration when I read the morning papers and realize that many of our efforts at changing things through education are being undermined by short-sighted Knesset members bent on legislating Judaism, still I feel alive. I am angry, I am pained, but I am energized by the excitement of fighting to shape a nation that doesn't yet know who it wants to be or how to appropriate the Judaic tradition in the modern world.

Israel is the public face of the Jewish people, and aliyah is a call to shape that public face. *Time* magazine follows us wherever we go. Whatever happens in Jerusalem is immediately broadcast on CNN worldwide. With the establishment of Israel, Jews can no longer hide. For better or for worse, Jews have gone public. We can no longer be "Jews at home" and "human beings in public."

Anyone who cares about the legacy of Jewish history must realize one thing: the future of Jews in America and everywhere else will be defined by the type of Jewishness we build in Israel. If we fail, diaspora Jewry will be ashamed to show its public face. If fundamentalism and delegitimization of others grow here, we won't be able to talk about the ethical legacy of the Jewish people.

We won't be able to repair the public shame of Yigal Amir's fanaticism.

The issue of aliyah, then, is: how are Jews to act when they return home to Israel? Who are we going to be? Jews who value pluralism and tolerance, and who understand the meaning of freedom of conscience; or Jews who, when returning home to their own country, act as if they had never heard about democracy or the rights of minorities?

Israel is not only a call to normalcy, to be like the nations. Israel is a call to fulfill the vision of Moses—"And you shall be to Me...a holy nation" (Exod. 19:6)—in a new way. Aliyah is a call to the individual to arise, to assume a dramatic role in history, to participate in nation building.

If we can overcome the embarrassment of the biblical and prophetic understanding of the role of Israel in history, and if the Jewish spiritual legacy can become personal conviction, then aliyah will regain the compelling power of an ideal worth striving for.

Aliyah must first address Israelis and educate them to appreciate the crucial role they can play in determining the future of Jewish life throughout the world. Israelis are asked to address not only the persecuted and frightened Jew but also, and above all, Jews who have lost their sense of memory and history, whose Jewishness has ceased being necessary and self-evident. It is not speeches and proclamations that will move diaspora Jews, but rather a Jewish quality of life that inspires the individual to want to participate in the three-thousand-year-old legacy of the Jewish nation.

Israeli society must convey the excitement and importance of living as modern Jews who combine a sense of history and tradition with a profound belief in new human possibilities. The final chapter of our people's spiritual drama has not yet been written.

The destiny of Israel is to awaken Jews to become active participants in shaping the future of the Jewish people's moral and spiritual legacy.

15

AUSCHWITZ OR SINAI?

IN THE AFTERMATH OF THE ISRAELI-LEBANESE WAR

THERE IS A healthy spirit of serious self-evaluation and criticism in Israeli society today. The triumphant ecstasy of the Six-Day War no longer dominates the consciousness of many Israelis.

In retrospect, the jubilant sense of victory created by the Six-Day War was a mixed blessing. Along with the positive effect of awakening the Jewish world to the centrality and importance of Israel, it also gave rise to national self-adulation and hubris.

Widespread in Israeli society today are a sober appreciation of political and moral complexities and a serious sense of responsibility for the unintended consequences of our actions. These elements made themselves felt during the recent war in Lebanon and are positive and hopeful signs of a mature orientation to life. The fact that our country tolerates serious and often heated disagreement is a sign of its internal health and strength. There is no doubt that Israeli society contains the vital moral forces needed for regeneration and renewal.

In the Judaic tradition, belief in renewal resulted from respect for mature and intelligent self-criticism. *Heshbon ha-nefesh* (self-examination) is a necessary condition for *teshuvah* (repentance and renewal). Honesty to oneself and to others is a precondition for authentic human growth and creativity. Self-praise and -adulation are deceptive and lead to moral sloppiness and to reveling in the status quo. Breakthroughs in the human spirit are facilitated by the courage to admit to moral failures.

Belief in the power of renewal is a central motif in Judaism. Such concepts as psychological determinism, historical inevitability, and fatalism are alien to our tradition's understanding of human action. Belief in radical freedom, in an open future, in surprise and novelty are crucial elements of normative Judaism.

There is, however, a fundamental difference between the yearning for a new future that reflects wishful romantic dreams and the judicious hope that has been tested by suffering, failure, and tragedy. Although we are a young nation, the intensity of our political reality and our long historical memories provide us with the experiences and insights necessary for finding new and mature directions for the future.

One of the fundamental issues facing the new spirit of maturity in Israel is this: Should Auschwitz or Sinai be the orienting category that shapes our understanding of the rebirth of the State of Israel? Important differences result from the relative emphasis we place on these two models.

In the twentieth century, we have again become a traumatized nation. The ugly demonic forces of anti-Semitism have horrified our sensibilities. We can never forget the destruction of millions of Jews during World War II. Many, therefore, justify and interpret the significance of our rebirth in terms of Jewish suffering and persecution. One often hears, in speeches in the Knesset and in rabbinic sermons, statements such as this: "Never again will we be vulnerable. Never again will we expose our lives to the ugly political forces in the world. Our powerful army has eliminated the need to beg for pity and compassion from the nations of the world. We will never forget the horrifying picture of refugees being refused entry into Palestine or Western liberal democracies."

While I respect and share in the anguish expressed in these sentiments, I believe it is destructive to make the Holocaust the dominant organizing category of modern Jewish identity. It is both politically and morally dangerous for our nation to perceive itself essentially as the suffering remnant of the Holocaust. It is pointless and often vulgar to argue that the Jewish people's suffering is unique in history.

Our bodies and minds have tasted the bitter consequences of human indifference and inhumanity. We have witnessed, in our own flesh, moral evil and social injustice. But this should not tempt us to become morally arrogant. Our suffering should lead us not to self-righteousness and self-pity but to an increased understanding and sensitivity to all human suffering.

Nonetheless, there are political leaders obsessed with the trauma of the Holocaust who proclaim that no one can judge the Jewish people. "No nation has the right to call us to moral judgment. We need not take the moral criticism of the world seriously because our suffering places us above the moral judgment of an immoral world." In making such statements, they willingly judge others while refusing to be judged themselves. In so doing, they violate a basic talmudic principle: you may not judge others if you refuse to be judged yourself.

Although it is morally legitimate to appreciate the dignity that comes with power and statehood, with freedom from the inconsistent and fragile goodwill of the nations of the world, it is a serious mistake to allow the trauma of Jewish suffering to be the exclusive frame of reference for understanding our national renaissance.

Israel is not only a response to modern anti-Semitism; above all it is a modern expression of the eternal Sinai covenant that has shaped Jewish consciousness throughout the millennia. It was not only the Holocaust that brought us back to Zion, but also, and more important, the eternal spirit of Sinai—the refusal to abandon our historical memories and destiny. One need not visit Yad Vashem in order to understand our love for Jerusalem. It is dangerous to our growth as a healthy people if Holocaust memorials replace the living message of Torah.

The model of Sinai awakens the Jewish people to their obligation to become a holy people. At Sinai, we discover the absolute demand of God; we discover who we are by what we do. Sinai calls us to action, to moral awakening, to living constantly with challenges of building a moral and just society that mirrors the sanctifying power of God in history. Sinai creates humility and openness to the demands of self-transcendence. In this respect, it is the antithesis of the moral narcissism that can result from suffering and from defining oneself as a victim.

The centrality of mitzvah in Judaism shatters egocentricity and demands of Jews that they judge themselves by the way they act and not by exaggerated national myths of the purity and uniqueness of the Jewish soul. *Na'aseh ve-nishma* (we will do and we will understand) was the response of our people at Sinai. We understand ourselves through our doing.

Sinai does not tell us about the moral purity of the Jewish soul, but about the significance of aspiring to live by the commandments. Sinai permanently exposes the Jewish people to prophetic aspirations and judgments. The Bible was never frightened of making Jews stand in judgment for their failure to implement their covenantal responsibilities.

Immediately after the account of the revelation at Sinai, we are reminded of Israel's unfaithfulness to the covenant in the vivid description of the Golden Calf incident. Sinai teaches us that there is no meaning to the election of Israel without judgment—there are no privileges without demands. Sinai requires that the Jew believe in the possibility of integrating the moral demands of the prophet with the realism required for political survival. Politics and morality were united when Israel was born as a nation at Sinai.

The rebirth of Israel can be viewed as a potential return to the fullness of the Sinai covenant—to Judaism as a way of life. The moral and spiritual aspirations of the Jewish tradition were not meant to be realized in Sabbath sermons or by messianic dreamers waiting passively on the margins of society for redemption to break miraculously into history. Torah study is not a substitute for actual life, nor are prayer and the synagogue moral holidays from the ambiguities and complexities of political life.

The Jewish world will have to learn that the synagogue is no longer the exclusive defining framework for Jewish communal life. Moral seriousness and political maturity and wisdom must come to our nation if we are to be judged by the way we struggle to integrate the Sinai covenant with the complexities of political realities.

The establishment of the modern State of Israel has removed us from the insulated world of the ghetto and has exposed Judaism and the Jewish people to the judgment of the world. We can no longer hide our weaknesses and petty failings. We live in total exposure.

We must therefore define who we are by what we do, not by any obsession with the long and noble history of Jewish suffering. In coming back to our land and rebuilding our nation, we have chosen to give greater moral weight to our actions in the present than to prophetic dreams of the future or to heroic memories of our past.

In choosing to act in the twentieth century rather than wait for perfect messianic conditions, we permanently run the risk of making serious mistakes in our moral and political judgments. We must therefore respond maturely to anyone who is critical of our shortcomings. The time has come for us to free ourselves from the exaggerated rhetoric of religious and moral superiority ("no one can teach us morality!") and to face the spiritually demanding task implicit in the Sinai covenant.

The prophets taught us that the state has only instrumental value for the purpose of embodying the covenantal demands of Judaism. When nationalism becomes an absolute value for Jews, and political and military judgments are not related to the larger spiritual and moral purpose of our national renaissance, we can no longer claim to continue the Judaic tradition. Rather, we have ironically become assimilated while speaking Hebrew in our own country.

In being open and appreciative of criticism, regardless of its source, we demonstrate that we endeavor to walk humbly and responsibly before the Lord of all creation, Who demands that Israel bear witness to the demands of justice within an imperfect world.

It is important to remember that the Jewish people did not go from the suffering conditions of Egypt directly into its own land. We first went to Sinai, made a covenant with God, and pledged absolute allegiance to the commandments. We spent years in the desert casting off the mentality of the suffering slave.

After we overcame the humiliating memory of slavery and persecution and understood that we were called to bear witness to God in history, only then did we enter the land. The memory of suffering in Egypt was absorbed by the covenantal normative demands of Sinai. We were taught not to focus on suffering outside of its normative and moral implications.

Because of Sinai, Jewish suffering did not create self-pity but moral sensitivity: "And you shall love the stranger because you were strangers in the land of Egypt."

Auschwitz, like all Jewish suffering of the past, must be absorbed and understood within the normative framework of Sinai. We will mourn forever because of the memory of Auschwitz. We will build a healthy new society because of the memory of Sinai.

16

YESHAYAHU LEIBOWITZ'S VISION OF

ISRAEL, ZIONISM, AND JUDAISM

THE WORLD IS familiar with Martin Buber, Franz Rosenzweig, Mordecai Kaplan, Abraham Joshua Heschel, and Joseph Soloveitchik; they are regarded as leading intellectual figures who shaped modern Jewish religious thought. By contrast, Yeshayahu Leibowitz is little known outside Israel. Yet, if one were to conduct a survey within Israel to determine which Jewish philosopher and religious thinker is most talked about and argued with, undoubtedly Leibowitz's name would appear at or near the top of the list.

Leibowitz's thinking is deeply anchored in the Israeli context. He was a Jewish patriot who, from his youth onward, rejected the Jewish people's subservience to alien political rule. Yet, one could scarcely find a harsher critic of chauvinistic manifestations within the Israeli establishment. When he denounced trends in Israel, it was not with the moral pathos of an alienated Jewish universalist intellectual but with the conviction of an unwavering Zionist who fought in Israel's War of Independence and was proud of his numerous grandchildren, who all lived in the land. He never harbored any thought of living outside of the land of Israel.

Every complexity and ambivalence of Israel, be it the moral and religious problematics of the country, the struggle to write a new chapter in Jewish history, the conflicts between messianists and antimessianists, religious and secularists, territorial maximalists and minimalists, the whole dynamism and confusion of Israeli intellectual and spiritual life—all these are reflected in the thought of Yeshayahu Leibowitz.

THE CHALLENGE TO JUDAISM

According to Leibowitz, Judaism is fundamentally a communal frame of reference. Its prime concern is not with saving the soul of the individual but with providing a way of life wherein a community can express its commitment to serve God. Halakhah gives expression to the way this community lives out its existence and defines its place in the world.

For long periods, the Jewish people was viewed by others and saw itself as a nation constituted by the rule of Torah. To Leibowitz, what made Jews different from other nations was not their theology; other religions share basic assumptions of Jewish monotheism, eschatology, and the like. Nor did their Bible distinguish them, for the Christians adopted it also. What made Jews unique was the Halakhah that governed their way of life. The laws governing what Jews could eat, which days they were allowed to work, when sexual relations were permitted, and the liturgical laws of daily and festive worship—all these structured and institutionalized the Jewish community and provided its distinct character.

To Leibowitz, the primacy of Halakhah in Judaism is not a theological judgment but an empirical description of what in fact occurred in history. He points out that the Jewish community could tolerate hostile theological tendencies in its midst. Maimonides, for example, regarded the theology of many of his fellow Jews as mythological and even pagan, while the critics of Maimonides claimed that his theology had been corrupted by ideas taken from Greek philosophy. There was, however, no comparable toleration of conflicting halakhic practice. Those who held minority halakhic views were allowed to state them, but in their practice they were required to conform to the established majority outlook. What made the Jews a distinct communal entity in history was their commitment to serve God through a shared form of disciplined life, irrespective of their competing and contradictory conceptions of God.

Such was the character of the Jewish community until the beginning of Jewish emancipation at the end of the eighteenth century. From then on, the Jewish community's self-understanding began to break down, giving rise to what Leibowitz saw as one of the crucial questions for Judaism in the modern world. Emancipation, when it afforded Jews the opportunity of merging completely into the surrounding non-Jewish culture, also provided competition with their traditional self-understanding. One attempt to meet that challenge was the emergence of trends within Judaism toward amending or even abandoning much of Halakhah, while preserving the synagogue as a place of worship. Secular Zionism constituted an even more powerful form of competition, since it was an ideology that aimed to redefine the Jewish people in wholly nonreligious terms as a national political community.

The challenge to Judaism in Israel is therefore very different from the challenge in the Western diaspora. In the latter, the assimilatory framework with which Judaism must compete is one that threatens to dissolve the Jewish ethnic group, to absorb the Jews in such a way that they are no longer identifiable as Jews. In Israel, there are two competing Jewish frameworks, both of which claim to be Jewish. One asserts that it continues Jewish history through a radical transformation of Jewish society and self-definition. The other maintains that the Jewish community is doomed if it abandons its religious roots.

In the diaspora, Jews can argue that mitzvot and the synagogue are necessary instruments for maintaining their identity as a particular community. That argument loses its force in the Israeli context, where there is another Jewish frame of reference, a total social and political framework that gives its members an identity as Jews. Hanging on to religion merely as an instrument for perpetuating Jewish identity makes no sense in a society whose total national political framework already gives Jews an anchorage for their identity. This distinction will be very important when we discuss Leibowitz's theology, where he argues strongly against making Judaism an instrumental value serving the perpetuation of the Jewish people.

In Israel, the religious framework is obliged to be self-justifying, not merely instrumental. It must have intrinsic significance if it is to claim the allegiance of Israelis. It is often impossible for diaspora Jews to understand why in Israel Judaism is talked about so much in terms of faith and religious commitment and so rarely in terms of the sociological identity frameworks that are so often discussed in the communities of the diaspora.

Leibowitz's constant argument against the Zionist secular option for defining the continuity of Jewish history is that it is a distortion of the historical framework of the Jewish people. His argument not only springs from the framework of faith but also is a purely empirical one. To claim continuity with the historical Jewish people and yet to abandon Halakhah, to abandon worship of God as the essential framework of Jewish identity, is a falsification of what in fact existed in history.

To Leibowitz, the halakhic way of life is a historical fact. Halakhah is primary for understanding the visible presence and action of this community in history. Leibowitz consequently disagrees both with the religious Zionists who joined the revolution to build political statehood and with the secular Zionists who claim to continue Jewish history while abandoning the halakhic framework. The next sections will deal with Leibowitz's criticisms of both these groups within Israeli society.

LEIBOWITZ'S CRITIQUE OF THE RELIGIOUS ZIONIST COMMUNITY

To Leibowitz, Judaism is a way of life for a community to demonstrate, in its actions and intentions, its willingness to worship God in an unredeemed world, a world that pursues its natural course. The essential subject of Judaism is not the individual but a community. Judaism is not meant to offer a way for the individual to overcome the problems of finitude, sin, and death and to find eternal salvation; it is a historical phenomenon through which a community expresses its commitment to worship God. This is axiomatic for Leibowitz and has enormous implications for his approach to the religious Zionist community and the religious opportunities that reborn Jewish statehood may afford. Hence, although he did not agree with them, Leibowitz understood those members of the religious community who saw the Zionist decision for national renewal and political independence as an act of Satan, a deviation from the religious value system of the Jewish people. To the anti-Zionist ultra-Orthodox religious community, autonomous political life will be legitimate for the Jewish people only in a future messianic reality. The laws of Judaism, as they see them, require Jews to live under the rule of alien political powers. Political subjugation; alienation; and lack of responsibility for the social, economic, and political conditions of society are part of the burden the Jew must carry as long as the era of exile is not replaced by the era of the Messiah.

Unlike the Haredi community, Leibowitz was one of the religious Jews who joined the political revolution to reestablish an autonomous, self-governing Jewish nation. He believed that no event in the last fifteen hundred years was comparable in scope with this bold move on the part of Jews to alter their political fate in history. In the darkest period of world history, the twentieth century, when diabolical evil triumphed in the world, when many Jews nearly lost all hope of any form of survival, and when despair was fed both by the forces of genocide and by the forces of assimilation, a group of people brought to completion the earlier Zionist revolution. They heroically defied the processes of disintegration and proclaimed with great vigor the Jewish people's renewed independent political existence.

Leibowitz was fully aware that this move was not motivated by a religious impulse. He claimed that the Jews who participated in this great political revolution did not intend their act to be an expression of worship of God. They did not found the state in order to establish the rule of the Torah in their lives. It was, he believed, a purely natural decision of a national community to abandon the condition of alienation and subservience to foreign political powers. This nationalist impulse is a legitimate and healthy impulse within a nation. But it had no religious significance because it did not grow from the intention of realizing a religious ideal. The observant Jews who participated in the creation of Israel did so out of the same natural impulse of patriotism present within the larger secular sector of the Jewish community.

This, however, is not how many members of the religious Zionist community understand the Zionist revolution. They celebrate Israel's Independence Day and the liberation of Jerusalem as religious holidays. They claim there is a redemptive process working itself out in the reborn Jewish state. In other words, they are prepared to participate in this secular revolution because they believe it has religious meaning. To those who embrace statehood from this perspective, Leibowitz poses the following questions: Can you in good conscience accept this new historical reality, yet maintain a *galut* (exilic) perspective on Judaism? Can you participate religiously in statehood while giving allegiance to a *galut* understanding of Halakhah that in no way authorized or prepared the religious community to assume responsibility for the maintenance and well-being of a total political community?

What religious perspective is needed to give integrity to the decision of the religious community to embrace political statehood? Far too many members of the religious establishment, Leibowitz claims, refused to realize the dishonesty of transferring to Israel the practice of relying on nonobservant members of the Jewish community to provide essential public services. If, in order to maintain their Judaism, the religious community must become a sect parasitical upon a majority of the Jews disloyal to Judaism, then Judaism has lost all its religious integrity.

Leibowitz offers a Jewish categorical imperative for the religious community: Act in such a way that you could wish all Jews to act in a similar fashion. If this principle were to guide the religious community, then halakhic Jews might begin to recognize what is needed in the new political reality of Israel. Judaism must so modify the Halakhah as to become capable of being lived by the total community of a modern state. Any Jewish perspective that does not imply the possibility of observance by the total community is a false application of the Judaic tradition. Halakhah

273

obligates every member of the community. Therefore, religious Jews who embrace the State of Israel must build a Judaism that can govern the entire community. They cannot desire statehood yet at the same time cling unyieldingly to laws of the Sabbath that were formulated under conditions where Jews were not responsible for the total society. If they adopt a halakhic framework in which Jews do not assume total responsibility for society, they are, in a sense, still in exile, and their religious affirmation of the creation of Israel is only a romantic illusion, a verbal cloak that lacks religious integrity.

One cannot but feel the depth of Leibowitz's anger over the timidity of the official rabbinate and the hypocrisy and failure of nerve of the religious Zionist community, as manifested in the pseudo-solutions offered for serious religious problems. He was appalled by the fact that the religious term "Rock of Israel" (*tzur yisrael*) was furtively inserted into Israel's Declaration of Independence as a compromise. The religious Zionists wanted a word denoting God, while the secularists could pretend that the term referred to the Israeli army.

Leibowitz constantly exposed the failure to recognize that something radically new and exciting had occurred in Jewish history. The past institutional frameworks of the Halakhah, he insisted, could not be the exclusive guiding frameworks for solving the religious problems of modern Israel. Leibowitz rejected exclusive reliance on legal precedents to deal with the modern situation. He was a halakhic existentialist who believed that our decision to participate in statehood could not derive legitimization from a halakhic framework that mirrored the past historical conditions of Jewish exile. There is a deeply independent spirit in Leibowitz's religious philosophy. We have a right, if our intention is to serve God, to be bold in our halakhic decisions.

What, then, is the fundamental difference between Leibowitz's call for halakhic change and the halakhic changes made by Conservative and Reform Jews in the diaspora? Leibowitz believed that the tendency toward change in the diaspora reflected a desire by Jews to accommodate themselves to a non-Jewish world, to overcome separateness by eliminating the dietary laws of *kashrut*, to minimize the laws of the Sabbath so that they could mingle socially and economically with non-Jews, to remove many of the laws that make Jews visibly different in the eyes of the Gentile community. Leibowitz did not believe that these changes expressed any authentic religious impulse. Historically, the Jewish people were always a distinct community. Modernity and the desire for social integration have no normative weight; these are not legitimate reasons to transform Halakhah. To make life easier and more pleasant, to express oneself psychologically in a more spontaneous way, to remove the halakhic laws of sexual inhibitions and enhance one's sexual life—all this was rejected by Leibowitz.

On the level of individual discipline, Leibowitz was uncompromising in his halakhic demands. He did not see psychological, social, and political reasons as legitimate justifications for change in the halakhic framework. On the other hand, the impulse for change that grows from the reestablishment of a Jewish national political community is indigenous to Judaism and thus can be legitimized without reference to the ethical, humanistic considerations that guided the Reform movement in the diaspora. Given the fact that Judaism was created to guide the Jewish people, and was meant to be lived by Jews in an autonomous Jewish society, it is false and inauthentic to claim that Judaism is possible only if it is not responsible for the total life of the community. The community's allegiance to Judaism demands that it share the burden of maintaining the physical well-being of a total Jewish society. Therefore, living under exilic political conditions is not the true expression of Judaism but a distortion, a dilution of the fullness of the halakhic challenge.

The important existential problem that Leibowitz poses for the religious community is the following: Is Judaism expected to be a way of life for the people's national political existence? If it is not, the religious Jew should join the anti-Zionist ultra-Orthodox. If one participates in the Zionist revolution and celebrates the birth of the State of Israel, then one must alter Halakhah so that Judaism can remain alive in its own autonomous political framework. This, to Leibowitz, was the only possible religious response to the rebirth of statehood. The most blatant manifestation of the desecration of Judaism in the modern world was the failure to show that a completely autonomous Jewish society, responsible for the normal secular tasks of a modern nation, can live by Halakhah.

Here one sees the difference between Leibowitz and other leading Jewish religious thinkers of the twentieth century. The difference is one of basic motivation. Rosenzweig and Hermann Cohen sought ways of legitimizing Judaism in a Christian society. According to Rosenzweig, Judaism bore witness to the eschatological moment in history. According to Hermann Cohen, Judaism bore witness to the messianic impulse of universality. Mordecai Kaplan tried to create a Judaism unencumbered by the problems of supernaturalism and divine election, to make Judaism possible in a modern democratic, pluralistic society.

Soloveitchik and Heschel attempted to revive the courageous qualities of the faith posture in a secular society. Fundamentally, Soloveitchik attempted to renew the halakhic option for the individual by showing that halakhic Judaism was a bold existential drama; Heschel tried to rehabilitate the sensibility and perspective of faith. Their common aim was to enable the individual in a modern society to see Judaism as a serious spiritual option.

For Leibowitz, the urgent issue was not competing with Christianity or refuting secular philosophical critiques of religion, but ensuring that Judaism would be a viable and authentic possibility for an autonomous political community. In Israel, he felt no need to convince Jews not to assimilate; rather, he had to convince them not to exchange a religious Jewish self-definition for a secular Jewish one. His problem was not with the rehabilitation of the "lonely man of faith" but with the rehabilitation of a close-knit, observant Jewish community that had decided to accept political independence, yet evaded the bold halakhic changes that such a decision properly entailed.

Soloveitchik and Heschel responded to the existential problems of the human condition. They demonstrated how Judaism overcomes anomie and provides personal dignity and uniqueness for the modern human being absorbed by a technological society. In the diaspora, Judaism must solve the problems facing the individual in mass society. In Israel, however, the community precedes the individual. In order for Judaism to be a serious option for the individual living in Israel, he or she has to be convinced of its viability as a framework for a total society. Soloveitchik and Heschel were existentialists who attempted to provide authenticity for the individual Jew. Leibowitz was an existentialist who strove to provide authenticity for the community.

THE CRITIQUE OF SECULAR ZIONISM

Gershom Scholem rightly observed that there is a deep dialectical tension within the Zionist secular revolution. Secular Zionists rebelled against their tradition but remained inside the national historical home of their parents. Zionism is like the young adult who rebels against his parents, cries out against their values, rejects nearly everything they stand for, and announces that he is going to leave home, never to return. He goes to the door, opens it with anger, and closes it with a bang—but forgets to leave the house.

The attachment to the biblical land, to the land upon which Jewish prayers were focused throughout history, indicates that the new revolution was tied to something very old. In building their revolution within the land, Zionists both revolted against Jewish history and saw themselves as continuing it. The option of establishing a Jewish homeland in Uganda never captured the imagination of the Jewish people. It would never have succeeded, because it represented a complete break with the Jewish historical tradition.

There is a profound traditional sentiment that accompanies the Zionist revolution. The attachment to the ancient historical past of the Jewish people goes together with the yearning for the creation of a new Jew. There was a deep need among secular Zionist ideologists to find historical legitimization for their revolution. They could not find legitimization through Halakhah, through the official religious community, or from an immediate continuity of tradition. They went back to the earliest frameworks of Jewish history where the Jewish people developed and grew in their own land. The "new" must be an expression of something deep within the Jewish tradition if it is to succeed as a Jewish revolution in modern times. If Zionism were a complete break with the Jewish past, if the modern Israeli could not be discovered in any way in the patterns of Jewish historical memory, then in a deep sense Zionism would represent the end of Jewish history, the total assimilation of the Jewish people to the non-Jewish world.

This option could not have inspired the early Zionist ideologists. They tried to rebel, but they sought continuity as well. This explains the subtle changes introduced into Jewish education in Israeli society. The Talmud was viewed as a creation of exile. The early pioneers rejected the legalistic minutiae of Halakhah, the classical emphasis on the study of Jewish law, the rapturous joy of the student in the talmudic academy. They found their heroic figures not in the talmudic sages but in early biblical leaders such as

Joshua, Gideon, and David. The books of Joshua, Judges, Samuel, and Kings became central to Jewish self-understanding. The important biblical narrative was not Exodus with its commandments and the miraculous journeying of the Jewish people in the desert, but the story of the bravery of Joshua and the judges who fought to defend Israel's nationalist aspirations.

The new Israelis see the Bible as the source not of miracle but of human courage. The biblical books that emerged from the land mirror their existential needs. The secular Zionist refuses to accept the Bible as read by the traditional religious community but reads the Bible in its own historical context. This was the meaning of Ben-Gurion's call for a return to the Bible. Love for the biblical land, the study of biblical archaeology, walking through the country accompanied by the Bible—these became substitutes for the traditional study of Bible and Talmud. The early Zionists looked to the Bible to discover how their return to the land continued the earlier love of the land. The natural beauty of the land inspired them. They loved the mountains, the rich pastures, and the panoramic desert. The bible was not the book in which they sought norms for daily life or a way of understanding God's covenantal love for Israel. It was, instead, a historical document of an ancient community that was being reborn in the modern world.

This is what distinguishes the modern secular Israeli love of the Bible from the love of it as Torah, as the basis of Halakhah. One cannot appreciate Leibowitz's critique of the Israeli love of the Bible without knowing how the Bible had been used by secular Zionists to legitimize their revolution against the tradition and to justify themselves as successors of ancient biblical Israel.

The Bible also served the Zionist concern with building a new society imbued with social and political justice. The biblical prophets were important figures to Zionists seeking a deep utopian vision for the new state. Whereas Halakhah seemed obsessed with dietary laws and the like, for these Zionists Judaism had to be taken out of the kitchen. Citing the prophetic critique of ritual, they claimed that the essentials of Judaism had to be sought not in Halakhah's disciplined way of life but in the prophetic political call for justice and social equality. Judaism was identified through the prophets as a political vision for the Jewish community.

Early Zionists used the Bible to reject the Talmud. Zionism claimed to be able to heal the diseased religious anthropology stemming from two thousand years of exile. Students in Israeli schools know the history of the Bible. The majority, however, are ignorant of the broader spiritual process that resulted from the creation of the Talmud. To the early Zionist educators, there were no great creative achievements during the many centuries of Israel's exile. The way of life that grew out of the interpretive talmudic tradition was rejected as an emasculated form of human existence.

In his writings, Leibowitz constantly referred to Hanukkah in an attempt to correct what he believed was the distortion of making the Maccabees of Hanukkah a symbol of contemporary Israeli military courage. The modern Israeli soldier cannot use the Maccabees as historical Jewish precedents. They fought to reestablish the reign of Torah; the Israeli army fights for the security of a secular state. To Leibowitz, the Israeli army resembles the Hellenists more than they resemble the Maccabees.

Leibowitz was repelled by what he saw as the attempt of secular Israelis to distort tradition in order to legitimize secular nationalist aspirations. Jewish history up to the Emancipation testifies to the Jewish community's covenantal identity and loyalty to God expressed through Halakhah. To remove God and Judaism from Jewish history is to empty it of authentic content. Similarly, to make the prophets into social revolutionaries and the Bible into a historical document legitimizing the modern secular community is to distort the meaning of a literary document that constantly proclaims its religious purpose. Leibowitz abhorred the attempt to change the prayer *Shema Yisrael* into "Hear, Israel, Israel is our people. Israel is one." The secular Zionist revolutionaries, he believed, must recognize that nothing in preemancipation Jewish history can be used honestly to legitimize the building of a secular Jewish society.

RELIGION AND STATE

To Leibowitz, the same dangers inherent in all nationalist revolutions are also present in our own national renaissance. If history teaches us anything, it is that patriotic sentiments can be used to justify every human folly and brutality. We Jews who have decided to embrace the political, national rebirth of the Jewish people are not immune to the corruption that affects other nations. The attempt on the part of the religious community to put a religious label on the creation of Israel by calling it the "beginning of the messianic redemption" is especially problematic. It creates the illusion that we are doing God's work and are thus immune to the corruption inherent in all human activities. Let us not imagine that what we do in Israel has nothing to do with the universal human hunger for power and domination, that our actions have a purity expressive of the divine imperative to redeem human history.

To Leibowitz, the major religious and moral imperative for Jews living in Israel is to keep Jewish nationalism free of all religious interpretations and legitimization. The religious establishment, however, failed to exercise the critical function demanded by Leibowitz. Instead, it sought political accommodation with the secularists. Worse still, it acquiesced in a Chief Rabbinate appointed under secular law. Religious Zionists thus lost the autonomous power of the religious institutions they possessed in exile. The religious community has become totally dependent on government aid, and therefore susceptible to its control.

Leibowitz repeatedly quoted a discussion with Ben-Gurion in which the latter opposed Leibowitz's call to separate religion and state, because religion would then become too powerful. He preferred having the rabbinate within the state framework in order to control it. Religious Zionists have no dignity because they have no autonomous power. For a seat in the cabinet, they may sell their soul. Leibowitz described the religious Zionists as the well-kept whore of the government. He never tired of ascribing all moral and political failures of the government to the fact that the religious Zionist community gave religious legitimacy to the state.

There is nothing wrong with the normal natural desire for a state, but one must know of the dangers that may result from the misuse of power. Nationalism has the potential of becoming a dangerous evil impulse, *yetzer ha-ra*. As long as we know that it is potentially the *yetzer ha-ra*, we can deal with it. To subsume it under categories of redemption, however, and to interpret our political aspirations as part of a historical process leading to a messianic society, is to deceive ourselves about our own intrinsic human fallibility. Leibowitz saw a most revealing example of the misuse of religious categories in the service of nationalist purposes in the use of the term *kiddush ha-shem*, the sanctification of God's name, to describe the valor of Israeli soldiers who have fallen in battle. The talmudic term *kiddush ha-shem* was used to describe the willingness of the Jewish people to suffer martyrdom for the sake of their loyalty to God and His Torah. How can we use this same term to describe the heroic fighting qualities of Israeli soldiers, however laudable those qualities may be?

Judaism and the Jewish people are inseparably connected. In embracing the faith of Judaism, a convert must equally pledge solidarity with all of the Jewish people. As in Ruth 1:16, "Your people shall be my people" must come before "Your God shall be my God." There is no embracing the God of Israel without also embracing the community of Israel. The organic connection between peoplehood and faith in Judaism contains, however, the danger that the Jewish faith commitment may be turned into absolute loyalty to the Jewish people. This brings Leibowitz back to the theme of idolatry, because putting Jewish peoplehood in the place of God is idolatry.

As long as Halakhah defined the community, there was no danger of substituting loyalty to peoplehood for loyalty to God. Solidarity with Jewish peoplehood and commitment to the Torah were able to work together as long as the Jewish community saw its own existence and history as instruments for serving God. In the modern period, however, secular Zionism aims to perpetuate Jewish existence and history, but not necessarily Judaism. Jews who join this secular drama are liable to turn involvement with the survival needs of Israel into the new Judaism. The post-Holocaust generation can make loyalty to Israel the new Jewish religion.

It would be a mistake, however, to define Leibowitz's religious critique only as a polemical response to the social and political reality of Israel. It is, I believe, deeply rooted in his general philosophical outlook. Leibowitz has a coherent, systematic religious philosophy that goes beyond the exigencies of his political critique.

LEIBOWITZ'S RELIGIOUS PHILOSOPHY

To Leibowitz, God is not to be understood in personalist, theistic terms. All attempts to describe God from the perspective of human concerns are tantamount to idolatry. In this respect, Leibowitz is religiously very close to the position articulated by Maimonides in his negative theology. Because of God's radical otherness from the human world, Maimonides claims, all descriptive language about God is false, inadequate, or idolatrous. One cannot subsume God under any genus or species, and therefore one cannot apply to God categories used to describe human reality. Biblical religious descriptions of God are, to Maimonides, a concession to human beings who cannot think about the divine reality in noncorporeal terms. Similarly, Leibowitz's theology: one cannot talk about God; one can only act in the presence of God. Judaism does not describe the reality of God, nor should one imagine that it is possible to make intellectual sense of the existence of God. Rather, religious language is prescriptive: it tries to direct Jews in their worship of God.

Maimonides based himself on philosophical considerations in insisting on the transcendence of God, inasmuch as all attempts to describe God violate the uniqueness and unity of God. In the case of Leibowitz, however, the reason for insisting on radical divine transcendence is not metaphysical but religious. It is not that human descriptions of God are false; rather, they are religiously inappropriate. To think of God in order to satisfy human needs, to legitimize ethical categories, or to enhance and secure political structures so as to give order and coherence to human society is to make God subservient to the needs of human beings.

Is humanity the center of value, or is God? To Leibowitz, the choice is either/or. If you choose the human as the center, you adopt an atheistic posture. And ethics, he claims, places the human being at the center of value. The religious impulse requires that acting in the presence of God be the center of value. Human action achieves significance only because God wills it and it is performed in God's presence.

Worship endows human activity with value. It is a mistake to imagine that Leibowitz does not recognize the importance of social and ethical actions within a religious framework. What Leibowitz rejects is the primacy of the ethical as an autonomous category that gives the ethical ultimate significance. Religion, in Leibowitz's view, rejects and denies the primacy of the ethical. In the religious framework, it is not "Love thy neighbor as thyself" but rather "Love thy neighbor; I am the Lord." Love of your neighbor takes place within the context of the worship of God. It is being in God's presence that lifts human beings out of their natural creatureliness. One is dignified in Judaism when called upon to act in the presence of God because Judaism enables the individual to subordinate all natural instincts and desires to the service of God. To transcend all human needs is the essence of the religious impulse.

Leibowitz completely rejects any attempt to justify religion by arguing that it provides the basis for an ethical universe. To Leibowitz, an atheistic society can create a very serious ethical personality. Ethics is possible without faith in God. One chooses a religious worldview not to discover rules for ethics but because one recognizes that God is the ultimate principle of reality and that the meaning of life is expressed in worshipping God, which, in Judaism, is expressed through the framework of Halakhah.

The centrality of mitzvah in Judaism implies that God is a source of demand, not a guarantor of success and liberation in history. Here is where Leibowitz distinguishes Judaism from Christianity. Christianity is a religion in which God redeems and liberates human beings from finitude and sin. Judaism, on the other hand, offers no promise of resolution and redemption; it does not offer solace, peace, security, meaning, or human happiness. Whereas Christianity promises to serve human needs, Judaism calls upon the individual to strive to worship God within the world as it is.

The seriousness of a Jew's quest to worship God is what gives significance and purpose to reality. Leibowitz's radical negative theology grows from a religious impulse to guard the concepts of worship and transcendence of God. It is an obscene violation of Leibowitz's sense of worship to think of God as manipulating the human world in a specific way. To think of God as the Being who provides for my wealth, benefit, and health is to reduce God (to use Leibowitz's metaphor) to being the super-administrator of the public health-care fund. To relate to God as the Guardian upon whom we rely when human efforts fail is to make God the grand administrator of the world. Such a view robs Judaism of its essential thrust of worship.

The essence of Leibowitz's religious philosophy is expressed in his essays on the commandments, on prayer, and on Job and Abraham. Leibowitz sees two approaches to prayer within the Jewish religious tradition. One approach treats prayer as growing from human crisis and human needs; prayer expresses the longing to have God look on my suffering and aid me in my troubles. According to the second approach, however, prayer is not rooted in personal need and the existential human condition of crying out for divine attentiveness, but rather in the disciplined commitment to stand before God in worship, irrespective of one's personal human conditions. Leibowitz rejects spontaneous prayer; he is wholly content to regard prayer as a regimen and discipline that obligates a Jew to stand before God regardless of the psychological or social circumstances. The irrelevance of such factors is, for Leibowitz, shown by the fact that the mourner who has just buried a child and the groom who has just married his beloved are called upon to recite the same prayers.

To Leibowitz, consequently, there is no problem of petitional prayer in the modern world because the essence of prayer is the symbolic act of expressing the commitment to fulfill the mitzvot. The essence of prayer is to accept the obligation to stand in worship of God. Therefore, by tautology, all prayer is answered, because the very meaning of prayer is the willingness to accept the discipline of the mitzvot irrespective of history and human suffering.

To Leibowitz, the paradigm of the religious life, the archetype of the love of God and the model of genuine worship of God, is Abraham at the *akedah*, at the moment he was prepared to sacrifice his son Isaac. Abraham's ability to submit to God's command, although it violated all his natural impulses of love for

286

his child and contradicted all his dreams of building a religious community in history, created a moment when Abraham's worship transcended all human strivings, longings, and aspirations. Whatever happens in the world does not detract from the demand of worship, since in the worship of God the anthropocentric world is transcended completely. One who is prepared to follow in the path of Abraham must be prepared to think in wholly theocentric categories. The triumph of the *akedah* is the triumph of theocentrism.

The living faith community of Israel mediates Leibowitz's understanding of Judaism. In the classical tradition of Judaism, the oral tradition of the Talmud defines how one is to respond to the biblical tradition. Leibowitz takes this approach to its extreme by claiming that the Bible no longer has any autonomous validity. To him, the revelatory movement of God in history, which the Bible depicts, has been replaced by the prayerful human movement toward God of the talmudic tradition. Leibowitz loved to refer to the fact that in contrast to the Bible, the descriptions of revelation and miracles in the Talmud ceased to be essential elements of the Jewish story; yet, it was the rabbis, not the prophets, who contributed most to strengthening the Jewish people as a religious community.

As an example of this, he cites the capacity of talmudic Judaism to combat idolatry. In the biblical world, God is described as very active and constantly interfering in human history. Yet, when God acts miraculously, the community reacts by turning to idolatry. The miraculous liberation of the Jews from Egypt is followed immediately by rebellion. The great spectacle of revelation at Sinai is followed immediately by the Golden Calf incident. The biblical narrative apparently teaches us that miracles and direct revelation do not create religious communities. Israel remained an idolatrous community despite all the miraculous interventions of God and the revelatory passion of the prophets.

The Jewish people became resolutely loyal when the discipline of talmudic Halakhah was internalized and institutionalized in Jewish life. When Jews became a prayer community and adopted a life disciplined by the normative framework of Halakhah, Judaism finally succeeded in becoming a committed religious community. This living religious community shaped Leibowitz's perception of Judaism. He is not interested in the theology of the Bible but is drawn to make religious sense of Judaism as mediated by a living people. Mitzvah and its concretization in Halakhah constitute the community's way of expressing its commitment to God.

How, then, does Leibowitz deal with the biblical descriptions of God? He interprets the Exodus from Egypt and the miraculous interventions in the desert within the conceptual framework of the legal tradition rather than as factual historical descriptions. The sanctity of the Bible in Jewish life is not a result of revelation but rather of the rabbis' decision to endow the twenty-four books of the Bible with sanctity. The normative authority of the Talmud, not divine intervention in history, established the canon. If you regard the Bible as authoritative only within the framework of the legal authority of the Jewish tradition, you are not forced to regard the Bible as a source of factual information but rather as a source of normative direction—that is, as Torah and mitzvah. Thus, Leibowitz neutralized the problem of the Bible's factual truth claims by asserting that factuality is the business of science and has no intrinsic religious significance. Judaism is concerned with how we act in the presence of God.

The theistic vision found in the Bible reflects a specific stage in the community's normative religious development. Before the community of Israel could truly enter a theocentric framework, it is portrayed in the Bible as having an anthropocentric perspective of God. This is what the Talmud calls *she-lo li-shemah*: the service of God not for its own sake, since it is service of God motivated by human psychological concerns and needs. *She-lo li-shemah* was accepted and legitimized by the Judaic tradition, but only as a stage on the road to *li-shemah*: the service of God for its own sake. Although the authentic paradigm of Judaism is Abraham at the *akedah*, there is a great gulf separating normal human beings from the ideal archetype of Abraham.

In striving for a theocentric consciousness, Judaism accepts actions that mirror an anthropocentric frame of worship as a preliminary stage. This is how Leibowitz understands the general communal approach to petitional prayer, the biblical descriptions of God, and the stories that deal with God's promises of reward and punishment. All these personalist descriptions mirror the anthropocentric focus, the *she-lo li-shemah* level of religious life. Ultimately, however, the tendency of Judaism and the essence of its religious power lie in its demand to love God unconditionally and to perform mitzvot motivated by pure, disinterested love of God. For philosophical reasons of this kind, Leibowitz cannot use concepts drawn from biblical anthropocentrism, or from messianism and eschatology, to ascribe religious significance to the mere historical fact that Israel has been reborn as an independent polity. Reborn Israel will be significant religiously only when this community demonstrates that all of life in an autonomous Jewish society is dedicated to the worship of God.

A THEOCENTRIC VERSUS A COVENANTAL THEOLOGY

Because he viewed belief in a personal God and attributing human relevance to mitzvot as being within the framework of *she-lo li-shemah*, Leibowitz took strong issue with my covenantal view of Judaism.

Hartman does not at all realize that equating faith in the Lord with faith in "the God of history" constitutes a devaluation of religion. It is to know and to worship the Lord, not in the sense of "The Lord is God," but as the manager of human deeds and events, just as one may conceive of the prime minister as one whose status is essentially defined by the function of running the affairs of the citizens of the state. In other words, a human collectivity, or even humankind as a whole, becomes the supreme goal and value, while God becomes the manager of their affairs, a kind of supreme prime minister or supreme judge; that is, a God who fulfills a function with regard to the world and man....

The faith that leads to the worship of God for its own sake never was and never will be the product of a particular historical reality or specific events in the history of man. Faith is anchored only in man's readiness to worship the Lord in the world as it is; directing the believing person's consciousness toward "redemption" is a trick of the evil impulse, which diverts man's attention from the task laid upon him.

Thus, as he saw it, expecting God to respond to human situations in history is *she-lo li-shemah*. Indeed, in accordance with his claim that the biblical narrative indicates the total failure of God's dramatic involvement in history to bring about faith and loyalty to God, Leibowitz held that the first passage of the Shema (Deut. 6:4–9), which commands Jews to love God, captures the essential meaning of true spirituality. My interpretation of the difference between rabbinic and biblical approaches to history— that it involves the difference between conceiving of God as a victor in history or a silent, waiting God, and that historical memory of

God's manifestations in history informed daily, normative, rabbinic practices—seemed meaningless to him: his black-and-white approach had no room for this kind of interpretation.

To me it seems obvious that historical events, both present and past, awaken people to dimensions of spirituality that would otherwise remain dormant. My connections with the covenant of Abraham and with the community of Israel are factors that influence my halakhic life. But to Leibowitz, the idea that, as I once wrote, "making contact with the Land of Israel, one is led to make contact with the God of Israel," was "horrifying" and represented nothing less than "the idolatry of nationalism, statehood, and earthliness, which threatens to replace the Judaism of worshiping the Lord." Leibowitz did not appreciate the role of memory, community, or historical consciousness in the life of faith, and he therefore misunderstood the symbolic, religious significance I attributed to living in the land of Israel. For him, worshipping God is the result of the decision to live by the Halakhah; it is solely an act of will unrelated to whether you live in New York or Jerusalem. He was prepared to acknowledge the religious value of my approach to Judaism, but only within the framework of *she-lo li-shemah* ("not for its own sake," religious practice motivated by extraneous reasons), and not of *li-shemah* ("for its own sake").

Such an either/or division between *li-shemah* and *she-lo li-shemah* seems altogether too stark. A human act may be based on many reasons; the presence of a *she-lo li-shemah* reason does not preclude the coexistence of a *li-shemah* reason.

In the Talmud and in many places in Maimonides' writings, *she-lo li-shemah* refers to an act motivated by reasons extraneous to the purpose of the commandment. If I give *tzedakah* (charity) so that my sick child will become healthy, or if I study Torah to receive honor or to become wealthy, or if I fulfill mitzvot so that God will reward me with wealth or political victory, then my reasons for doing these mitzvot are extraneous to their religious normative purposes. Such acts of *she-lo li-shemah* differ markedly from religious acts done for reasons associated with the implicit significance of particular commandments. For example, my observance of the laws of the Sabbath may awaken in me a sense of creatureliness, which is a way of internalizing and acknowledging my belief in God as the creator of the universe. By abstaining from those acts prohibited on the Sabbath, I dramatically express my allegiance to the God of creation and to the implied idea that on the Sabbath human beings are not masters of the universe.

The religious meaning of performing a mitzvah is not constituted exclusively by deliberate submission to God, irrespective of the content of the mitzvah. What one considers to be the significance of a mitzvah will determine how one decides whether particular reasons for doing a mitzvah are intrinsic or extraneous. The reason for observing the Sabbath described above is implicit in the mitzvah of the Sabbath. By equating this approach to the Sabbath with that of soccer fans who observe the Sabbath so that their favorite team will win, Leibowitz reduces the category of *she-lo li-shemah* to absurdity. This category ceases to be religiously useful if it fails to discriminate between the religious values of such different forms of behavior.

Leibowitz reaches this untenable position because a fundamental premise of his philosophy of Judaism is that there can be no human significance to mitzvot. Accordingly, it is pointless to try to uncover how a Jew's commitment to God and Halakhah expresses an understanding of human psychology and human values. Any attempt to elucidate the human significance of mitzvot is futile and may be justified only as an educative instrument meant to be superseded by what Leibowitz understands as *li-shemah*: pure worship of God. Leibowitz's religious Jew is not unlike the mystic who aspires to the annihilation of the self in the quest for mystic union. The goal of religious life involves a negation of the total human self. By contrast, my covenantal approach never negates the human self in the life of worship.

Since Leibowitz refused to admit human significance into his analysis of Halakhah, he attacked my views whenever they suggested that Halakhah has a bearing on human character. Because I maintain that the entire human person, not only the will, enters into the worship of God, I am concerned with formulating a characterology of Halakhah, that is, an analysis of the attitudes, sensibilities, and traits that inform characteristic Judaic postures to life. Although I do not make psychology into a necessary or sufficient condition for explaining religious behavior, I argue that unless certain attitudes of life develop in a person, that person will lack the necessary conditions for living fully according to Halakhah. One who believes in God as creator, for instance, should reflect on the meaning of human finitude and limitations, should relate to life as a gift, should acknowledge the "other" beyond the self, and should try to reject a manipulative attitude to other human beings. In other words, belief in creation not only entails a cognitive commitment to a belief in the origin of the universe but also involves an attitudinal orientation that organizes one's relationship to oneself, other human beings, and the natural world.

This is how I understand the talmudic association of arrogance and anger with idolatry. One who is arrogant or subject to violent fits of rage lacks the proper character for entering into a genuine relationship with God. I do not claim that humility, self-control, and gentleness are equivalent to faith. Indeed, I reject the religious tyranny of those who paternalistically subsume all ethical individuals under the category of "believer." My approach is to seek out some of the necessary human conditions of faith and thus to indicate to spiritual and ethical people that we may have a great deal in common. If the halakhic community were to formulate a characterology of its worldview by emphasizing the type of personality Halakhah attempts to realize, it would contribute to creating a universe of discourse in which mutual understanding between halakhic and nonhalakhic Jews could take place.

But because his theology draws such a sharp distinction between theocentric and anthropocentric perspectives on Judaism, Leibowitz insisted that there could be no real dialogue between religious and nonreligious Jews.

> The halakhic Jew accepts the yoke of Torah and commandments with its obligatory way of life because he sees it as the worship of God, and in the worship of God he sees the normative component in the Jewish person's life. The halakhic way of life will not be accepted by an individual who does not see the worship of God as the central value, because he will not acknowledge God and His worship, nor will it be accepted by the person who does not regard the observance of Torah and commandments (a life according to the teachings of the Halakhah) as a concrete expression of the worship of God. Indeed, psychologically he is incapable of accepting it because it deprives him of some of those pleasures to which, according to the modern system of values, the individual is entitled. Moreover, it forces upon him obligations whose significance he cannot understand. The two lifestyles remain alien to each other and not parallel; those who pursue them cannot live together even if "dialogue" leads them to "understand" one another.

I am fully aware of the differences that distinguish one community from another because of a commitment to Halakhah. Nevertheless, such differences in practice need not create unbridgeable divisions between people who do not share a common way of life. The situation today, however, is informed by mutual suspicion and estrangement, with little or no possibility for discourse. And demonization and violence invariably erupt when communication is believed to be impossible.

LEIBOWITZ'S LEGACY

To Leibowitz, God does not act on behalf of any specific ethnic community. Jewish particularity grows from the Jewish community's decision to live according to the mitzvot. What makes the Jewish people unique is not God's election of Israel but the way of life that constitutes the Jewish community's particular framework of worship.

Halakhic concretization of the mitzvot can change. Indeed, Leibowitz calls for bold, innovative halakhic changes in Israel. If these changes come, if the religious community demonstrates its power to build a society dedicated to the service of God, if it demonstrates how the halakhic theocentric passion can have vital significance in the modern world, then Judaism has a future. If, however, the religious community cannot offer that vision, or if it fails to persuade the larger community to shift its focus from a secular, humanistic framework to a halakhic perspective, Leibowitz sees little hope for the continued existence of Judaism or the Jewish people.

Leibowitz offers no theological promise that guarantees the eternity of Judaism. He knows only of a living community in the past, which because of its effort, commitment, and courage developed and sustained Judaism under all conditions in history. Judaism's strength and continuity depend on the way the community lives. History is filled with uncertainty. The future is open-ended. Leibowitz, as a profound realist, did not underestimate the forces of assimilation or the disintegration of the religious community that followed Jewish emancipation. He was greatly concerned about the tendency in the Jewish people to religious and communal disintegration in the modern world.

He cried out bitterly against the distorted image of Judaism found in many religious circles in Israel, whereby God is made an instrument serving the political, nationalist hungers of groups like Gush Emunim. To view God as instrument and guarantor of the success of our political, nationalist aspirations is the height of idolatry. Will Israel change its course? Will we uproot the incipient idolatry in our midst? Will we have the courage to build a society that mirrors the new spirit needed for the renewal of Halakhah? Will the community awaken to the internal dangers of assimilation and spiritual decadence? Is there hope?

Leibowitz would have replied that we know only the present task. We are shaped by what we do in the present. What we do as a community defines who we are. Neither memory nor prayerful hope counts, only present action. The past and the future are beyond human or divine control and are therefore insignificant from a religious perspective. A community that lives only off its memories or its messianic anticipations is a community that has sown the seeds of its own spiritual destruction.

Leibowitz offered Israelis and Jews throughout the world no hope, no promise, no prayer. He offered only the voice of an honest, critical thinker who lived in Israel with great trepidation regarding the future, but who nevertheless persisted, with great passion and sincerity, to march across the country with the dedication of a young man, speaking to all who were willing to listen and to learn.

INDEX

About JEWISH LIGHTS Publishing

People of all faiths and backgrounds yearn for books that attract, engage, educate, and spiritually inspire.

Our principal goal is to stimulate thought and help all people learn about who the Jewish People are, where they come from, and what the future can be made to hold. While people of our diverse Jewish heritage are the primary audience, our books speak to people in the Christian world as well and will broaden their understanding of Judaism and the roots of their own faith.

We bring to you authors who are at the forefront of spiritual thought and experience. While each has something different to say, they all say it in a voice that you can hear.

Our books are designed to welcome you and then to engage, stimulate, and inspire. We judge our success not only by whether or not our books are beautiful and commercially successful, but by whether or not they make a difference in your life.

We at Jewish Lights take great care to produce beautiful books that present meaningful spiritual content in a form that reflects the art of making high quality books. Therefore, we want to acknowledge those who contributed to the production of this book.

Stuart M. Matlins, Publisher

PRODUCTION
Bronwen Battaglia, Bridgett Taylor & David Wall

EDITORIAL
Jennifer Goneau & Martha McKinney

COVER DESIGN
Bronwen Battaglia

COVER / TEXT PRINTING & BINDING
Lake Book, Melrose Park, Illinois

Spirituality

The Dance of the Dolphin
Finding Prayer, Perspective and Meaning in the Stories of Our Lives
by *Karyn D. Kedar*

Helps you decode the three "languages" we all must learn—prayer, perspective, meaning—to weave the seemingly ordinary and extraordinary together.
6 x 9, 176 pp, HC, ISBN 1-58023-154-3 **$19.95**

Does the Soul Survive?
A Jewish Journey to Belief in Afterlife, Past Lives & Living with Purpose
by *Rabbi Elie Kaplan Spitz*; Foreword by *Brian L. Weiss, M.D.*

Spitz relates his own experiences and those shared with him by people he has worked with as a rabbi, and shows us that belief in afterlife and past lives, so often approached with reluctance, is in fact true to Jewish tradition.
6 x 9, 288 pp, Quality PB, ISBN 1-58023-165-9 **$16.95**; HC, ISBN 1-58023-094-6 **$21.95**

The Gift of Kabbalah
Discovering the Secrets of Heaven, Renewing Your Life on Earth
by *Tamar Frankiel, Ph.D.*

Makes accessible the mysteries of Kabbalah. Traces Kabbalah's evolution in Judaism and shows us its most important gift: a way of revealing the connection between our "everyday" life and the spiritual oneness of the universe. 6 x 9, 256 pp, HC, ISBN 1-58023-108-X **$21.95**

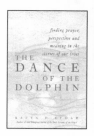 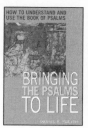   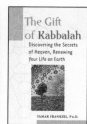

God Whispers: *Stories of the Soul, Lessons of the Heart*
by Karyn D. Kedar 6 x 9, 176 pp, Quality PB, ISBN 1-58023-088-1 **$15.95**

Bringing the Psalms to Life: *How to Understand and Use the Book of Psalms*
by Rabbi Daniel F. Polish
6 x 9, 208 pp, Quality PB, ISBN 1-58023-157-8 **$16.95**; HC, ISBN 1-58023-077-6 **$21.95**

The Empty Chair: *Finding Hope and Joy—*
Timeless Wisdom from a Hasidic Master, Rebbe Nachman of Breslov AWARD WINNER!
4 x 6, 128 pp, Deluxe PB, 2-color text, ISBN 1-879045-67-2 **$9.95**

The Gentle Weapon: *Prayers for Everyday and Not-So-Everyday Moments*
Adapted from the Wisdom of Rebbe Nachman of Breslov
4 x 6, 144 pp, Deluxe PB, 2-color text, ISBN 1-58023-022-9 **$9.95**

Or phone, fax, mail or e-mail to: **JEWISH LIGHTS** Publishing
Sunset Farm Offices, Route 4 • P.O. Box 237 • Woodstock, Vermont 05091
Tel: (802) 457-4000 • Fax: (802) 457-4004 • www.jewishlights.com
Credit card orders: **(800) 962-4544** (9AM–5PM ET Monday–Friday)
Generous discounts on quantity orders. SATISFACTION GUARANTEED. Prices subject to change.

Spirituality & More

The Jewish Lights Spirituality Handbook
A Guide to Understanding, Exploring & Living a Spiritual Life
Ed. by *Stuart M. Matlins, Editor-in-Chief, Jewish Lights Publishing*

Rich, creative material from over fifty spiritual leaders on every aspect of Jewish spirituality today: prayer, meditation, mysticism, study, rituals, special days, the everyday, and more.
6 x 9, 456 pp, Quality PB, ISBN 1-58023-093-8 **$18.95**; HC, ISBN 1-58023-100-4 **$24.95**

The Story of the Jews: *A 4,000-Year Adventure*
Written and illustrated by *Stan Mack*

Through witty cartoons and accurate narrative, illustrates the major characters and events that have shaped the Jewish people and culture. For all ages.
6 x 9, 304 pp, Quality PB, ISBN 1-58023-155-1 **$16.95**

Cast in God's Image
Discover Your Personality Type Using the Enneagram and Kabbalah
by *Rabbi Howard A. Addison*

With more than twenty hands-on spiritual exercises, will help you understand your own personality type and those of the people around you—enriching your relationships, your work...your life. 7 x 9, 176 pp, Quality PB, ISBN 1-58023-124-1 **$16.95**

 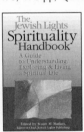 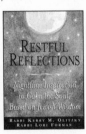  

The Enneagram and Kabbalah: *Reading Your Soul*
by Rabbi Howard A. Addison 6 x 9, 176 pp, Quality PB, ISBN 1-58023-001-6 **$15.95**

Mystery Midrash: *An Anthology of Jewish Mystery & Detective Fiction* AWARD WINNER!
Ed. by Lawrence W. Raphael 6 x 9, 304 pp, Quality PB, ISBN 1-58023-055-5 **$16.95**

Criminal Kabbalah: *An Intriguing Anthology of Jewish Mystery & Detective Fiction*
Ed. by Lawrence W. Raphael; Foreword by Laurie R. King
6 x 9, 256 pp, Quality PB, ISBN 1-58023-109-8 **$16.95**

Six Jewish Spiritual Paths: *A Rationalist Looks at Spirituality*
by Rabbi Rifat Sonsino 6 x 9, 208 pp, HC, ISBN 1-58023-095-4 **$21.95**

Sacred Intentions: *Daily Inspiration to Strengthen the Spirit, Based on Jewish Wisdom*
by Rabbi Kerry M. Olitzky & Rabbi Lori Forman
4½ x 6½, 448 pp, Quality PB, ISBN 1-58023-061-X **$15.95**

Restful Reflections: *Nighttime Inspiration to Calm the Soul, Based on Jewish Wisdom*
by Rabbi Kerry M. Olitzky & Rabbi Lori Forman
4½ x 6½, 448 pp, Quality PB, ISBN 1-58023-091-1 **$15.95**

Embracing the Covenant: *Converts to Judaism Talk About Why & How* Ed. by Rabbi Allan Berkowitz & Patti Moskovitz 6 x 9, 192 pp, Quality PB, ISBN 1-879045-50-8 **$16.95**

Wandering Stars: *An Anthology of Jewish Fantasy & Science Fiction* Ed. by Jack Dann; Intro. by Isaac Asimov 6 x 9, 272 pp, Quality PB, ISBN 1-58023-005-9 **$16.95**

Israel—A Spiritual Travel Guide: *A Companion for the Modern Jewish Pilgrim* AWARD WINNER!
by Rabbi Lawrence A. Hoffman 4¾ x 10, 256 pp, Quality PB, ISBN 1-879045-56-7 **$18.95**

Spirituality/Jewish Meditation

Aleph-Bet Yoga
Embodying the Hebrew Letters for Physical and Spiritual Well-Being
by *Steven A. Rapp*
Foreword by *Tamar Frankiel* and *Judy Greenfeld*; Preface by *Hart Lazer*
Blends aspects of hatha yoga and the shapes of the Hebrew letters. Connects yoga practice with Jewish spiritual life. Easy-to-follow instructions, b/w photos.
7 x 10, 128 pp, Quality PB, ISBN 1-58023-162-4 **$16.95**

Discovering Jewish Meditation
Instruction & Guidance for Learning an Ancient Spiritual Practice
by *Nan Fink Gefen*
Gives readers of any level of understanding the tools to learn the practice of Jewish meditation on your own. 6 x 9, 208 pp, Quality PB, ISBN 1-58023-067-9 **$16.95**

One God Clapping: *The Spiritual Path of a Zen Rabbi* AWARD WINNER!
by *Alan Lew* with *Sherril Jaffe*
A fascinating personal story of a Jewish meditation expert's roundabout spiritual journey from Zen Buddhist practitioner to rabbi. 5½ x 8½, 336 pp, Quality PB, ISBN 1-58023-115-2 **$16.95**

 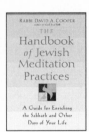 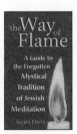  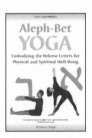

The Handbook of Jewish Meditation Practices
A Guide for Enriching the Sabbath and Other Days of Your Life
by *Rabbi David A. Cooper*
Jewish practices and traditions, easy-to-use meditation exercises, and contemplative study of Jewish sacred texts. 6 x 9, 208 pp, Quality PB, ISBN 1-58023-102-0 **$16.95**

Stepping Stones to Jewish Spiritual Living: *Walking the Path Morning, Noon, and Night*
by Rabbi James L. Mirel & Karen Bonnell Werth
6 x 9, 240 pp, Quality PB, ISBN 1-58023-074-1 **$16.95**

Meditation from the Heart of Judaism: *Today's Teachers Share Their Practices, Techniques, and Faith* Ed. by Avram Davis
6 x 9, 256 pp, Quality PB, ISBN 1-58023-049-0 **$16.95**; HC, ISBN 1-879045-77-X **$21.95**

The Way of Flame: *A Guide to the Forgotten Mystical Tradition of Jewish Meditation*
by Avram Davis 4½ x 8, 176 pp, Quality PB, ISBN 1-58023-060-1 **$15.95**

Minding the Temple of the Soul: *Balancing Body, Mind, and Spirit through Traditional Jewish Prayer, Movement, and Meditation* by Tamar Frankiel and Judy Greenfeld
7 x 10, 184 pp, Quality PB, Illus., ISBN 1-879045-64-8 **$16.95**

Entering the Temple of Dreams: *Jewish Prayers, Movements, and Meditations for the End of the Day* by Tamar Frankiel and Judy Greenfeld
7 x 10, 192 pp, Illus., Quality PB, ISBN 1-58023-079-2 **$16.95**

Healing/Wellness/Recovery

Jewish Paths toward Healing and Wholeness
A Personal Guide to Dealing with Suffering
by *Rabbi Kerry M. Olitzky*; Foreword by *Debbie Friedman*

Why me? Why do we suffer? How can we heal? Grounded in personal experience with illness and Jewish spiritual traditions, this book provides healing rituals, psalms and prayers that help readers initiate a dialogue with God, to guide them along the complicated path of healing and wholeness. 6 x 9, 192 pp, Quality PB, ISBN 1-58023-068-7 **$15.95**

Healing of Soul, Healing of Body
Spiritual Leaders Unfold the Strength & Solace in Psalms
Ed. by *Rabbi Simkha Y. Weintraub, CSW*, for The National Center for Jewish Healing

For those who are facing illness and those who care for them. Inspiring commentaries on ten psalms for healing by eminent spiritual leaders reflecting all Jewish movements make the power of the psalms accessible to all.
6 x 9, 128 pp, Quality PB, Illus., 2-color text, ISBN 1-879045-31-1 **$14.95**

Jewish Pastoral Care
A Practical Handbook from Traditional and Contemporary Sources
Ed. by *Rabbi Dayle A. Friedman*

Gives today's Jewish pastoral counselors practical guidelines based in the Jewish tradition.
6 x 9, 464 pp, HC, ISBN 1-58023-078-4 **$35.00**

Twelve Jewish Steps to Recovery: *A Personal Guide to Turning from Alcoholism & Other Addictions . . . Drugs, Food, Gambling, Sex . . .* by Rabbi Kerry M. Olitzky & Stuart A. Copans, M.D. Preface by Abraham J. Twerski, M.D.; "Getting Help" by JACS Foundation 6 x 9, 144 pp, Quality PB, ISBN 1-879045-09-5 **$13.95**

One Hundred Blessings Every Day: *Daily Twelve Step Recovery Affirmations, Exercises for Personal Growth & Renewal Reflecting Seasons of the Jewish Year* by Rabbi Kerry M. Olitzky 4½ x 6½, 432 pp, Quality PB, ISBN 1-879045-30-3 **$14.95**

Recovery from Codependence: *A Jewish Twelve Steps Guide to Healing Your Soul* by Rabbi Kerry M. Olitzky 6 x 9, 160 pp, Quality PB, ISBN 1-879045-32-X **$13.95**

Renewed Each Day: *Daily Twelve Step Recovery Meditations Based on the Bible* by Rabbi Kerry M. Olitzky & Aaron Z. *Vol. I: Genesis & Exodus; Vol. II: Leviticus, Numbers and Deuteronomy*
Vol. I: 6 x 9, 224 pp, Quality PB, ISBN 1-879045-12-5 **$14.95**
Vol. II: 6 x 9, 280 pp, Quality PB, ISBN 1-879045-13-3 **$14.95**

Life Cycle/Grief

Against the Dying of the Light
A Parent's Story of Love, Loss and Hope
by Leonard Fein

The sudden death of a child. A personal tragedy beyond description. Rage and despair deeper than sorrow. What can come from it? Raw wisdom and defiant hope. In this unusual exploration of heartbreak and healing, Fein chronicles the sudden death of his 30-year-old daughter and reveals what the progression of grief can teach each one of us.
5½ x 8½, 176 pp, HC, ISBN 1-58023-110-1 **$19.95**

Mourning & Mitzvah, 2nd Ed.: *A Guided Journal for Walking the Mourner's Path through Grief to Healing* with *Over 60 Guided Exercises*
by Anne Brener, L.C.S.W.

For those who mourn a death, for those who would help them, for those who face a loss of any kind, Brener teaches us the power and strength available to us in the fully experienced mourning process. Revised and expanded. 7½ x 9, 304 pp, Quality PB, ISBN 1-58023-113-6 **$19.95**

Grief in Our Seasons: *A Mourner's Kaddish Companion*
by Rabbi Kerry M. Olitzky

A wise and inspiring selection of sacred Jewish writings and a simple, powerful ancient ritual for mourners to read each day, to help hold the memory of their loved ones in their hearts. Offers a comforting, step-by-step daily link to saying Kaddish.
4½ x 6½, 448 pp, Quality PB, ISBN 1-879045-55-9 **$15.95**

Tears of Sorrow, Seeds of Hope
A Jewish Spiritual Companion for Infertility and Pregnancy Loss
by Rabbi Nina Beth Cardin   6 x 9, 192 pp, HC, ISBN 1-58023-017-2 **$19.95**

A Time to Mourn, A Time to Comfort
A Guide to Jewish Bereavement and Comfort
by Dr. Ron Wolfson   7 x 9, 336 pp, Quality PB, ISBN 1-879045-96-6 **$18.95**

When a Grandparent Dies
A Kid's Own Remembering Workbook for Dealing with Shiva and the Year Beyond
by Nechama Liss-Levinson, Ph.D.
8 x 10, 48 pp, HC, Illus., 2-color text, ISBN 1-879045-44-3 **$15.95**   **For ages 7–13**

Children's Spirituality

Cain & Abel AWARD WINNER!
Finding the Fruits of Peace
by *Sandy Eisenberg Sasso*
Full-color illus. by *Joani Keller Rothenberg*

For ages 5 & up

A sensitive recasting of the ancient tale shows we have the power to deal with anger in positive ways. Provides questions for kids and adults to explore together. "Editor's Choice"—American Library Association's *Booklist*

9 x 12, 32 pp, HC, Full-color illus., ISBN 1-58023-123-2 **$16.95**

For Heaven's Sake AWARD WINNER!

For ages 4 & up

by *Sandy Eisenberg Sasso*; Full-color illus. by *Kathryn Kunz Finney*
Everyone talked about heaven, but no one would say what heaven was or how to find it. So Isaiah decides to find out. 9 x 12, 32 pp, HC, Full-color illus., ISBN 1-58023-054-7 **$16.95**

God Said Amen AWARD WINNER!

For ages 4 & up

by *Sandy Eisenberg Sasso*; Full-color illus. by *Avi Katz*
Inspiring tale of two kingdoms: one overflowing with water but without oil to light its lamps; the other blessed with oil but no water to grow its gardens. The kingdoms' rulers ask God for help but are too stubborn to ask each other. Shows that we need only reach out to each other to find God's answer to our prayers. 9 x 12, 32 pp, HC, Full-color illus., ISBN 1-58023-080-6 **$16.95**

God in Between AWARD WINNER!

For ages 4 & up

by *Sandy Eisenberg Sasso*; Full-color illus. by *Sally Sweetland*
If you wanted to find God, where would you look? This magical, mythical tale teaches that God can be found where we are: within all of us and the relationships between us.
9 x 12, 32 pp, HC, Full-color illus., ISBN 1-879045-86-9 **$16.95**

A Prayer for the Earth: *The Story of Naamah, Noah's Wife*

For ages 4 & up

by *Sandy Eisenberg Sasso*; Full-color illus. by *Bethanne Andersen* AWARD WINNER!
Opens religious imaginations to new ideas about the story of the Flood. When God tells Noah to bring the animals onto the ark, God also calls on Naamah, Noah's wife, to save each plant on Earth. 9 x 12, 32 pp, HC, Full-color illus., ISBN 1-879045-60-5 **$16.95**

But God Remembered AWARD WINNER!
Stories of Women from Creation to the Promised Land

For ages 8 & up

by *Sandy Eisenberg Sasso*; Full-color illus. by *Bethanne Andersen*
Vibrantly brings to life four stories of courageous and strong women from ancient tradition; all teach important values through their actions and faith.
9 x 12, 32 pp, HC, Full-color illus., ISBN 1-879045-43-5 **$16.95**

Children's Spirituality

In Our Image
God's First Creatures AWARD WINNER!
by *Nancy Sohn Swartz*
Full-color illus. by *Melanie Hall*

For ages 4 & up

A playful new twist on the Creation story—from the perspective of the animals. Celebrates the interconnectedness of nature and the harmony of all living things. "The vibrantly colored illustrations nearly leap off the page in this delightful interpretation." —*School Library Journal*
9 x 12, 32 pp, HC, Full-color illus., ISBN 1-879045-99-0 **$16.95**

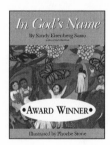

God's Paintbrush AWARD WINNER!
by *Sandy Eisenberg Sasso*; Full-color illus. by *Annette Compton*

For ages 4 & up

Invites children of all faiths and backgrounds to encounter God openly in their own lives. Wonderfully interactive; provides questions adult and child can explore together at the end of each episode. 11 x 8½, 32 pp, HC, Full-color illus., ISBN 1-879045-22-2 **$16.95**

Also available: **A Teacher's Guide: A Guide for Jewish & Christian Educators and Parents**
8½ x 11, 32 pp, PB, ISBN 1-879045-57-5 **$8.95**

God's Paintbrush Celebration Kit 9½ x 12, HC, Includes 5 sessions/40 full-color Activity Sheets and Teacher Folder with complete instructions, ISBN 1-58023-050-4 **$21.95**

In God's Name AWARD WINNER!
by *Sandy Eisenberg Sasso*; Full-color illus. by *Phoebe Stone*

For ages 4 & up

Like an ancient myth in its poetic text and vibrant illustrations, this award-winning modern fable about the search for God's name celebrates the diversity and, at the same time, the unity of all people. 9 x 12, 32 pp, HC, Full-color illus., ISBN 1-879045-26-5 **$16.95**

What Is God's Name? (A Board Book)

For ages 0–4

An abridged board book version of award-winning *In God's Name.*
5 x 5, 24 pp, Board, Full-color illus., ISBN 1-893361-10-1 **$7.95** A SKYLIGHT PATHS Book

The 11th Commandment: *Wisdom from Our Children*
by *The Children of America* AWARD WINNER!

For all ages

"If there were an Eleventh Commandment, what would it be?" Children of many religious denominations across America answer this question—in their own drawings and words. "A rare book of spiritual celebration for all people, of all ages, for all time."—*Bookviews*
8 x 10, 48 pp, HC, Full-color illus., ISBN 1-879045-46-X **$16.95**

Children's Spirituality

Because Nothing Looks Like God

For ages 4 & up

by *Lawrence and Karen Kushner*
Full-color illus. by *Dawn W. Majewski*
MULTICULTURAL, NONDENOMINATIONAL, NONSECTARIAN
What is God like? The first collaborative work by husband-and-wife team Lawrence and Karen Kushner introduces children to the possibilities of spiritual life. Real-life examples of happiness and sadness—from goodnight stories, to the hope and fear felt the first time at bat, to the closing moments of life—invite us to explore, together with our children, the questions we all have about God, no matter what our age.

11 x 8½, 32 pp, HC, Full-color illus., ISBN 1-58023-092-X **$16.95**

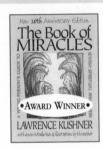

Where Is God?
What Does God Look Like?
How Does God Make Things Happen? (Board Books)

For ages 0–4

by *Lawrence and Karen Kushner*; Full-color illus. by *Dawn W. Majewski*
Gently invites children to become aware of God's presence all around them. Three board books abridged from *Because Nothing Looks Like God* by Lawrence and Karen Kushner.
Each 5 x 5, 24 pp, Board, Full-color illus. **$7.95**   SKYLIGHT PATHS Books

Sharing Blessings
Children's Stories for Exploring the Spirit of the Jewish Holidays

For ages 6 & up

by *Rahel Musleah* and *Rabbi Michael Klayman;* Full-color illus.
What is the spiritual message of each of the Jewish holidays? How do we teach it to our children? Through stories about one family's life, *Sharing Blessings* explores ways to get into the *spirit* of thirteen different holidays.
8½ x 11, 64 pp, HC, Full-color illus., ISBN 1-879045-71-0 **$18.95**

The Book of Miracles   AWARD WINNER!
A Young Person's Guide to Jewish Spiritual Awareness

For ages 9 & up

by *Lawrence Kushner*
Introduces kids to a way of everyday spiritual thinking to last a lifetime. Kushner, whose award-winning books have brought spirituality to life for countless adults, now shows young people how to use Judaism as a foundation on which to build their lives.
6 x 9, 96 pp, HC, 2-color illus., ISBN 1-879045-78-8 **$16.95**

Women's Spirituality

The Women's Torah Commentary: *New Insights from Women Rabbis on the 54 Weekly Torah Portions* Ed. by *Rabbi Elyse Goldstein*

For the first time, women rabbis provide a commentary on the entire Five Books of Moses. More than twenty-five years after the first woman was ordained a rabbi in America, these inspiring teachers bring their rich perspectives to bear on the biblical text. In a week-by-week format; a perfect gift for others, or for yourself. 6 x 9, 496 pp, HC, ISBN 1-58023-076-8 **$34.95**

Moonbeams: *A Hadassah Rosh Hodesh Guide*
Ed. by *Carol Diament, Ph.D.*

This hands-on "idea book" focuses on *Rosh Hodesh*, the festival of the new moon, as a source of spiritual growth for Jewish women. A complete sourcebook that will initiate or rejuvenate women's study groups, it is also perfect for women preparing for *bat mitzvah*, or for anyone interested in learning more about *Rosh Hodesh* observance and what it has to offer. 8½ x 11, 240 pp, Quality PB, ISBN 1-58023-099-7 **$20.00**

In 2 Vols.

In 2 Vols.

•AWARD WINNER•

•AWARD WINNER•

Lifecycles In Two Volumes AWARD WINNERS!
V. 1: *Jewish Women on Life Passages & Personal Milestones*
Ed. and with Intros. by Rabbi Debra Orenstein
V. 2: *Jewish Women on Biblical Themes in Contemporary Life*
Ed. and with Intros. by Rabbi Debra Orenstein and Rabbi Jane Rachel Litman
V. 1: 6 x 9, 480 pp, Quality PB, ISBN 1-58023-018-0 **$19.95**; HC, ISBN 1-879045-14-1 **$24.95**
V. 2: 6 x 9, 464 pp, Quality PB, ISBN 1-58023-019-9 **$19.95**

ReVisions: *Seeing Torah through a Feminist Lens* AWARD WINNER!
by Rabbi Elyse Goldstein 5½ x 8½, 224 pp, Quality PB, ISBN 1-58023-117-9 **$16.95**; 208 pp, HC, ISBN 1-58023-047-4 **$19.95**

The Year Mom Got Religion: *One Woman's Midlife Journey into Judaism*
by Lee Meyerhoff Hendler 6 x 9, 208 pp, Quality PB, ISBN 1-58023-070-9 **$15.95**

Ecology

Torah of the Earth: *Exploring 4,000 Years of Ecology in Jewish Thought*
In 2 Volumes Ed. by *Rabbi Arthur Waskow*

An invaluable key to understanding the intersection of ecology and Judaism. Leading scholars provide a guided tour of Jewish ecological thought.
Vol. 1: *Biblical Israel & Rabbinic Judaism,* 6 x 9, 272 pp, Quality PB, ISBN 1-58023-086-5 **$19.95**
Vol. 2: *Zionism & Eco-Judaism,* 6 x 9, 336 pp, Quality PB, ISBN 1-58023-087-3 **$19.95**

Ecology & the Jewish Spirit: *Where Nature & the Sacred Meet* Ed. and with Intros.
by Ellen Bernstein 6 x 9, 288 pp, Quality PB, ISBN 1-58023-082-2 **$16.95**

The Jewish Gardening Cookbook: *Growing Plants & Cooking for Holidays & Festivals*
by Michael Brown 6 x 9, 224 pp, Illus., Quality PB, ISBN 1-58023-116-0 **$16.95**;
HC, ISBN 1-58023-004-0 **$21.95**

Spirituality—The Kushner Series
Books by Lawrence Kushner

The Way Into Jewish Mystical Tradition
Explains the principles of Jewish mystical thinking, their religious and spiritual significance, and how they relate to our lives. A book that allows us to experience and understand the Jewish mystical approach to our place in the world.
6 x 9, 224 pp, HC, ISBN 1-58023-029-6 **$21.95**

Jewish Spirituality: *A Brief Introduction for Christians*
Addresses Christian's questions, revealing the essence of Judaism in a way that people whose own tradition traces its roots to Judaism can understand and appreciate.
5½ x 8½, 112 pp, Quality PB, ISBN 1-58023-150-0 **$12.95**

Eyes Remade for Wonder: *The Way of Jewish Mysticism and Sacred Living*
A Lawrence Kushner Reader Intro. by *Thomas Moore*
Whether you are new to Kushner or a devoted fan, you'll find inspiration here. With samplings from each of Kushner's works, and a generous amount of new material, this book is to be read and reread, each time discovering deeper layers of meaning in our lives.
6 x 9, 240 pp, Quality PB, ISBN 1-58023-042-3 **$16.95**; HC, ISBN 1-58023-014-8 **$23.95**

   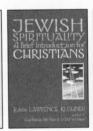 

Invisible Lines of Connection: *Sacred Stories of the Ordinary* AWARD WINNER!
5½ x 8½, 160 pp, Quality PB, ISBN 1-879045-98-2 **$15.95**

Honey from the Rock: *An Introduction to Jewish Mysticism* SPECIAL ANNIVERSARY EDITION
6 x 9, 176 pp, Quality PB, ISBN 1-58023-073-3 **$15.95**

The Book of Letters: *A Mystical Hebrew Alphabet* AWARD WINNER!
Popular HC Edition, 6 x 9, 80 pp, 2-color text, ISBN 1-879045-00-1 **$24.95**; *Deluxe Gift Edition,* 9 x 12, 80 pp, HC, 4-color text, ornamentation, slipcase, ISBN 1-879045-01-X **$79.95**; *Collector's Limited Edition,* 9 x 12, 80 pp, HC, gold-embossed pages, hand-assembled slipcase. With silkscreened print. Limited to 500 signed and numbered copies, ISBN 1-879045-04-4 **$349.00**

The Book of Words: *Talking Spiritual Life, Living Spiritual Talk* AWARD WINNER!
6 x 9, 160 pp, Quality PB, 2-color text, ISBN 1-58023-020-2 **$16.95**; HC, ISBN 1-879045-35-4 **$21.95**

God Was in This Place & I, i Did Not Know: *Finding Self, Spirituality and Ultimate Meaning*
6 x 9, 192 pp, Quality PB, ISBN 1-879045-33-8 **$16.95**

The River of Light: *Jewish Mystical Awareness* SPECIAL ANNIVERSARY EDITION
6 x 9, 192 pp, Quality PB, ISBN 1-58023-096-2 **$16.95**

Because Nothing Looks Like God
by Lawrence and Karen Kushner; Full-color illus. by Dawn W. Majewski
11 x 8½, 32 pp, HC, Full-color illus., ISBN 1-58023-092-X **$16.95** For ages 4 & up

Life Cycle & Holidays

How to Be a Perfect Stranger, 2nd Ed. In 2 Volumes
A Guide to Etiquette in Other People's Religious Ceremonies
Ed. by *Stuart M. Matlins* & *Arthur J. Magida* AWARD WINNER!

What will happen? What do I do? What do I wear? What do I say? What are their basic beliefs? Should I bring a gift? Explains the rituals and celebrations of North America's major religions/denominations, helping an interested guest to feel comfortable. *Not* presented from the perspective of any particular faith. SKYLIGHT PATHS Books

Vol. 1: *North America's Largest Faiths,* 6 x 9, 432 pp, Quality PB, ISBN 1-893361-01-2 **$19.95**
Vol. 2: *Other Faiths in North America,* 6 x 9, 416 pp, Quality PB, ISBN 1-893361-02-0 **$19.95**

The Book of Jewish Sacred Practices
CLAL's Guide to Everyday & Holiday Rituals & Blessings
Ed. by *Rabbi Irwin Kula* & *Vanessa L. Ochs, Ph.D.*

A meditation, blessing, profound Jewish teaching, and ritual for more than one hundred everyday events and holidays. 6 x 9, 368 pp, Quality PB, ISBN 1-58023-152-7 **$18.95**

Celebrating Your New Jewish Daughter: *Creating Jewish Ways to Welcome Baby Girls into the Covenant—New and Traditional Ceremonies*
by Debra Nussbaum Cohen; Foreword by Rabbi Sandy Eisenberg Sasso
6 x 9, 272 pp, Quality PB, ISBN 1-58023-090-3 **$18.95**

The New Jewish Baby Book AWARD WINNER!
Names, Ceremonies & Customs—A Guide for Today's Families
by Anita Diamant 6 x 9, 336 pp, Quality PB, ISBN 1-879045-28-1 **$18.95**

Parenting As a Spiritual Journey
Deepening Ordinary & Extraordinary Events into Sacred Occasions
by Rabbi Nancy Fuchs-Kreimer 6 x 9, 224 pp, Quality PB, ISBN 1-58023-016-4 **$16.95**

Putting God on the Guest List, 2nd Ed. AWARD WINNER!
How to Reclaim the Spiritual Meaning of Your Child's Bar or Bat Mitzvah
by Rabbi Jeffrey K. Salkin 6 x 9, 224 pp, Quality PB, ISBN 1-879045-59-1 **$16.95**

The Bar/Bat Mitzvah Memory Book: *An Album for Treasuring the Spiritual Celebration* by Rabbi Jeffrey K. Salkin and Nina Salkin
8 x 10, 48 pp, Deluxe HC, 2-color text, ribbon marker, ISBN 1-58023-111-X **$19.95**

For Kids—Putting God on Your Guest List
How to Claim the Spiritual Meaning of Your Bar or Bat Mitzvah
by Rabbi Jeffrey K. Salkin 6 x 9, 144 pp, Quality PB, ISBN 1-58023-015-6 **$14.95**

Bar/Bat Mitzvah Basics, 2nd Ed.: *A Practical Family Guide to Coming of Age Together*
Ed. by Cantor Helen Leneman 6 x 9, 240 pp, Quality PB, ISBN 1-58023-151-9 **$18.95**

Hanukkah, 2nd Ed.: *The Family Guide to Spiritual Celebration*—The Art of Jewish Living
by Dr. Ron Wolfson 7 x 9, 240 pp, Quality PB, Illus., ISBN 1-58023-122-5 **$18.95**

The Shabbat Seder—The Art of Jewish Living
by Dr. Ron Wolfson 7 x 9, 272 pp, Quality PB, Illus., ISBN 1-879045-90-7 **$16.95**

The Passover Seder—The Art of Jewish Living
by Dr. Ron Wolfson 7 x 9, 352 pp, Quality PB, Illus., ISBN 1-879045-93-1 **$16.95**

Spirituality

My People's Prayer Book: *Traditional Prayers, Modern Commentaries*
Ed. by Dr. Lawrence A. Hoffman

Provides a diverse and exciting commentary to the traditional liturgy, helping modern men and women find new wisdom in Jewish prayer, and bring liturgy into their lives. Each book includes Hebrew text, modern translation, and commentaries *from all perspectives* of the Jewish world.
Vol. 1—*The Sh'ma and Its Blessings*, 7 x 10, 168 pp, HC, ISBN 1-879045-79-6 **$23.95**
Vol. 2—*The Amidah*, 7 x 10, 240 pp, HC, ISBN 1-879045-80-X **$23.95**
Vol. 3—*P'sukei D'zimrah* (Morning Psalms), 7 x 10, 240 pp, HC, ISBN 1-879045-81-8 **$24.95**
Vol. 4—*Seder K'riat Hatorah* (The Torah Service), 7 x 10, 264 pp, HC, ISBN 1-879045-82-6 **$23.95**
Vol. 5—*Birkhot Hashachar* (Morning Blessings), 7 x 10, 240 pp, HC, ISBN 1-879045-83-4 **$24.95**

Becoming a Congregation of Learners
Learning as a Key to Revitalizing Congregational Life by Isa Aron, Ph.D.;
Foreword by Rabbi Lawrence A. Hoffman, Co-Developer, Synagogue 2000
6 x 9, 304 pp, Quality PB, ISBN 1-58023-089-X **$19.95**

Self, Struggle & Change
Family Conflict Stories in Genesis and Their Healing Insights for Our Lives
by Dr. Norman J. Cohen 6 x 9, 224 pp, Quality PB, ISBN 1-879045-66-4 **$16.95**

Voices from Genesis: *Guiding Us through the Stages of Life*
by Dr. Norman J. Cohen 6 x 9, 192 pp, Quality PB, ISBN 1-58023-118-7 **$16.95**;
HC, ISBN 1-879045-75-3 **$21.95**

Ancient Secrets: *Using the Stories of the Bible to Improve Our Everyday Lives*
by Rabbi Levi Meier, Ph.D. 5½ x 8½, 288 pp, Quality PB, ISBN 1-58023-064-4 **$16.95**

The Business Bible: *10 New Commandments for Bringing Spirituality & Ethical Values into the Workplace*
by Rabbi Wayne Dosick 5½ x 8½, 208 pp, Quality PB, ISBN 1-58023-101-2 **$14.95**

Being God's Partner: *How to Find the Hidden Link Between Spirituality and Your Work*
by Rabbi Jeffrey K. Salkin; Intro. by Norman Lear AWARD WINNER!
6 x 9, 192 pp, Quality PB, ISBN 1-879045-65-6 **$16.95**; HC, ISBN 1-879045-37-0 **$19.95**

God & the Big Bang
Discovering Harmony Between Science & Spirituality AWARD WINNER!
by Daniel C. Matt 6 x 9, 224 pp, Quality PB, ISBN 1-879045-89-3 **$16.95**

Soul Judaism: *Dancing with God into a New Era*
by Rabbi Wayne Dosick 5½ x 8½, 304 pp, Quality PB, ISBN 1-58023-053-9 **$16.95**

Finding Joy: *A Practical Spiritual Guide to Happiness* AWARD WINNER!
by Rabbi Dannel I. Schwartz with Mark Hass
6 x 9, 192 pp, Quality PB, ISBN 1-58023-009-1 **$14.95**; HC, ISBN 1-879045-53-2 **$19.95**

Theology/Philosophy

Love and Terror in the God Encounter: *The Theological Legacy of Rabbi Joseph B. Soloveitchik*
by *Dr. David Hartman*

Renowned scholar David Hartman explores the sometimes surprising intersection of Soloveitchik's rootedness in halakhic tradition with his genuine responsiveness to modern Western theology. An engaging look at one of the most important Jewish thinkers of the twentieth century.
6 x 9, 240 pp, HC, ISBN 1-58023-112-8 **$25.00**

These Are the Words: *A Vocabulary of Jewish Spiritual Life*
by *Arthur Green*

What are the most essential ideas, concepts and terms that an educated person needs to know about Judaism? From *Adonai* (My Lord) to *zekhut* (merit), this enlightening and entertaining journey through Judaism teaches us the 149 core Hebrew words that constitute the basic vocabulary of Jewish spiritual life. 6 x 9, 304 pp, Quality PB, ISBN 1-58023-107-1 **$18.95**

Broken Tablets: *Restoring the Ten Commandments and Ourselves*
Ed. by *Rabbi Rachel S. Mikva;* Intro. by *Rabbi Lawrence Kushner* AWARD WINNER!

Twelve outstanding spiritual leaders each share profound and personal thoughts about these biblical commands and why they have such a special hold on us.
6 x 9, 192 pp, Quality PB, ISBN 1-58023-158-6 **$16.95**; HC, ISBN 1-58023-066-0 **$21.95**

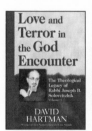  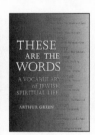 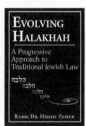 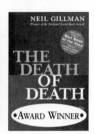

A Heart of Many Rooms: *Celebrating the Many Voices within Judaism* AWARD WINNER!
by Dr. David Hartman 6 x 9, 352 pp, Quality PB, ISBN 1-58023-156-X **$19.95**; HC, ISBN 1-58023-048-2 **$24.95**

A Living Covenant: *The Innovative Spirit in Traditional Judaism* AWARD WINNER!
by Dr. David Hartman 6 x 9, 368 pp, Quality PB, ISBN 1-58023-011-3 **$18.95**

Evolving Halakhah: *A Progressive Approach to Traditional Jewish Law*
by Rabbi Dr. Moshe Zemer 6 x 9, 480 pp, HC, ISBN 1-58023-002-4 **$40.00**

The Death of Death: *Resurrection and Immortality in Jewish Thought* AWARD WINNER!
by Dr. Neil Gillman 6 x 9, 336 pp, Quality PB, ISBN 1-58023-081-4 **$18.95**; HC, ISBN 1-879045-61-3 **$23.95**

The Last Trial: *On the Legends and Lore of the Command to Abraham to Offer Isaac as a Sacrifice* by Shalom Spiegel 6 x 9, 208 pp, Quality PB, ISBN 1-879045-29-X **$17.95**

Tormented Master: *The Life and Spiritual Quest of Rabbi Nahman of Bratslav*
by Dr. Arthur Green 6 x 9, 416 pp, Quality PB, ISBN 1-879045-11-7 **$18.95**

The Earth Is the Lord's: *The Inner World of the Jew in Eastern Europe*
by Abraham Joshua Heschel 5½ x 8, 128 pp, Quality PB, ISBN 1-879045-42-7 **$14.95**

A Passion for Truth: *Despair and Hope in Hasidism* by Abraham Joshua Heschel
5½ x 8, 352 pp, Quality PB, ISBN 1-879045-41-9 **$18.95**

Your Word Is Fire: *The Hasidic Masters on Contemplative Prayer* Ed. by Dr. Arthur Green and Dr. Barry W. Holtz 6 x 9, 160 pp, Quality PB, ISBN 1-879045-25-7 **$15.95**

  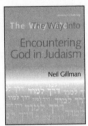